HyperCard® 2
QuickStart

Rebecca Gold

HyperCard 2 QuickStart.

Copyright © 1992 by Que® Corporation.

Library of Congress Catalog No.: 91-67628

ISBN: 0-88022-852-0

94 93 92   6 5 4 3 2 1

Interpretation of the printing code: the rightmost double-digit number is the year of the book's printing; the rightmost single-digit number, the number of the book's printing. For example, a printing code of 92-1 shows that the first printing of the book occurred in 1992.

HyperCard 2 QuickStart is based on HyperCard 2.0 and 2.1.

Screen reproductions in this book were created using Exposure Pro from Baseline Publishing, Memphis, TN.

Publisher: Lloyd J. Short

Acquisitions Manager: Rick Ranucci

Product Development Manager: Thomas H. Bennett

Managing Editor: Paul Boger

Book Designer: Scott Cook

Production Team: Jeff Baker, Claudia Bell, Brad Chinn, Brook Farling, Denny Hager, Audra Hershman, Carrie Keesling, Phil Kitchel, Bob LaRoche, Laurie Lee, Anne Owen, Caroline Roop, Kevin Spear, Bruce Steed, Susan VandeWalle, Phil Worthington

Product Director
Kathie-Jo Arnoff

Production Editor
Pamela Wampler

Editor
Jill D. Bond

Technical Editor
David W. Keller

Composed in Garamond and MCP Digital
by Que Corporation

About the Author

Rebecca Gold, a native of Newport, Rhode Island, has been a computer consultant in technical documentation, software quality assurance, and training since 1980. She was the founder of a computer training company based in Long Beach, and she is currently teaching in an alternative elementary school in Manhattan Beach. She also writes fiction for children and adults.

She lives with her husband and daughter in Redondo Beach, California.

Acknowledgments

I would like to thank a few people who have helped greatly in making this book possible.

First, my friend and fellow Que author, Mark Bilbo, for playing matchmaker with Que and me.

My brother-in-law, David Sardinha, for all his help with the screen shots, again and again.

Roger Bloxberg of Nova Development for his assistance and for allowing me to use his products as examples.

And my dear friend Joe Will for creating the HyperRes stack used in Chapter 10 . . . and for taking me to lunch when I thought I couldn't write another word.

I would also like to acknowledge the terrific people at Que who have turned my manuscript into a book! Chris Katsaropoulos, for getting me on board and checking in with me periodically to see that I was maintaining my sanity; Kathie-Jo Arnoff, whose suggestions and guidance improved the end result drastically; and Pamela Wampler, whose editorial "eye" has been invaluable.

Most especially I would like to thank my husband, Osvaldo, and my daughter, Necia, for their continued love and support through the good, the bad, and the crazy days of this writer's life.

Trademark Acknowledgments

Que Corporation has made every effort to supply trademark information about company names, products, and services mentioned in this book. Trademarks indicated below were derived from various sources. Que Corporation cannot attest to the accuracy of this information.

Apple, LaserWriter, and Macintosh are registered trademarks of Apple Computer, Inc.

Claris and MacPaint are registered trademarks of Claris Corporation.

CompuServe is a registered trademark of CompuServe, Inc. and H&R Block, Inc.

GEnie is a trademark of General Electric Company.

HyperCard and HyperTalk are registered trademarks of Apple Computer, Inc., licensed to Claris Corporation.

Contents at a Glance

Table of Contents

Introduction

The only difficult thing about HyperCard is defining *exactly* what it is. Simply stated, HyperCard is whatever you want it to be.

Think of someone handing you a set of tools you can use separately or together to organize and display information. Any kind of information. Any way at all. And along with these tools comes a bunch of applications other people created using the same set of tools. You can either use an application "as is," or use your tools to open an application and take out a piece, put in a different piece, or spruce up the application to suit your own taste. Or, maybe you prefer to use the tools to create your own application from scratch. All of this, in essence, is HyperCard.

HyperCard has become as well known in the Macintosh community as the mouse. It has been referred to as a "software erector set." There are thousands of Macintosh "software erectors" who have used HyperCard's building tools to create useful, fun, and innovative HyperCard applications, called *stacks*.

There are stacks to keep electronic address or appointment books; store collections of graphic or scanned images; run self-paced training programs, tutorials, or demos; create animated or audio presentations; check grammar or spelling in a document; design architectural layouts; play games; talk to other computers over a network; create labels for disks, videos, or books; create and organize libraries for books or electronic media; create graphic presentations from numerical data; create invoices or expense reports; maintain company inventory, and so on.

What do you want HyperCard to be for you? You have programs, tools, and power. Now just use your imagination.

Who Should Use This Book

If you're in the process of unbundling your new Macintosh computer and wondering what the program disk labeled "HyperCard" is all about, this book is for you. Or, if you have purchased HyperCard Version 2.0 or 2.1 (or have been using HyperCard 1.x and have just upgraded to 2.1), this book is for you, too. Version 2.1 is a major upgrade to HyperCard; it offers many new features you will want to learn about and use right away.

What's in This Book

This book will take you through each of the five levels of HyperCard. You will learn how to use HyperCard to access information in the many stacks that came with your program, and you will learn how to add, edit, and delete information from the stacks. You also will learn how to customize a stack to your own particular needs, create graphics, and even change the function of a stack. Best of all, by the end of the book, you will be able to create your own HyperCard programs from start to finish.

The fifth level of HyperCard, called *Scripting*, is not covered in its entirety in this book. You will be introduced to Scripting and learn how to write simple scripts for buttons and cards, but the entire HyperTalk language is not covered.

Conventions Used in This Book

This book uses special typefaces for different kinds of text. User input, or text you type, appears in blue and bold:

Type **set userlevel to 5** in the message box.

On-screen text appears in a special font:

Click the right button labeled `Documents`.

In procedures, keyboard characters appear as icons:

Hold down ⌘ and press 4.

A hyphen between keyboard characters means that you hold down the first key, press the second key, and then release both keys.

Pull down the Go menu and select Message, or press ⌘-M.

How This Book Is Organized

This book is a step-by-step guide you can use to teach yourself HyperCard 2 at your own pace. With each chapter, you build on your knowledge of Hyper-Card. You can move to the next level of the program and the book when you're ready. On the right side of each chapter opening, you see a list of topics covered in the chapter. You can use these lists to find quickly the information you need.

HyperCard is divided into five levels. The chapters in this book begin with the most introductory level of the program and gradually include more complex material. The last three chapters are devoted to creating sample HyperCard stacks you will find useful and fun. Following the chapters are two appendixes that provide installation instructions and information on acquiring more HyperCard stacks.

The book is broken into the following chapters:

Chapter 1 gives you an overview of the Macintosh computer and the Hyper-Card program. The basic Macintosh principles and operations that you should be familiar with before you start the exercises in this book are discussed. Chapter 1 also addresses how to enable the HyperCard program that is delivered with your new Macintosh computer.

Chapter 2 introduces you to the first level of HyperCard, called *Browsing*. You will learn how to move through cards and stacks and take a look at some of the stacks that came with your program. You will also learn how to use the HyperCard Help system and take the HyperCard Tour.

Chapter 3 brings you to the second level of HyperCard, called *Typing*. Here you will add, edit, and delete cards and textual information in a stack.

Chapter 4 covers the printing and reporting features of HyperCard. Many of these features are new in HyperCard 2.0.

Chapter 5 brings you to the third level of HyperCard, called *Painting*. It will introduce you to each of the HyperCard Painting tools to create and enhance graphics in any card or stack.

Chapter 6 covers the fourth level of HyperCard, called *Authoring*. You will be able to customize stacks by creating and modifying buttons and fields and linking cards and stacks to others. In this chapter you will modify a stack template for an invoice stack.

Chapter 7 introduces you to another new feature in HyperCard 2.0, the Icon Editor. The Icon Editor allows you to create and modify icons to add to your card or stack buttons.

Chapter 8 will take you through, step by step, the design and creation of a new stack to use as a client database. You will also learn how to work with multiple windows so that you can work with more than one stack at the same time. All of the button and field and linking techniques that you have been introduced to previously will be used in this chapter.

Chapter 9 will introduce you to the fifth level of HyperCard, called *Scripting*. You will learn how to open existing scripts for buttons, cards, and stacks, and modify them to accommodate changes to the stack. You will also learn how to create your own scripts for buttons to perform various functions in a stack. You will create another stack in this chapter for a book library where you will create the scripts for buttons and use many of the features you have been introduced to up to this point.

In Chapter 10 you will build another stack, step by step, from scratch. This stack is an automated résumé stack, and it acts similar to a self-running demo. You will write all of the button and card scripts for the stack.

Appendix A contains instructions on installation.

Appendix B contains information on where to get more HyperCard stacks.

An Overview of HyperCard and the Macintosh

1

Bill Atkinson, one of the original Macintosh "gurus" and the author of MacPaint, had a distinct goal in mind when he first created HyperCard. Atkinson wanted to develop a program that would enable any Macintosh user to access and share information with other Macintosh users, regardless of their computer experience. HyperCard certainly meets that goal, and goes way beyond.

At its most basic level, HyperCard is an information manager, whether that information is in the form of text, graphics, scanned images, animation, or sound. You can use HyperCard to access information assembled by others, modify or add to what's already there, customize the order and display, search for a specific piece of information, and link any piece of information to any other piece so that you can simply *click* from one level of detail to the next.

Solely as an information manager, HyperCard is a very useful tool. Not only is it extremely easy to use, but it is quite powerful and fun. Anyone, regardless of programming experience or even Macintosh experience, can start using HyperCard at its most basic level in a matter of minutes.

Learning about your Macintosh

Using bundled HyperCard

Learning HyperCard terms and concepts

1

The real mastery behind HyperCard is its use as a development tool, or "software erector set," as it has been called. Without any prior programming experience, you can construct new HyperCard applications (called *stacks*) simply by modifying the stacks that have been provided for you. And with a little imagination, you can design and develop your own stacks before you're even aware that you're programming!

This chapter will introduce you to the basics of your Macintosh computer and give you an overview of the HyperCard program. The Macintosh and Hyper-Card are simple to learn and fun to use. Before long you will be a master at both!

Key Terms in This Chapter

Desktop	The screen, disk icons, Trash Can icon, and menu bar you see when you first start your Macintosh.
Icon	A graphic representation (or picture) of a file, folder, disk, or application.
Finder	The Macintosh operating system. The program that creates your desktop, shows you where your files are located, copies files from icon to icon, dictates what your desktop looks like, and much more.
Menu	A list of commands available to use. A menu can be revealed, or pulled down, by placing the mouse pointer on the menu title at the top of the screen and holding down the mouse button.
Bundled HyperCard	The HyperCard program included with your Macintosh computer purchased from Apple, as opposed to the HyperCard program (or the HyperCard upgrade kit) you can purchase separately from Claris.
User level	The setting on the Preferences card in the Home stack that gives you access to the various HyperCard tools and capabilities. HyperCard is organized into five user levels: Browsing, Typing, Painting, Authoring, and Scripting.
Card	HyperCard's basic unit of information. A card can contain text information, graphics, sound, animation, or any combination thereof.

Background	The area on a card that is shared by more than one card. The background of a card can be thought of as the card's "template." The background can contain buttons, fields, text, or pictures.
Field	The field is the area (or areas) on a card that contains textual information that most likely changes from card to card. There are two basic kinds of fields: background fields and card fields.
Button	An area on the card (or in the card's background) that initiates an action when you click it.
Stack	A named group of cards that usually contain related information. Each stack is actually a separate Macintosh disk file.
Browse tool	The little hand with the pointing finger you see when you move the mouse through cards and stacks. The Browse tool can change its appearance, depending on its location in a card.

How HyperCard Is Organized

HyperCard is divided into five user levels. The levels are Browsing, Typing, Painting, Authoring, and Scripting. You will begin at the most basic level, Browsing, where you will learn about the program by looking at stacks others have created. Essentially, you can "look but not touch" at this level. Browsing is covered in Chapter 2.

At the next level, called *Typing*, you actually use the stacks for your own needs. You can add, edit, and delete text information in any card, or add or remove a card from a stack. Typing is introduced in Chapter 3.

The Painting user level, where you can access HyperCard's Painting tools to create and edit graphics in a stack, is covered in Chapter 5. And in Chapter 6 you are introduced to the Authoring user level, where you can change the function of a card or stack, and even create a new stack from scratch.

The fifth level, called *Scripting*, is the most advanced level of HyperCard. At the Scripting level, you can write and edit programs written in HyperTalk, the language of HyperCard. Although you will modify and create a few simple scripts in Chapter 9, scripting and the HyperTalk language are not covered extensively in this book.

1 What Do You Need To Run HyperCard?

To run HyperCard 2.1, you must have the following equipment:

- A Macintosh with two 800K floppy disk drives or one 800K floppy disk drive and one hard disk drive
- At least 1M of memory
- Either a monochrome or color display
- System and Finder, version 6.0.5 or greater

If you are unsure of the version of the System and Finder you are using, pull down the Apple menu (the left-most menu on the menu bar, indicated by the little apple) and select About The Finder. If you are not running System 6.0.5 or later, consult your local Apple dealer to obtain a set of system disks.

The following equipment, although not necessary, is strongly recommended:

- A hard disk, either internal or external
- A printer

Learning about Your Macintosh

If this is the first time you are turning on your Macintosh, it is a good idea to learn a few standard Macintosh operations before you continue with this book. Specifically, you should be able to open, close, and move icons and windows, and select menu items.

Starting Your Macintosh

To start your Macintosh, turn on the power switch located on the back left side of your Macintosh. On a Mac II, the switch is either on the right side on the back of the machine or on the keyboard. If you have an external hard drive, turn it on first.

After a few seconds, you will hear a beep telling you that your Mac is on. Then, a little, smiling Mac will appear on your screen.

If instead of a smiling Mac, a frowning Mac appears on your screen, you need to do one of two things:

- If you have an external hard drive, turn off your Mac, turn on the external hard drive, and then turn your Mac back on.

8

1

- If you don't have a hard drive, insert into the disk drive slot the System disk that came with your Macintosh, then restart your Mac.

You cannot proceed until the smiling Mac appears.

Looking at Your Desktop

After the smiling Mac goes away, you will see the opening Macintosh screen, or *desktop*. The desktop contains icons, or pictures, that represent either your floppy diskette or your hard disk and the Trash Can (which is used to delete files or eject disks). There are also five menus across the top of the screen (Apple, File, Edit, View, and Special). If you are running System 7, an additional menu, Label, will appear.

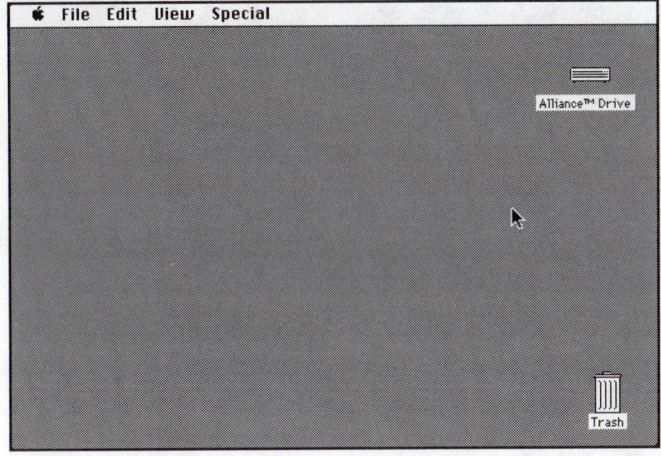

This is what a typical desktop might look like.

The Macintosh operating system is called the Finder. The Finder is the program that creates your desktop, shows you where your files are located, copies files from icon to icon, dictates what your desktop looks like, and much more. Although you may be unaware of it, you are continually using the Finder every time you work with your Macintosh.

Using the Mouse

The mouse is used to select menu items or icons on your desktop, as well as perform several other functions. If you are using your Macintosh for the first time, it may take you a little while to get used to the mouse, but don't worry. Before long the mouse will feel like an extension of your hand!

1

Practice moving the mouse around a flat surface or on a mouse pad if you have one. As you move the mouse, the mouse pointer (the arrow you see on the screen) moves in the same direction. To perform some basic operations using the mouse, follow these steps:

1. Position the mouse pointer onto the disk icon. Press and release the mouse button once very fast. This technique is called *clicking* the mouse. The icon becomes darkened, meaning that it is selected. When you select an icon, your next action will apply to that icon.

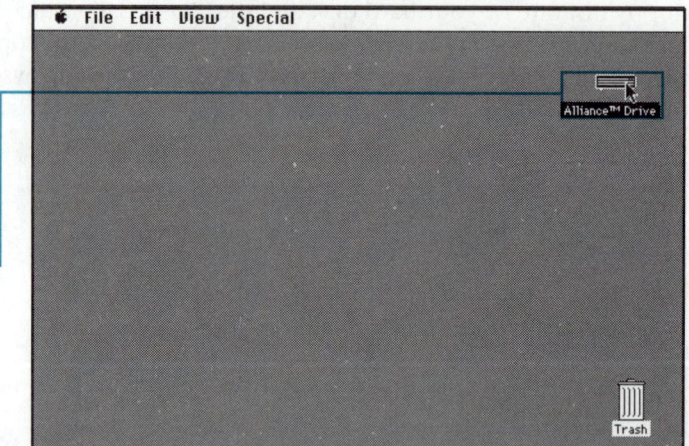

Here, the hard disk icon is selected.

2. Move the mouse pointer off the icon. Click the mouse again to deselect the icon.

3. Click the mouse twice in rapid succession on the disk icon. This technique is called *double-clicking*. When you double-click the mouse, it performs a different function. For example, double-clicking an icon opens its window (see "Opening and Closing Windows").

Using Menus

When you first start your Macintosh, the desktop will have five menus (or six with System 7) across the top of the screen. These menus include the Apple menu, the File menu, the Edit menu, the View menu, the Label menu under System 7, and the Special menu. These menus contain options you can use with items on your desktop.

10

To view a menu's contents, position the mouse pointer over the menu title, and then press and hold down the mouse button. This process is called *pulling down* a menu. Available menu choices appear in black letters, and unavailable ones appear in grey. Depending on the exact location of your mouse pointer or the process you are in, certain menu items will be available and others will not.

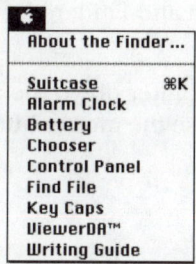

This is the Apple menu.

This is the File menu.

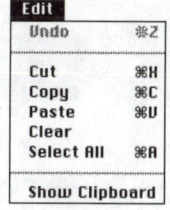

This is the Edit menu.

This is the View menu.

1

This is the Special
menu.

Depending on what version of the System and Finder you have, these menus
can contain slightly different items.

To select a menu item, drag the mouse pointer down the menu until the
item you want is highlighted. Then, release the mouse button. Dragging is
described in the text that follows.

Moving or Dragging Icons

Dragging is an essential operation when working with the Macintosh, and with
HyperCard in particular. You can drag (or move) icons, windows, or other
objects anywhere on your desktop. To drag an icon, follow these steps:

1. Position the mouse pointer on top of the Trash Can icon. Click the
   mouse once to select the icon.

2. Press and hold down the mouse button. Move the mouse while
   holding down the button. As you move the mouse, the icon's outline
   moves. This process is called *dragging*.

Here, the Trash
Can icon is
dragged across
the screen.

3. Release the mouse button. The icon appears in a new location.

Opening and Closing Windows

When you open an icon, the icon's window appears. Inside the window, you see more icons representing the files stored on that disk. You can have several windows open on the screen at one time.

Follow these steps to open and then close a window:

1. To open the disk icon window, you can double-click the icon itself, as explained previously. Or, click the icon to select it, then pull down the File menu and select Open.

2. To close a window, pull down the File menu and select Close. Or, move the mouse pointer inside the little box in the upper left corner of the window and click the mouse once. This box is called the close box.

Click the mouse inside the close box to close the window.

Moving a Window

To move a window, position the mouse pointer on the lined title bar at the top of the window. Press and hold down the mouse button, and then drag the window wherever you want.

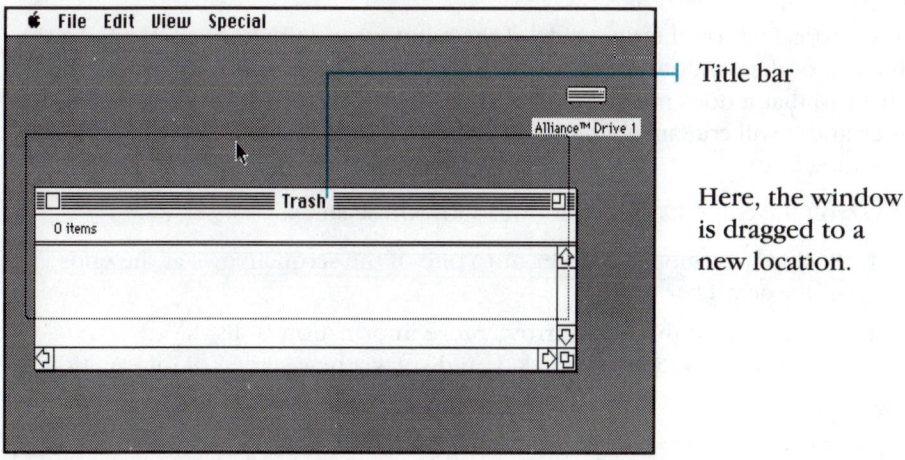

Title bar

Here, the window is dragged to a new location.

1

Changing a Window's Size

You can make any window on your desktop smaller or larger by clicking the *zoom box* in the upper right corner of the window. You also can use the *size box* in the lower right corner of the window.

To change a window's size, position the mouse pointer onto the size box in the lower right corner of the window. Press and hold down the mouse button, and then drag the window in any direction to change its size. When you click the zoom box, the window's size alternates between the maximum size possible and the size you have set.

Use the size box to make a window smaller or larger.

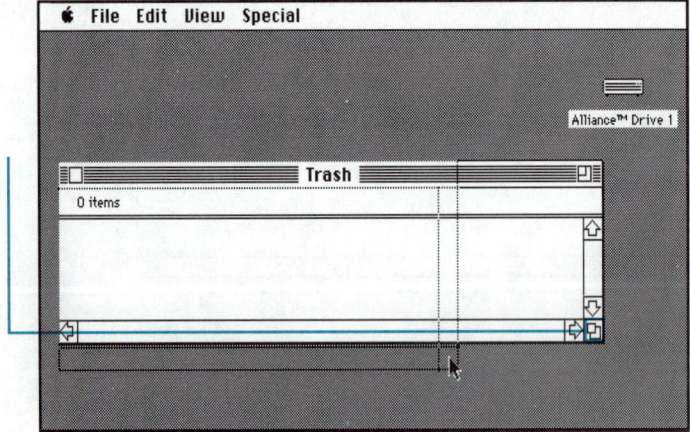

Scrolling

The vertical bar on the right side of the window and the horizontal bar on the bottom of the window are called the *scroll bars*. If you make a window too small so that it does not show all of its contents, the scroll bar will become grey and it will contain a white box (called the *scroll box*) below the upward-pointing arrow.

To scroll the contents of a window, follow these steps:

1. Position the mouse pointer onto one of the scroll arrows at the ends of the scroll bar.

2. Click once on the scroll arrow. More information is displayed in the window. Each time you click, you display a new screen of information.

You also can position the mouse pointer on the scroll arrow and hold down the mouse button to scroll continuously. The upward-pointing arrow scrolls backward through the contents, and the downward-pointing arrow scrolls forward.

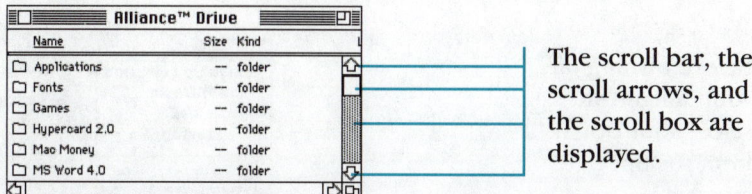

The scroll bar, the scroll arrows, and the scroll box are displayed.

3. You also can drag the scroll box up or down on the vertical scroll bar or to the right or left on the horizontal scroll bar. The information in the window moves in the same direction in an amount relative to the distance you drag the scroll box.

Opening Multiple Windows

You can have several windows open on your desktop at one time (limited by the amount of memory your Macintosh has). When you click inside one window, that window becomes "active," meaning that you can work with the icons in that window. Only one window can be active at one time. You can tell which window is currently active by the greyed title bar. The title bars of inactive windows are white.

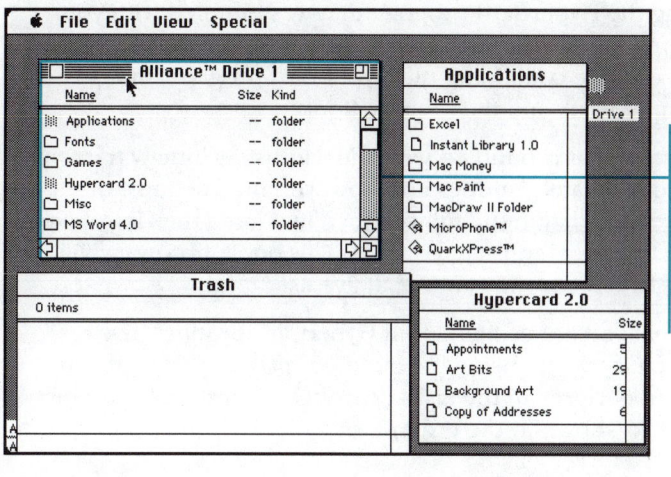

You can have several windows open at one time, but only one window can be "active" at one time.

1

Ending Your Session

It's always a good idea to end your work session by quitting the program in which you are working. Then, pull down the Special menu and select Shut Down.

Before turning off
your Macintosh,
select Shut Down
from the Special
menu.

Using Bundled HyperCard

If you purchased HyperCard 2.0 (or greater) from Claris (or an Apple dealer), you received a set of five diskettes:

- HyperCard Program
- HyperCard Tour
- HyperCard Stacks
- HyperCard More Stacks
- HyperCard Help

Since 1987, Apple has been shipping HyperCard with every new Macintosh. The materials (stacks) included with HyperCard have changed slightly over the years. If you are using the HyperCard program that was bundled with your Macintosh and you purchased your Mac after October 1990, you received one HyperCard program diskette containing the HyperCard program and two stacks: the Appointment Book and the Address Book.

The HyperCard program that is bundled with a Macintosh is exactly the same as the one that is sold separately. It does not, however, include most of the sample stacks that are included in the full product, including the Help stack. Also, only two of the five user levels are enabled. This book, however, will show you some "magic" so that you can use all five user levels.

This book assumes that you are using the full HyperCard product (five diskettes). However, even if you are using the bundled version of HyperCard, you will still be able to perform all the tasks described in this book; you just won't have all the stacks shown in the examples.

1

If you are using the bundled version, you can purchase the complete set of disks for about $50. Contact your local Claris dealer (1-800-628-2100) and ask for the HyperCard upgrade kit.

In the meantime, to enable your bundled version of HyperCard, perform the following steps:

1. If HyperCard is not yet installed, install HyperCard as explained in Appendix A of this book.

2. Double-click the HyperCard icon to start the program.

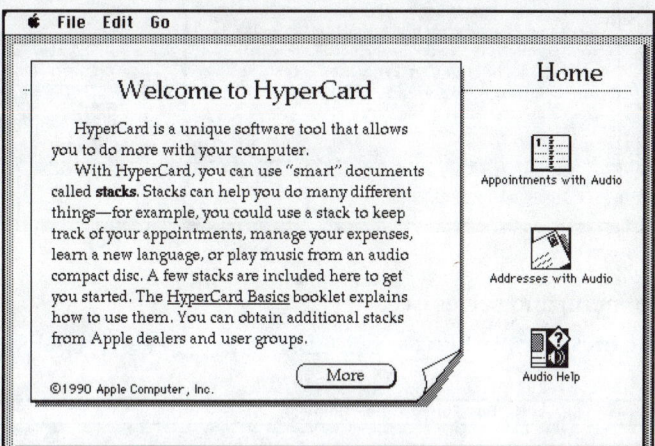

The HyperCard opening screen, or Home card, will appear. This Home card is different from the Home card of the complete product.

3. Pull down the Go menu and select Message.

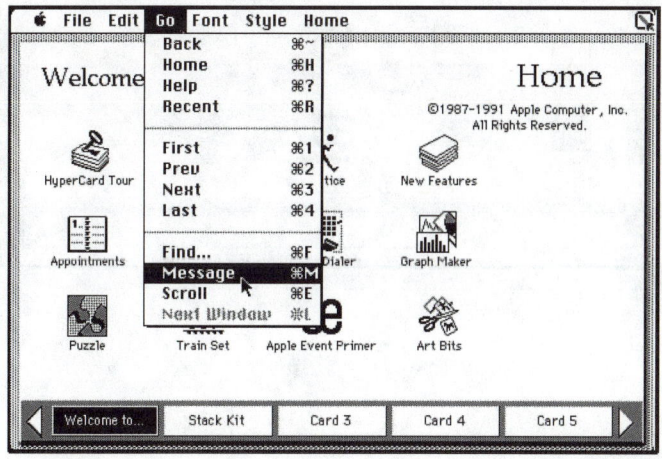

Here, the Message option is selected from the Go menu.

1

4. Type **set userlevel to 5** in the message box that appears. Press Return

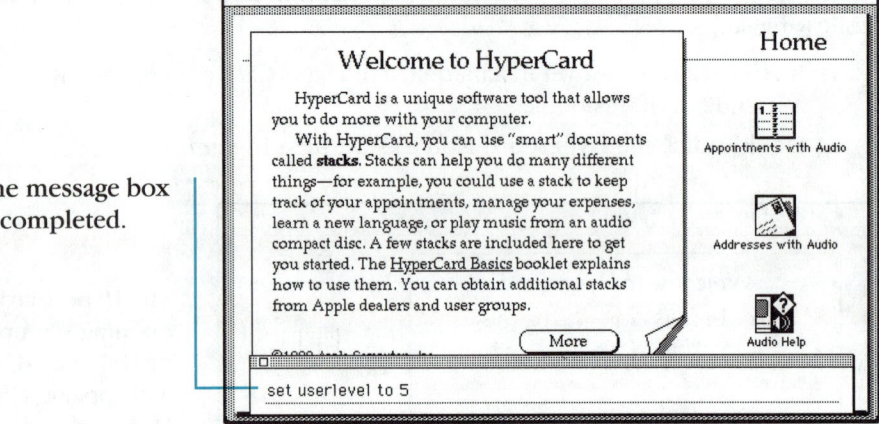

The message box is completed.

5. Pull down the Go menu and select Last.

6. Type **magic** in the message box. Press Return

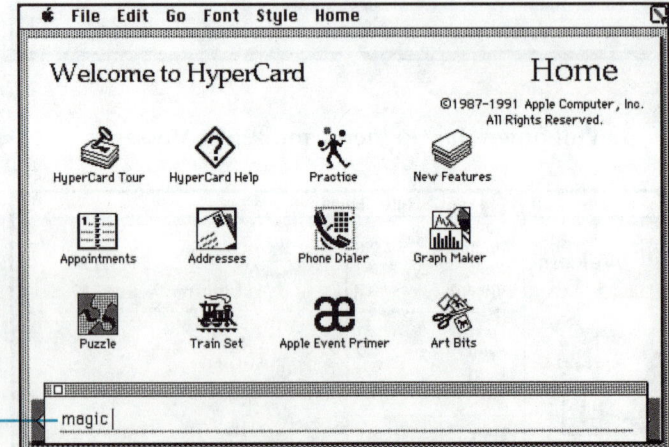

The message box is completed.

1

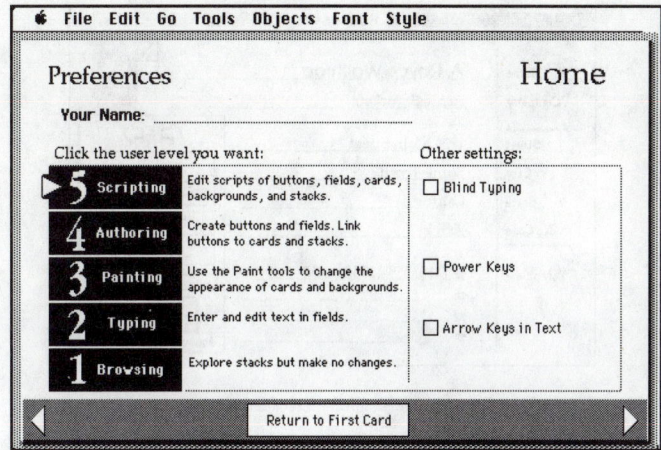

Your program is now fully enabled, and the User Preference levels are revealed.

7. Pull down the Go menu and select Home.

You are back to the opening screen of HyperCard, the Home card. Now that you have enabled your program, you have full access to HyperCard's tools and capabilities so that you can perform the tasks described throughout this book.

Learning Basic HyperCard Terms and Concepts

Before you launch into the world of HyperCard, you need to understand a few key terms used throughout the program and this book. Don't be concerned if you don't fully understand these terms right now. As you move through the exercises in this book, the terms will become clearer.

What Is a Card?

A card is HyperCard's basic unit of information. A card is much like a 3-by-5-inch index card. A card in HyperCard, however, can contain text information, graphics, sound, animation, or any combination thereof. A card can fill the entire screen, or you can display a card on just part of the screen in a window. Each card consists of three basic components: a background, fields, and buttons.

1

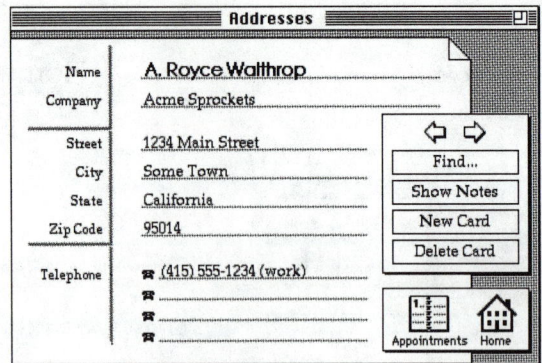

Here is an example of what a card might look like.

What Is a Background?

Every card has a background. The background of a card is what you see before you enter any information on the card. The background contains a set of elements (buttons, fields, text, or pictures) that is shared by more than one card in the stack.

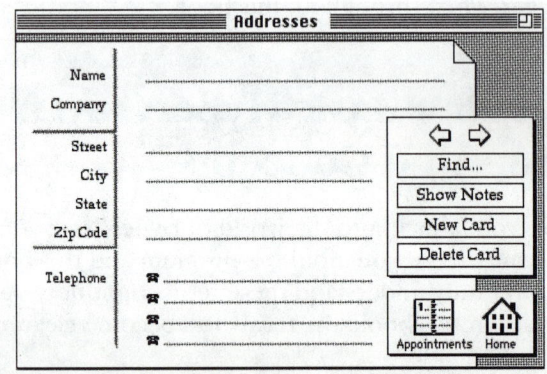

For example, on a company inventory stack, the background might contain the company name and address, or even a picture.

With the company name and address in the background, you don't have to reenter the same information on every card in the stack.

The background might also contain a button to take you to another stack regardless of which card you may be viewing.

What Is a Field?

A field is the area (or areas) on a card that contains textual information that most likely changes from card to card.

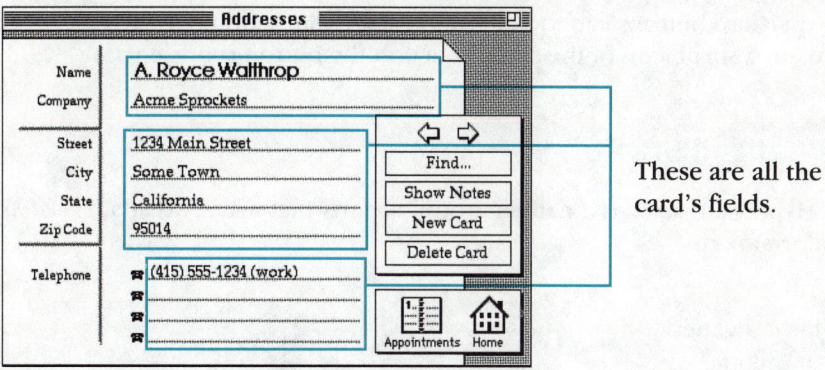

These are all the card's fields.

Fields can be included on all cards that share the same background (a "background field"), or they can be unique to a certain card. Text typed into a card field is always unique to that card. Text typed into a background field can be unique to a particular card in that background or shared by all the cards in the background.

Text fields, in general, are rectangular areas on a card. You can use one of five field styles: transparent, opaque, rectangle, shadow, and scrolling.

What Is a Button?

At least one button usually appears on each card. When you click a button, something happens. (Unlike most other Macintosh programs, you only need to click *once* to activate buttons.) You might go to another card or stack, or the button might perform a separate function on its own, such as dialing a phone or calculating a figure.

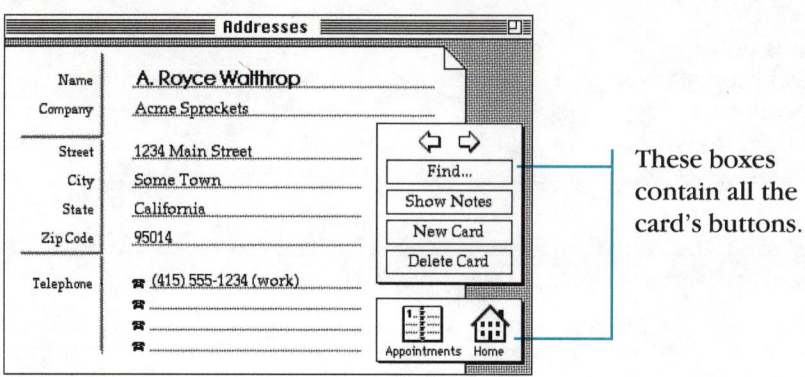

These boxes contain all the card's buttons.

21

1

HyperCard buttons can look like almost anything, from a conventional check box to a small icon of the stack or action the button represents.

What Is a Stack?

A HyperCard stack is a named group of cards that usually contain related information.

This is a generic stack icon.

Each stack is actually a separate Macintosh disk file and is represented by a stack icon in the Finder.

A stack can contain several backgrounds. A background can contain several cards. A card can contain several buttons and several fields.

What Is the Browse Tool?

The Browse tool is the little hand with the pointing finger you see when you move the mouse through cards and stacks. The Browse tool may change its appearance depending on its location in a card. For example, when the Browse tool is on a text entry field in a card, it turns into an I-beam cursor, which tells you that you can type text. When the Browse tool is moved up to the menu line, it turns into a pointing arrow so that you can select a menu item.

This is how the Browse tool appears on a card's buttons.

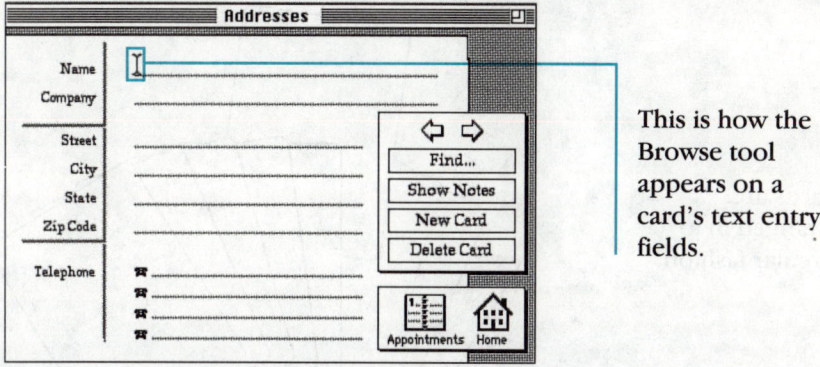

This is how the Browse tool appears on a card's text entry fields.

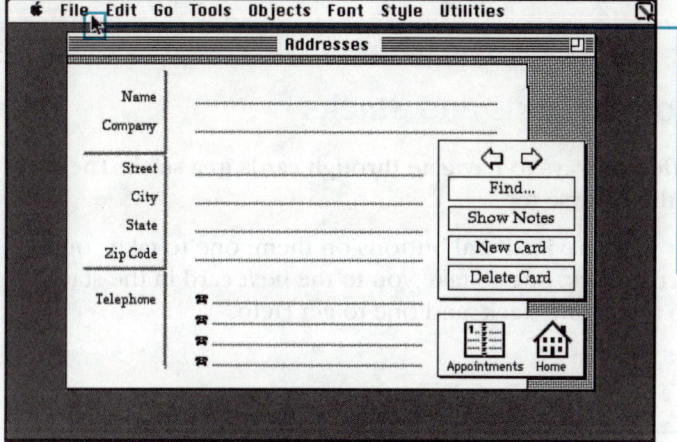

This is how the Browse tool appears on menu line items.

How Cards Are Arranged

Cards are arranged in a stack in a circular fashion. This means that moving from one card to the next will eventually bring you back to the first card. Think of your stack of 3-by-5-inch cards. After you look at the first card, you put it on the bottom of the stack and look at the second card, and so on. After you have looked at all the cards in the stack, the first card appears again on the top of the stack. Cards are in the order in which they were entered, unless the cards have been sorted.

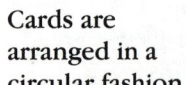

Cards are
arranged in a
circular fashion.

Navigating through Cards and Stacks

There are several different ways to navigate through cards in a stack. The most convenient is using the Browse tool.

Most cards have four main navigational buttons on them: one to take you to the previous card in the stack, one to take you to the next card in the stack, one to return you to the Home stack, and one to get Help.

Help button ——————————————

Home button ——————————————

These are the four
main buttons on
most cards.

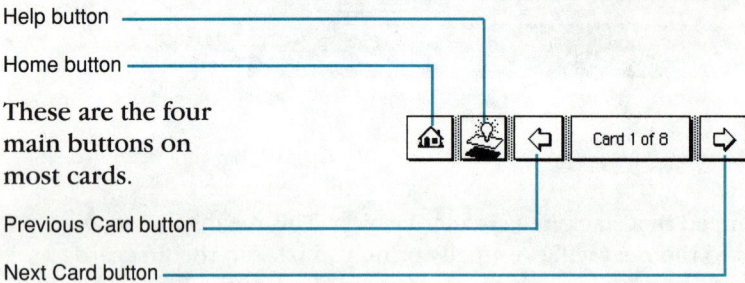

Previous Card button ———————————————

Next Card button ———————————————

What Is HyperTalk?

HyperTalk is the programming language of HyperCard. You can use the HyperTalk language to write programs (called *scripts*) for more advanced stacks.

Summary

This chapter introduced you to the basics of HyperCard and your Macintosh computer. You learned how HyperCard is organized and how to enable the HyperCard program that was bundled with your new Macintosh. You learned the basic terms and concepts of HyperCard, as well as the basics of your desktop and how to work with icons and windows. You also learned how to use the mouse (or, in some cases, menus) to open, close, move, size, and scroll through windows.

Specifically, you learned the following key information about HyperCard and your Macintosh:

- HyperCard is divided into five user levels: Browsing, Typing, Painting, Authoring, and Scripting.

- When you first start your Macintosh, you must first see a smiling Mac in the center of your screen before you can proceed. After the smiling Mac goes away, you will see the opening Macintosh screen, or desktop. It contains icons, or pictures, that represent your floppy diskette or your hard disk and the Trash Can.

- The mouse is used to select menu items or icons on your desktop.

- To move or drag an icon, position the mouse pointer on top of the icon. Pressing and holding down the mouse button, move the mouse. As you move the mouse, the icon's outline moves with it.

- To open an icon's window, select the icon and then select Open from the File menu. Or, you can double-click the icon to open its window.

- To close a window, select the Close option from the File menu. Or, click the upper left corner box, the close box.

- To change a window's size, click the zoom box in the upper right corner of the window. Or, click the size box in the lower right corner of the window.

- To scroll through a window, click the scroll arrow. To scroll continuously, keep the mouse button pressed down.

- To make a window active when more than one window is open on your desktop, click anywhere in the window.

- To enable your bundled version of HyperCard, go to the last card, which is the Preferences card, and type set userlevel to 5 in the message box. Then, type magic in the message box.

- A card is HyperCard's basic unit of information. Each card is made up of three basic components: background, fields, and buttons. Cards are arranged in a stack in a circular fashion.

1

■ The background of a card is what you see before you enter any information on the card.

■ A field is the area (or areas) on a card that contains textual information.

■ A button is an area on the card that will perform an action when you click it.

■ A HyperCard stack is a named group of cards that usually contain related information.

■ The Browse tool is the little hand with the pointing finger you see when you move the mouse through cards and stacks. The Browse tool may change its appearance depending on its location in a card.

■ To navigate through cards and stacks, you can use the Browse tool to click a navigation button. Most cards have four main navigational buttons on them: one to take you to the previous card in the stack, one to take you to the next card in the stack, one to return you to the Home stack, and one to get Help.

Now that you have a general idea of what HyperCard is all about, it's time to move on and actually take a look at some of the stacks that came with your program. So turn on your Mac, relax, and move on to Chapter 2.

Getting Started with HyperCard

This chapter introduces you to the first level of HyperCard, Browsing. *Browsing* means that you have the ability to view any HyperCard stack, whether it is one that comes with the HyperCard program or one you acquire elsewhere. You do not, however, have the ability to make changes to the stack. So, for example, if you are browsing through the Address Book stack, you will not be able to enter any of your own addresses or edit the addresses already included. You will only be able to view the information that has already been entered for you.

In this chapter, you will learn how to move through cards and stacks. You also will take a look at some of the stacks that came with HyperCard, learn how to centralize your HyperCard activities through the Home stack, and learn to access Help.

You do not need to have any prior knowledge of Hyper-Card before beginning this chapter. However, you do need to have the program installed. If you have not yet installed HyperCard, go to Appendix A and install HyperCard. Then, return to this chapter.

Starting HyperCard

Using the Home stack

Opening more than one stack

Getting Help

Going Home

Taking the HyperCard tour

Browsing through the Address Book

2

Key Terms in This Chapter

Browsing	The first user level of HyperCard. Browsing means that you have the ability to view any HyperCard stack you may have. You cannot make any changes to the stack, however. Browsing means essentially "look but don't touch."
Home stack	The most important stack in HyperCard. The Home stack is where you first start out. It will most likely be your central base of operations while you are working with HyperCard. The Home stack consists of nine cards.
Home cards	There are five Home cards in the Home stack. These cards can function like indexes to your HyperCard environment. They contain icons (which are actually buttons) that take you to the stacks you use most often. Initially, three of the five Home cards are empty.
Search Paths cards	Whenever you tell HyperCard to open a particular stack, application, or document, HyperCard looks through your hard disk or floppy disk to locate the item you selected. The routing list (or path) is maintained automatically in the Search Paths cards.
Preferences card	Where you set your desired user level. Initially, the user level in the Preferences card is set to Typing.
Key combinations	Two or more keys pressed at the same time to perform a particular function. Nearly every menu item in Hyper-Card has a corresponding key combination that appears next to the menu item.
Recent command	A command found in the Go menu that enables you to display a miniaturized version of up to the last 42 cards you viewed (in any stack). Then, by clicking any card, you immediately go to that card.

Starting HyperCard

To start the HyperCard program after it has been installed, perform the following steps:

1. Move the mouse pointer onto the HyperCard icon and click once.

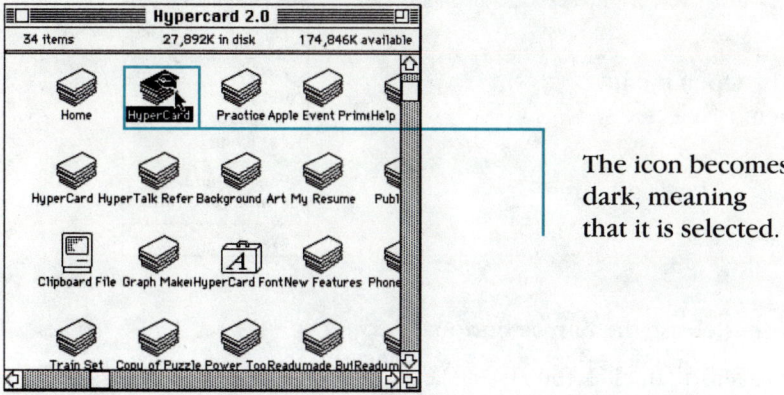

The icon becomes
dark, meaning
that it is selected.

2. Move the mouse pointer onto the word File at the top of the screen
   and hold down the mouse button to reveal the File menu. This
   process is called *pulling down* a menu.

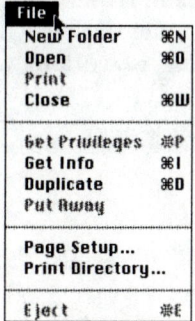

The File menu is
pulled down.

3. Holding the mouse button down, move the mouse pointer down the
   menu until the word Open is highlighted. This process is called *selecting* a menu item.

29

2

The Open menu
item is selected.

4. Release the mouse button.

As a shortcut, click the HyperCard icon twice in rapid succession to start the
program. This technique is called *double-clicking*.

Using the Home Stack

The Home stack is the most important stack in HyperCard. In fact, HyperCard
will not work without a Home stack. The Home stack is where you start. It will
be your central base of operations while you are working with HyperCard.

When you start
HyperCard, you
see the first card,
or the *Home
card*, of the
Home stack.

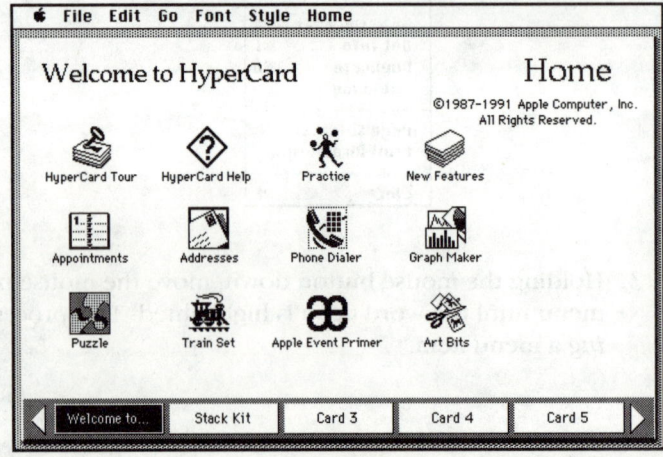

30

2

The little hand with the pointing finger that moves across the screen when you move your mouse is called the *Browse tool*.

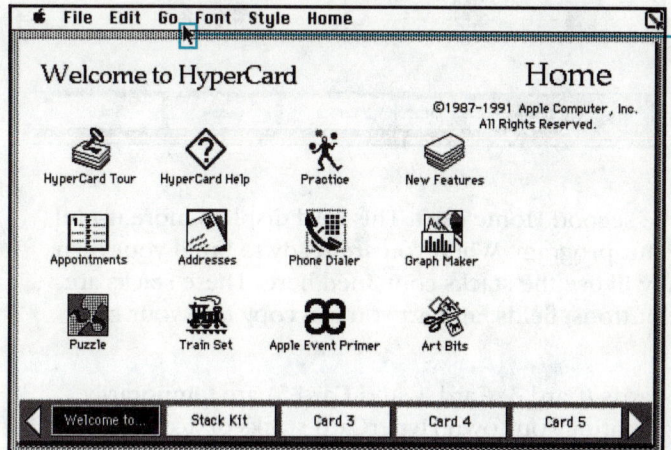

When you move the Browse tool over the menu line at the top of the screen, the little hand turns into a pointing arrow.

The Home stack consists of nine cards: five Home cards, three Search Paths cards, and the Preferences card. You will learn more about each of these cards as you continue reading this chapter.

Understanding the Home Cards

There are five Home cards supplied with HyperCard. The Welcome to Hyper-Card Home card is the first one (the one on your screen right now if you followed the preceding steps). This card displays icons for the stacks you use most often. Each icon is actually a button that will take you to the stack it represents. So, in essence, the Home cards function like indexes to your HyperCard stacks.

31

2

On the bottom of each Home card are rectangular buttons that will take you to the other Home cards.

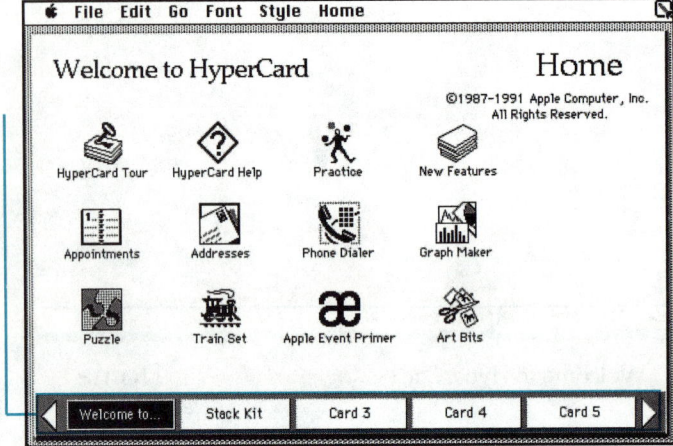

The Stack Kit card is the second Home card. This card displays more useful stacks provided with your program. When you are ready to build your own HyperCard stacks, you will use the stacks contained here. These stacks are filled with readymade buttons, fields, and art you can copy into your own stacks.

The next three Home cards (Card 3, Card 4, and Card 5) are temporarily blank. When you start creating your own HyperCard stacks or acquire other HyperCard stacks, you can copy your new stack icons into one of these cards so that you can access the new stacks quickly and easily. HyperCard has given you plenty of room for you to add your own stacks, but if you do run out of room, you can always add more Home cards to display more stacks.

Moving through a Stack

There are several different ways to move through cards in a stack. You can use the Browse tool and click the navigational buttons; you can pull down the Go menu and select one of the various options to move from card to card; you can use the left- and right-arrow keys on the keyboard to move from one card to the next in sequence; or, you can press certain keyboard combinations to move from one place to the next.

Using the Left- and Right-Arrow Buttons

The most convenient way to move through a stack is by using the left- and right-arrow buttons. These buttons are usually located near the bottom of a card. To move through the cards in the Home stack, perform the following steps:

1. Place the Browse tool onto the right-arrow button at the bottom of the card and click the mouse button once.

2

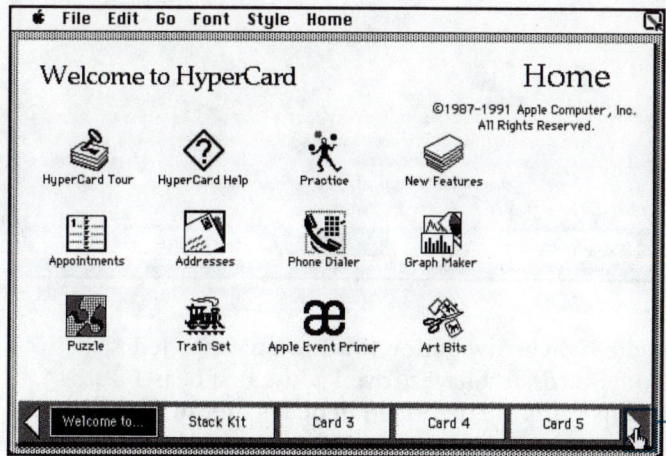

Here, the right-arrow button is being clicked.

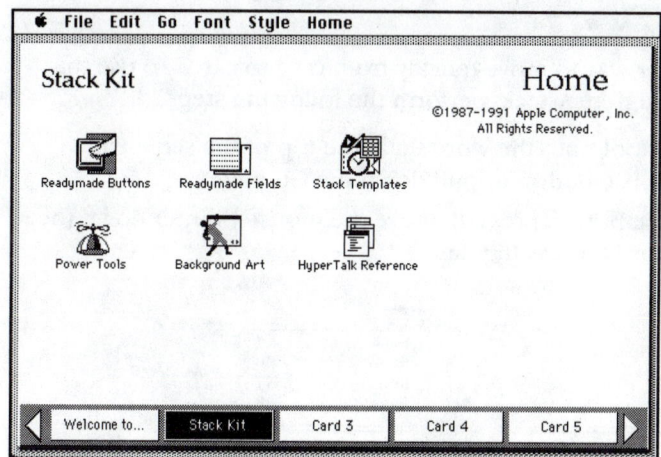

The second Home card, called *Stack Kit*, is displayed.

2. Click the Card 3 button at the bottom of the Stack Kit card to move to the third Home card.

2

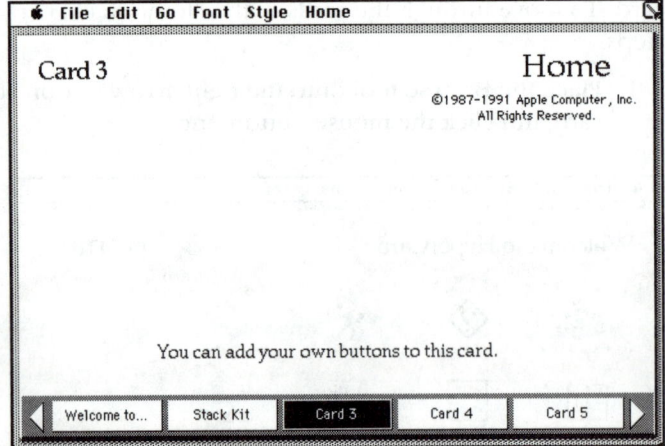

The third card is empty, but you will add buttons to it as you progress through this book.

3. Continue clicking the right-arrow button until you have cycled through all five Home cards and have arrived at the first Search Paths card. The Search Paths cards are described in detail later in this chapter.

Using the Go Menu

The Go menu is another way to move quickly from card to card. To use the Go menu to move through the stack, perform the following steps:

1. Move the Browse tool onto the word Go at the top of the screen and hold down the mouse button to pull down the Go menu.

2. Keeping the mouse button pressed, move the mouse pointer down the menu until the word Last is highlighted.

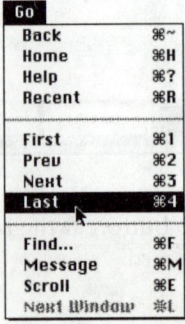

Here, the Last menu item is selected.

You will go to the last card in the Home stack, which is the Preferences card.

3. Pull down the Go menu again and select First to go back to the first card in the Home stack, which is the Home card.

4. Pull down the Go menu again and select Next to go to the next card in the Home stack, which is the Stack Kit card.

The Recent command in the Go menu is another handy way to see where you have been. With this command, you can go back quickly to a particular card. HyperCard keeps track of each card you go to and maintains in memory at all times the last 42 cards you have viewed. To use the Recent command, perform the following steps:

1. Pull down the Go menu and select Recent.

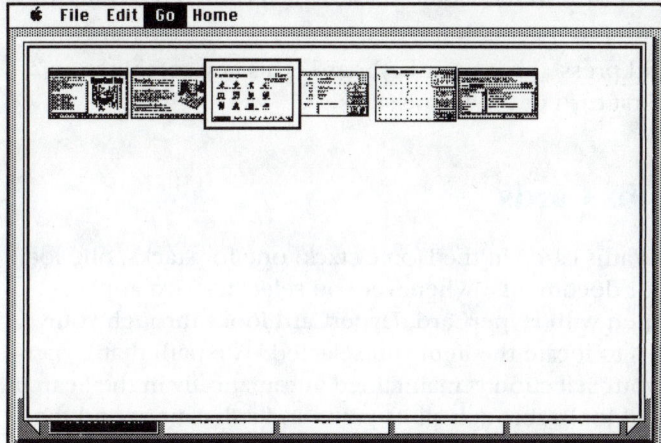

You see a minia-turized version of (up to) the last 42 cards you have viewed. The current card has a white box around it.

2. Click any miniature card in the display to go to that particular card.

3. Pull down the Go menu again and select Home to return to the first Home card.

Using Key Combinations

Nearly every menu item in HyperCard has a corresponding key combination that appears next to the menu line item. Key combinations are two or more keys pressed at the same time to perform a particular function. To use the key combinations in the Go menu, perform the following steps:

1. Pull down the Go menu.

2

The key combinations appear next to each menu line item.

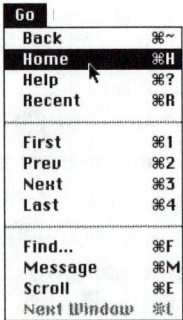

2. Release the mouse button to hide the Go menu.

3. Hold down ⌘ and press ④ on your keyboard. This key combination takes you to the Last card in the Home stack, which is the Preferences card.

4. Hold down ⌘ and press ① on your keyboard. This key combination takes you to the First card in the Home stack.

Using Search Paths Cards

There are three Search Paths cards in the Home stack: one for stacks, one for applications, and one for documents. Whenever you select a stack, application, or document to open with HyperCard, HyperCard looks through your hard disk or floppy disks to locate the item you selected. The path that Hyper-Card takes to look for your selection is maintained automatically in the Search Paths cards. If HyperCard looks through all its paths and still cannot find the stack, application, or document you want to open, a dialog box appears, and HyperCard asks you to help locate the item.

This is the dialog box that appears when HyperCard cannot find the stack, application, or document.

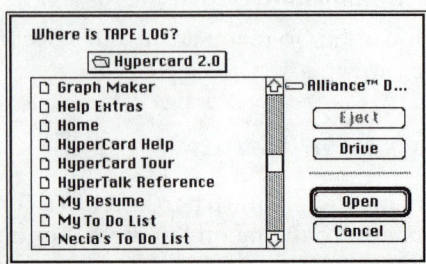

After you locate the item, HyperCard will remember where you found it and add that path to the list of path names in the appropriate Search Paths card. Next time you select the stack, application, or document, HyperCard will not need your assistance locating the item.

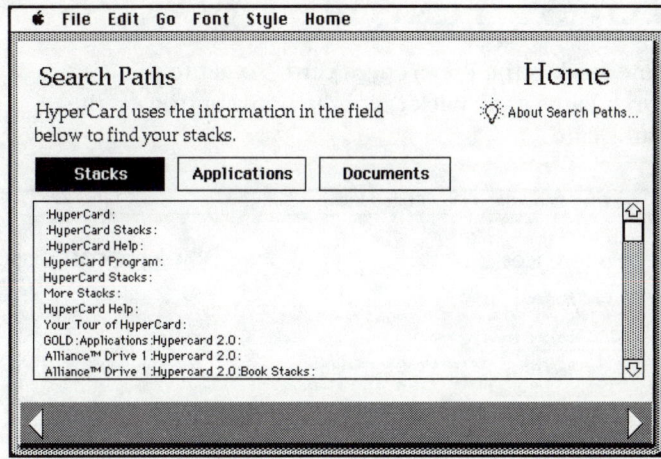

The Search Paths cards lists all the possible disks and folders Hyper-Card will search for your stacks, applications, and documents.

To read more about Search Paths, perform the following steps:

1. Move the Browse tool over the light bulb icon located in the upper right corner of the card.

Here, the Browse tool is positioned properly over the light bulb.

2. Click the light bulb and read the information displayed.

3. Click the area marked click here to go back to the Search Paths card.

To move through the Search Paths cards, perform the following steps:

1. Place the Browse tool onto the middle button labeled Applications and click the mouse button once to list all the disks and folders HyperCard will search for applications.

2. Click the right button labeled Documents to list all the disks and folders HyperCard will search for other documents.

2

This list of path names may be empty now. As you use your HyperCard program, the program will automatically generate and maintain these Search Paths lists.

Understanding the Preferences Card

The last card in the Home stack is the Preferences card. To get to the Preferences card from the Search Paths card, click the right-arrow button on the bottom of the Search Paths card.

The Preferences card is now displayed.

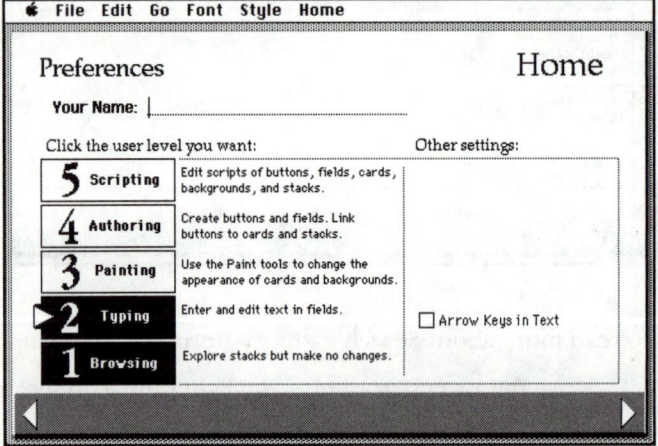

The Preferences card is where you set your user level. There are five different user levels of HyperCard. Initially, the user level is set to Typing, which is one of the most basic levels. As you grow comfortable with HyperCard, you can move on to the next level, revealing more menus, commands, and capabilities.

To change the user level, move the Browse tool over the button labeled 1 Browsing and click once. The user level is now set to Browsing, disabling all text editing capabilities.

Opening More Than One Stack

If your Macintosh has enough memory, you can open more than one stack at a time. Each stack you open will replace the one currently on your screen, unless you select the Open in New Window option. You may find it helpful to

2

keep the HyperCard Help stack open on one corner of your screen while you are working with another stack. To keep the HyperCard Help stack open, follow these steps:

1. Pull down the File menu and select Open Stack.

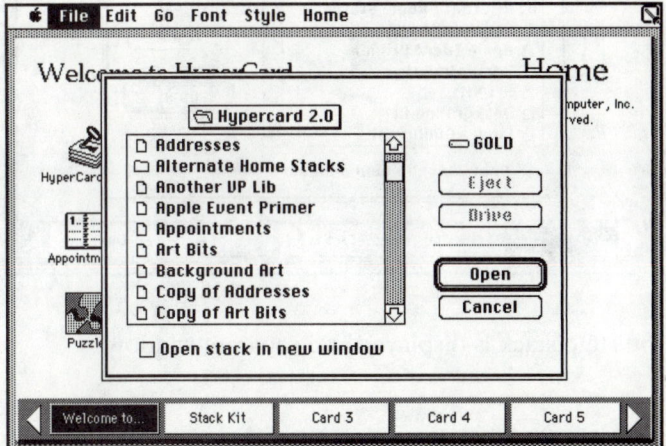

A list of the stacks in the current folder is displayed.

2. Move the mouse pointer down until the Help stack is selected. Or, press [H] on your keyboard to see the first entry in the list that starts with the letter H.

3. Click the box labeled Open stack in new window to open the stack in a new window and not replace the window you currently have open.

4. Click the Open button.

Note: If the stack you want to open is not in the current folder displayed, move the mouse pointer onto the Folder icon and, keeping the mouse button pressed, select the folder from which you want the stacks to be displayed.

2

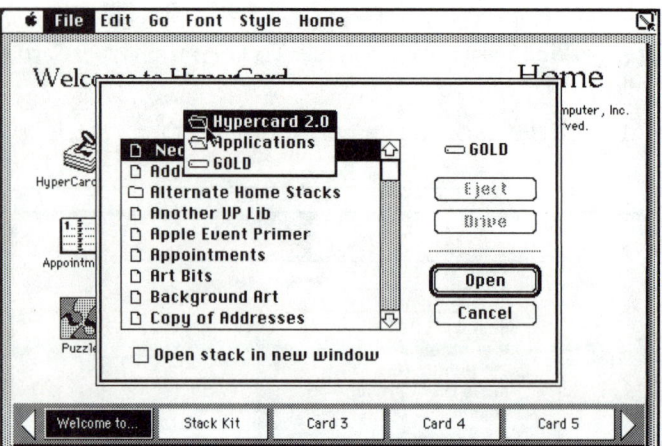

The Folder icon is shown here.

The first card of the Help stack is displayed in a separate window.

Getting Help

From anywhere in the HyperCard program, Help is one mouse click away. If you are on the Home card, you can click the HyperCard Help Stack icon. You also can open the Help stack by following the previous steps, pulling down the Go menu and selecting Help, or even using the ⌘-? key combination.

Each card in HyperCard Help is arranged in a similar manner. There is a list of topics on the left side of the card. When you click any one of the topics, a more detailed list (or information about the topic) appears on the right side.

The first card of the Help stack should now be on your screen. To use the Help stack, follow these steps:

1. Click the HyperCard Basics line on the left side of the card.

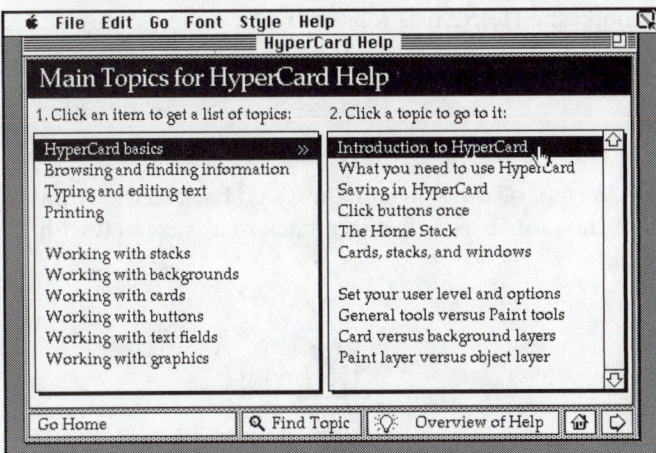

For each topic you click on the left side of the screen, an accompanying list of topics appears on the right.

2. Click the Introduction to HyperCard line on the right side of the card. The Introduction card appears.

3. When you have finished reading the Introduction card, click the right-arrow button on the bottom of the card to move to the next card. Or, click the Main Topics button to go back to the Main Topics card.

You also can click the Find Topic button at the bottom of the card. You can select from the list of subjects on the left side of the card by clicking the subject and then selecting the topic from the list displayed on the right side of the card. Also, you can type any subject in the Subject field, and then click the Find button to display the list of topics from which to choose.

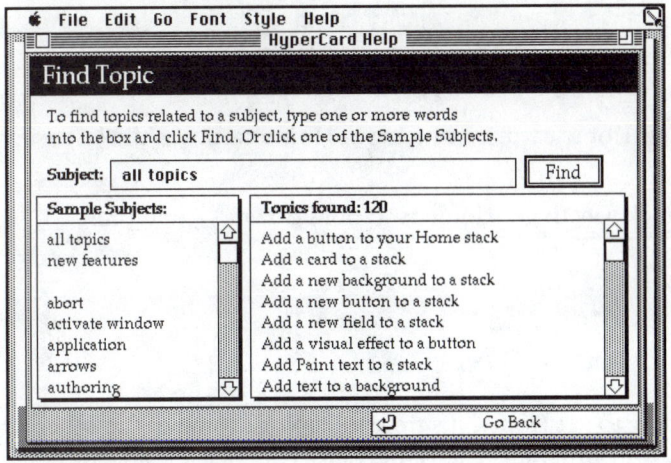

Alternatively, you can type **all topics**, as shown here.

Then, click your way through the Help cards related to the topic.

2 Going Home

No matter where you are in HyperCard, you can always go back to the Home stack with a single click of the mouse. Nearly every stack that is created with HyperCard has a Home button.

The Home button
is usually repre-
sented by an icon
of a house.

Even if the card you are viewing does not have a Home button, going Home is still just one click away. To go Home from where you are now, pull down the Go menu and select Home.

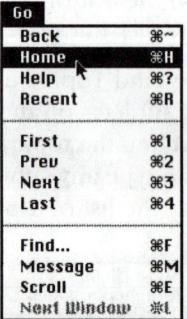

Here, the Home
menu item is
selected.

You are back at the first Home card, or whichever Home card was the last one you were viewing.

Shortcut: Another quick way to get Home is to hold down ⌘ and press Ⓗ on your keyboard.

Taking the HyperCard Tour

Now that you know how to get Home, it's time to explore some of the other stacks that came with your program. The HyperCard Tour stack is an excellent place to start. To open the HyperCard Tour stack, perform the following steps:

1. Click the HyperCard Tour Stack icon on your Home card.

HyperCard Tour

The HyperCard Tour Stack icon is shown here.

2. Go through the Tour, and don't be afraid to have a good time. When you have finished, go back Home.

Browsing through the Address Book

The next stack you will browse through is the Address Book stack that came with HyperCard. This is a very handy stack that you can use to maintain an electronic version of your address book.

Addresses

To open the Addresses stack, click the Addresses icon on your Home card.

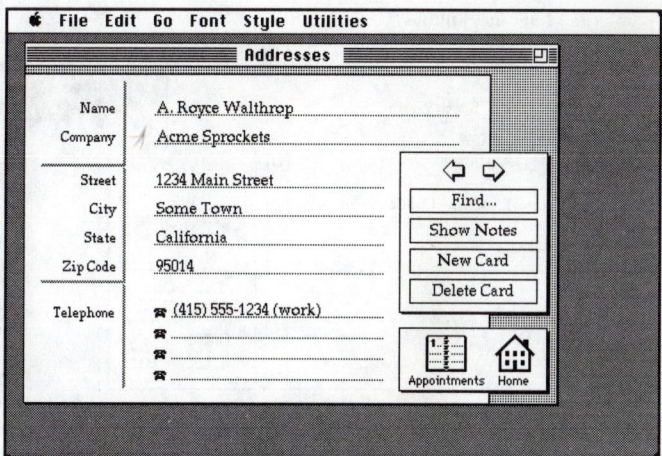

The first card of the Addresses stack appears.

2

The Address Book stack contains two cards with names, addresses, and phone numbers on them. Several buttons on the card serve functions you will learn about in the next chapter. Because your user level is set only to Browsing, you cannot edit or enter new information on these cards yet. To browse through the Addresses stack, follow these steps:

1. Click the right-arrow button to move to the next card.

This is the second card in the Address Book stack.

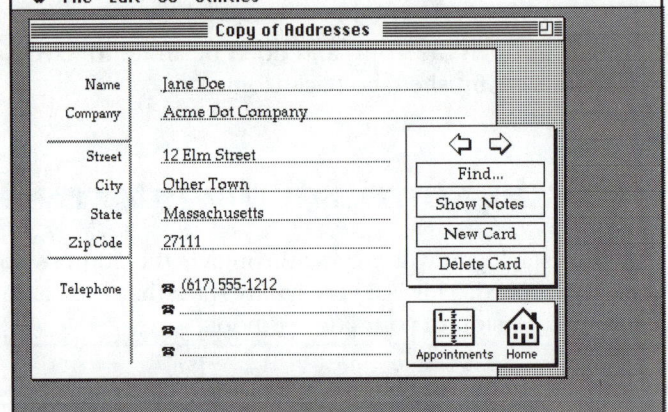

2. Click the Show Notes button. An additional window where you can store information appears.

Click the Hide Notes button to hide this window.

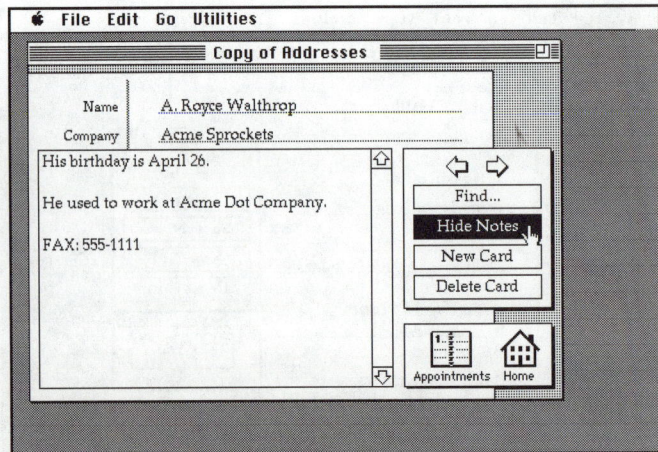

3. Click the Find button. The Find dialog box appears.

4. Type any text you want to look for. Then, click OK.

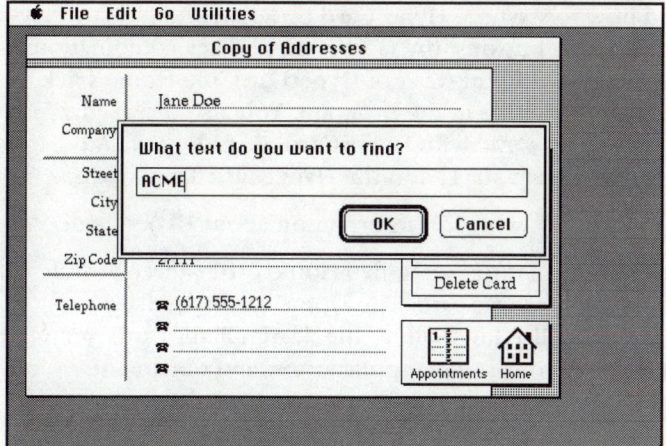

For example, type
ACME in the Find
dialog box.

HyperCard will look through the entire stack and find the first occurrence of the text you enter.

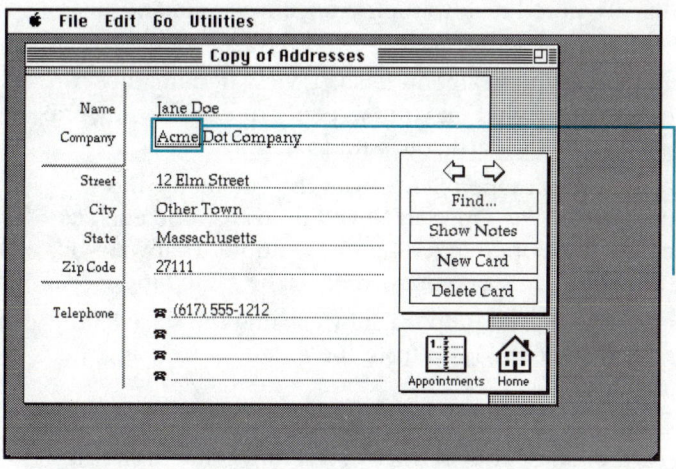

The "found" text
is enclosed in a
rectangle.

5. Each time you press [Return], you will go to the next occurrence of the text you entered, even if the text occurs in the Additional Notes field. Press [Return] until you are back at the first occurrence again.

6. When you are through browsing, click the Home button to go Home.

Summary

2

This chapter showed you how to use the first level of HyperCard, which is Browsing. You learned how to start the HyperCard program and how to move through cards and stacks using buttons, the Go menu, and key combinations. You learned about the most important stack of HyperCard, the Home stack, and how to go Home from anywhere in the program. You also browsed through some of the stacks that came with HyperCard, including the Addresses stack, the HyperCard Help stack, and the HyperCard Tour stack.

Specifically, you learned the following key information about HyperCard:

■ The Home stack consists of nine cards: five Home cards, three Search Paths cards, and the Preferences card. The Home cards are like indexes to the stacks you use most often; the Search Paths cards keep track of where you store your stacks, applications, and documents; and the Preferences card is where you set your user level.

■ To set the user level to Browsing, go to the last card in the Home stack, which is the Preferences card, and click the rectangle labeled Browsing.

■ To move through cards and stacks, you can use the left- and right-arrow buttons, the various options on the Go menu, and the key combinations that are noted next to their respective commands in the Go menu.

■ The Recent command in the Go menu lets you view in miniature (up to) the last 42 cards you viewed on your screen. To return to any one of the cards viewed, click the card you want to go to.

■ To open a new stack, select Open Stack from the File menu and choose the desired stack. The Open in New Window option enables you to have the new stack open in a different window. That way you can view more than one stack on your screen at the same time.

■ You can access the HyperCard Help stack by clicking the stack icon in the Home card, by selecting Help from the menu, or by using the ⌘-? key combination.

■ You can always return to the Home stack by clicking the Home button from whatever card or stack you are in, by selecting Home from the Go menu, or by pressing the ⌘-H key combination.

■ Using the Addresses stack, you can maintain an electronic version of your address book. With the user level set to Browsing, you can look through the cards in the Addresses stack and use the Find button to locate a name or address, but you are unable to make any changes.

Now that you're comfortable browsing through a few of the stacks that came with your HyperCard program (Help, Tour, and Addresses), you are ready to move on to the next level of HyperCard, called *Typing*. At this level, you will be able to enter or edit textual information in any stack you want. When you're ready, move on to Chapter 3, "Using a HyperCard Stack."

2

Using a HyperCard Stack

Up until now, you have been browsing through HyperCard, unable to change or add anything to the cards you view. In this chapter, you will use the second level of HyperCard, *Typing*, to edit, add, and delete cards in a stack. You will use both the Address Book and the Appointment Book stacks that came with HyperCard, and you will add cards to include your own information in these stacks. You also will learn how to change the appearance of text with different fonts and styles, and use HyperCard's searching and sorting capabilities.

3

Key Terms in This Chapter

Typing   The second user level in HyperCard. With your user level set to typing, you are able to edit, add, or delete cards in a stack.

Addresses stack   The Address Book stack came with your HyperCard program. With it, you can maintain an electronic version of your personal or professional address book.

Appointment Book stack   The Appointment Book stack came with your HyperCard program. With it, you can keep track of daily, weekly, or monthly appointments electronically. You also can set the Appointment Book stack to print pages for your physical appointment book.

Save a Copy   An important command found in the Hyper-Card File menu. This command enables you to save a copy of any stack you're working on under a new name.

Font menu   A menu that lists all the fonts you can use to change the appearance of text in your card.

Style menu   A menu that lists all the styles you can use to change the appearance of the selected fonts.

Setting the User Level to Typing

In Chapter 2 you were introduced to the Preferences card, where you set your user level to Browsing. To change the user level to Typing, follow these steps:

1. With the Home card on your screen, click the left-arrow button to go to the Preferences card (or select Last from the Go menu).

2. Move the Browse tool onto the button labeled Typing and click once.

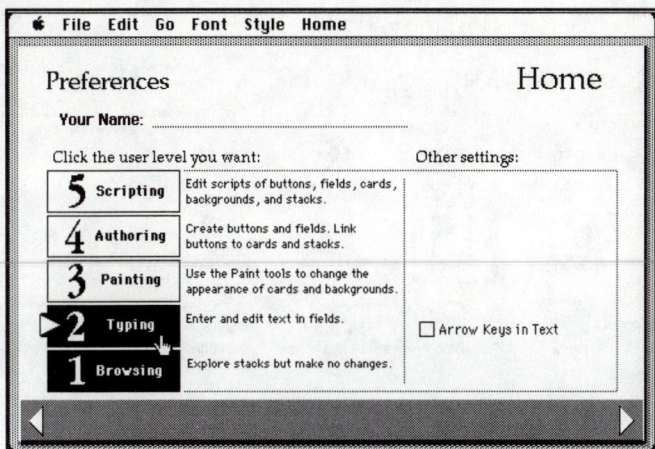

When the user level is set to Typing, two additional menus appear at the top of the screen: Font and Style. Also, an additional box, labeled Arrow Keys in Text, appears to the right.

3

3. Click the Arrow Keys in Text check box. This step enables you to use the left- and right-arrow keys on the keyboard, in addition to the mouse, to move the cursor to the left or right when you are entering or editing text.

   Note: If you do not choose the Arrow Keys in Text option, the left- and right-arrow keys on your keyboard will move you to the previous or next card in the stack.

4. Move the Browse tool to the line that says Your Name. Click the mouse once and type in your name.

5. Move the Browse tool to the right-arrow button and click to return to the Home card.

Using the Addresses Stack

The first stack in which you will test your Typing capabilities is the Addresses stack that came with HyperCard. This handy stack helps you maintain an electronic version of your address book.

51

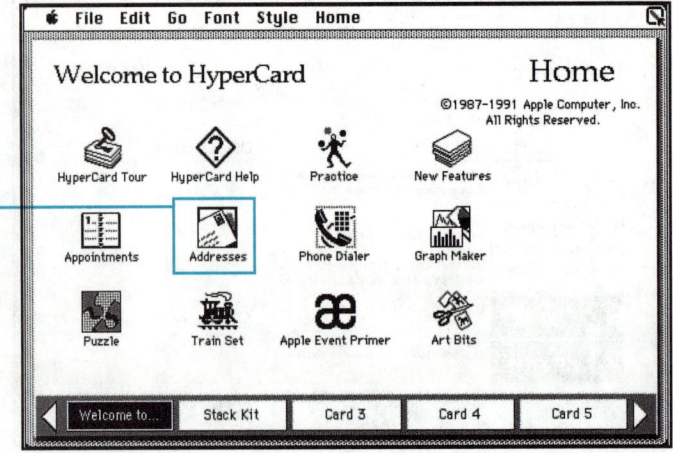

3

To open the Addresses stack, click the Addresses icon on your Home card.

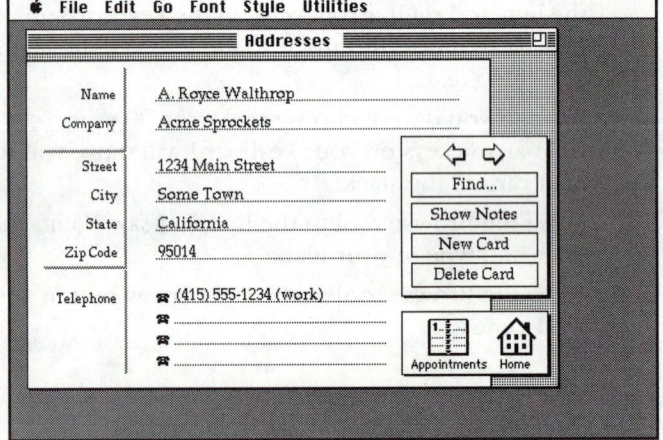

The first card of the Addresses stack appears.

Notice that when the Addresses stack is open, the Home menu on the top of the screen has been replaced with a Utilities menu.

In HyperCard the cards in a stack often look like the things they represent. Because the cards in the Address Book stack look like a physical address book or Rolodex, you see something familiar on your screen, and you assume that you would use it the same way—which is correct. The Address Book stack contains two cards with names, addresses, and phone numbers on them. The cards also contain several buttons you will learn about as you continue with this chapter.

Saving a Copy

Unlike changes you make in most programs, changes you make to a card or stack in HyperCard are saved automatically as you go along. This concept is very important to understand, especially when you are just starting out. When you are experimenting with the cards in the stacks, you are not given the option to abandon changes when you have finished. So, if you do not want to modify the original stack before you begin making changes to it, you should first save a copy of the original stack. To save a copy of the original stack, perform the following steps:

3

1. Pull down the File menu and select Save A Copy.

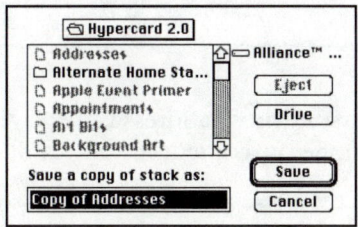

This dialog box appears.

2. Type **original address stack** as the new name.
3. Click the Save button.

You have just saved a copy of the original Addresses stack that was supplied with the HyperCard program. Now you are free to make changes to the Addresses stack, knowing that you can always return to the original one if you so desire.

Entering and Editing Information

Cards contain specific areas where you can add or edit textual information. Those areas are the card's *fields*. If you move the Browse tool around the Address card on the screen, you will see the hand change to an I-beam cursor when it is on a text-entry area, or field.

3

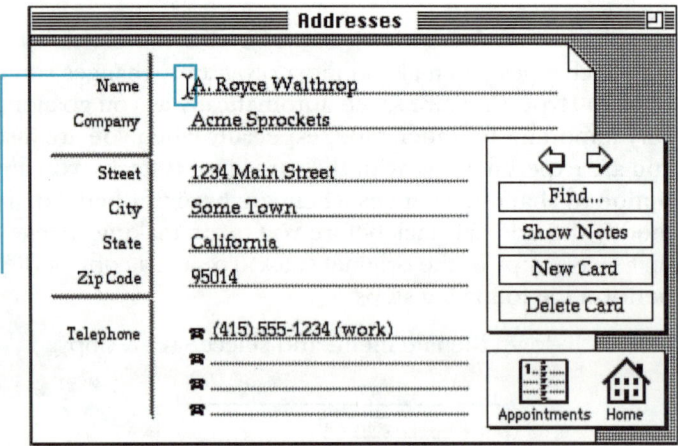

Here, the hand
has changed to an
I-beam cursor.

Assuming you do not know the person whose address is displayed on this first card, follow the steps below to change the contents of this card.

1. Move the I-beam cursor directly to the left of the name A. Royce Walthrop and, keeping the mouse button pressed down, drag the cursor to the right to highlight the entire name. Then, release the mouse button.

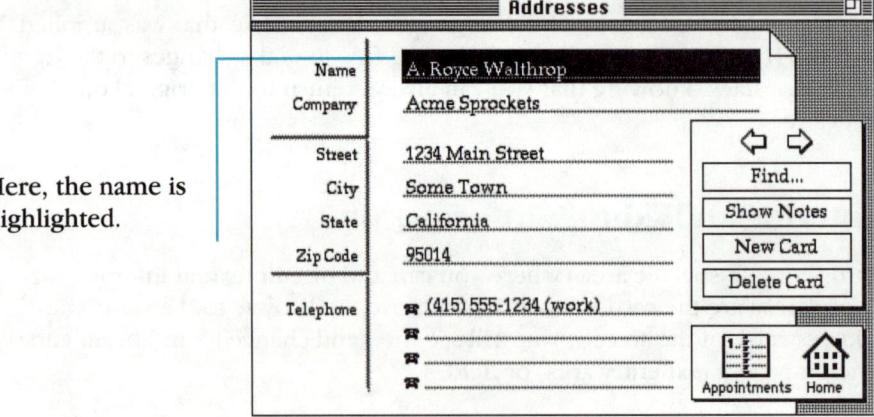

Here, the name is
highlighted.

2. Type the name of someone you know. For example, type Necia Mehling

As in other Macintosh programs, when text is selected, whatever new text you type replaces the selected text. You do not need to delete the old text first.

3. Press Tab ⇥ (or Return) to go to the Company Name field.

4. Replace Acme Sprockets with the correct company name. For example, type **Silver Enterprises, Inc.**

5. Tab to each of the remaining fields and enter the correct address, city, state, ZIP code, and phone number.

   For example, type:

   302 Morningside Drive

   Redondo Beach, CA 90278

   555-7326

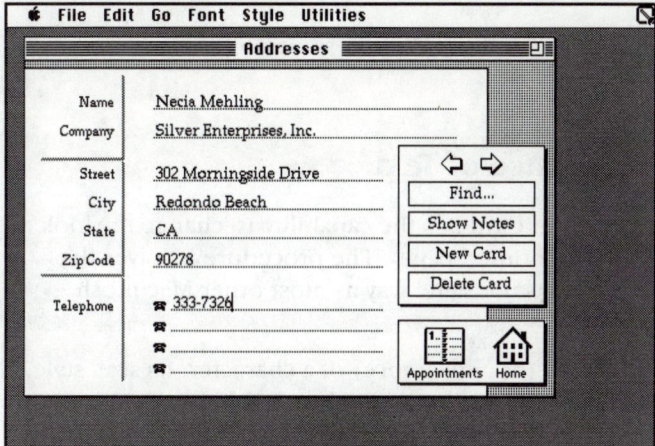

Your screen will look like this.

Note: If you click the Telephone icon located to the left of the phone number, your modem (if you have one) will dial the number you entered in that field.

6. Click the Show Notes button. Type any additional information you like in the pop-up field.

   For example, type:

   Birthday: June 10

   Anniversary: September 9

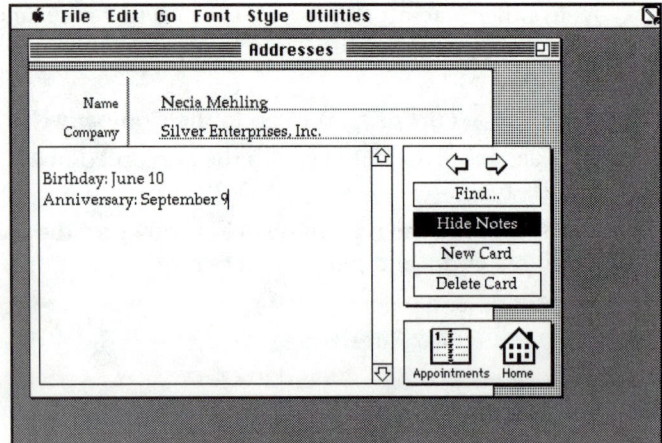

3

Your screen will
look like this.

7. When you have finished, click the Hide Notes button to return to the Address card.

Changing the Appearance of Text

One of the new features of HyperCard 2 is the capability to change the look of the text on the screen (and the printed page). The procedure involves the Font and Style menus, and works the same way as most other Macintosh programs.

A font is essentially the typeface (or appearance) of a character: its size, style, and weight. Type style refers to the attributes (such as **boldface**, outline, *italic*, shadow, or other options you see on many Macintosh applications) of the text. With HyperCard 2.1, you can change the font type and style of text in a card simply by selecting the text and choosing the font type, style, and size from the Font and Style menus.

Using the Font Menu

The Font menu lists all the fonts you currently have stored in your system. When you pull down the Font menu, you will see a checkmark next to the font that is currently in use on the selected text or the text your cursor is on. If all the font entries are gray, you don't have any text selected or you have not clicked in a field of text you can edit.

Now that you have entered information on an Address card, experiment a little. Try changing the font type in the Name field. To change the font type, follow these steps:

1. Move the I-beam cursor directly to the left of the Name field on the card and, keeping the mouse button pressed, drag the cursor to the right to highlight the entire name, and then release the mouse button.

2. Pull down the Font menu and select the font you want to use.

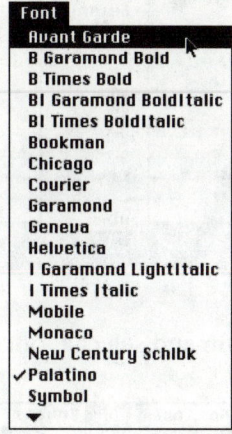

3

For example, select Avant Garde.

3. Release the mouse button. The selected text is displayed in the new font. Try a few different fonts in the menu until you find one you like.

Using the Style Menu

The *font style* refers to whether the text is displayed in boldface, italic, underline, outline, shadow, condense, or extend. Text can only have one font type associated with it, but it can have more than one style. In other words, the font type may be Avant Garde, and the style may be boldface, underline, shadow, and condense. When you choose any one of the styles listed, a checkmark will appear next to that style. You also can change the size of the font, which is measured in points. The Style menu lists the available point sizes of each font.

To change the font style, follow these steps:

1. Highlight the Name field, if it is not already highlighted.

2. Pull down the Style menu and select a style.

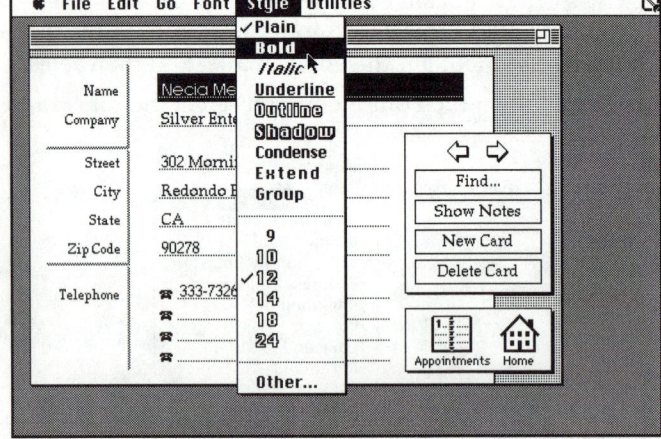

3

For example,
select Bold.

3. Pull down the Style menu again and select a font size.

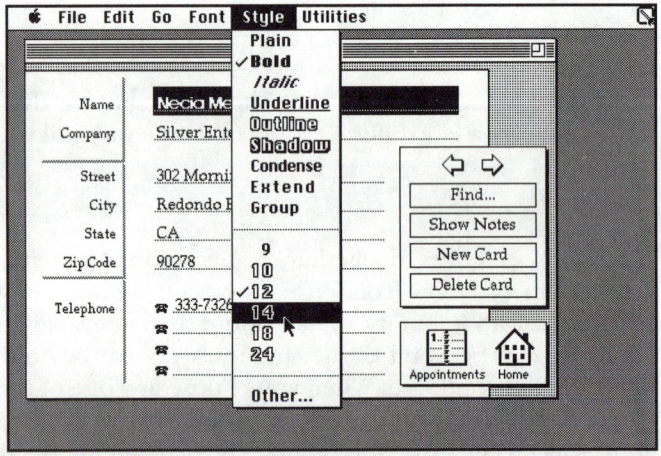

For example,
select 14 for the
font size.

4. Pull down the Style menu again and select Italic for an additional
effect.

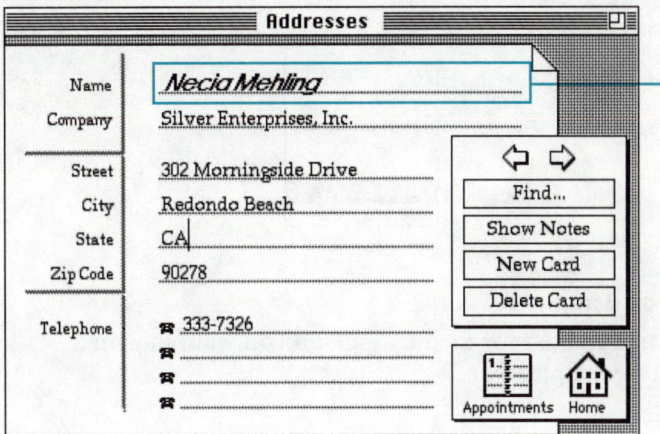

The name on the card is displayed in Avant Garde, Bold, Italic, and 14-point size.

3

Adding a New Card

When a stack is created as a template for others to use, it may come with one or two cards of information as examples. These stacks usually contain a button to add a new card, because adding new cards is one of the first things a user will want to do. If the stack does not contain a button to add a new card, you can add a new card to any stack by choosing New Card from the Edit menu.

The Address Book stack is made up of only two cards. After you have edited the names and addresses on the cards, you're ready to add new ones to the stack. To add a new card to the Address Book stack, follow these steps:

1. Click the New Card button.

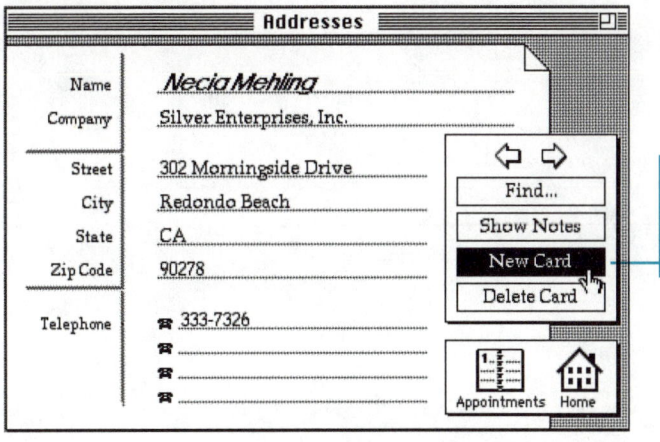

The New Card button is on the right side of the card.

59

Or, you can
choose New Card
from the Edit
menu.

3

A blank Address card appears.

2. Enter the name and address for the next person you want in your
Address Book. For example, type:

April Sardinha
Pineapple Music, Inc.
2302 Lees Ave
Newport, RI 02840
401-555-0305

Editing Cards

Like most other Macintosh programs, HyperCard gives you the ability to cut,
copy, and paste text from one card to the other. This is very helpful when
adding names of people who work for the same company, for example. To use
the Edit menu to copy text onto another card, follow these steps:

1. Select the text you want to copy. For example, select `Pineapple`
`Music, Inc.` in the Company field.

2. Pull down the Edit menu and select Copy Text.

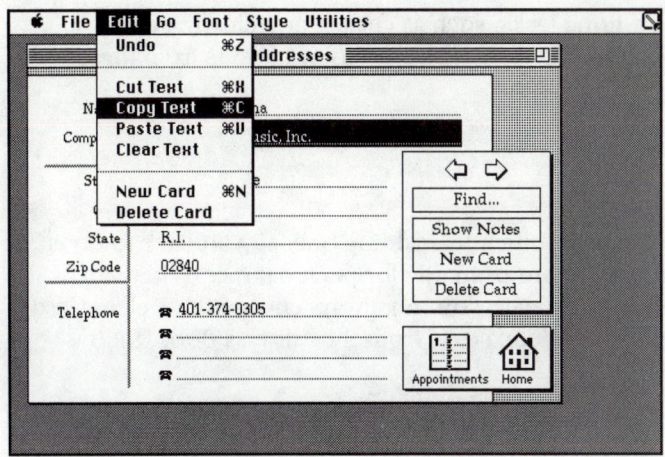

Copy Text is selected from the Edit menu.

3

3. Click the New Card button to add another card.
4. Type in another name. For example, type **Shane Hopkins**.
5. Press Tab⁺ to go to the Company field.
6. Pull down the Edit menu and select Paste Text.

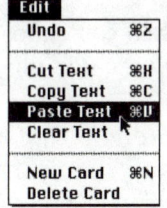

Paste Text is selected from the Edit menu.

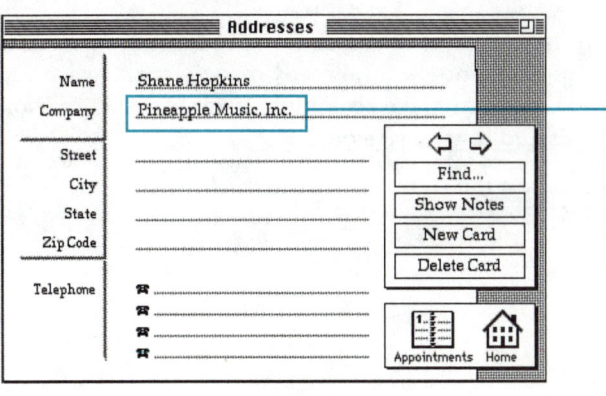

The Company name from the previous card is pasted in the field.

You can perform other editing tasks, such as cutting and clearing text, by following this basic procedure and selecting different options from the Edit menu.

Deleting a Card

3

Removing a card from a stack is much like adding one: all you have to do is click a button. Most stacks that are primarily for personal record keeping will have a Delete Card button. However, you can always choose the Delete Card option on the Edit menu. To delete a card from the Address Book, follow these steps:

1. Click the Delete Card button on the right side of the card.

A dialog box appears, asking you to confirm the deletion.

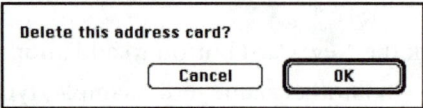

2. Click the OK button. (If you do not want to delete the card after all, click the Cancel button.)

   Note: This dialog box appears only when you choose the Delete Card button. If you choose Delete Card from the Edit menu, the card will be deleted without your confirmation.

3. When the card has been deleted, the previous card in the stack appears.

Searching for a Card

To find a particular card in a stack or to search for specific text, you can use the Find command in the Go menu. Several ready-made HyperCard stacks, however, include a Find button to make searching easier for you. To look for a particular name or address, follow these steps:

1. Click the Find button on the right side of the card.

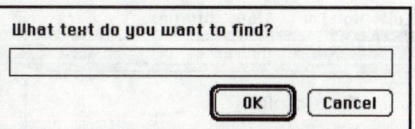

This dialog box
appears.

2. Type the first or last name of someone for whom you know you have an Address card. For example, if you followed the steps in "Adding a New Card" and added a card for someone named April, type April.

3. Click OK.

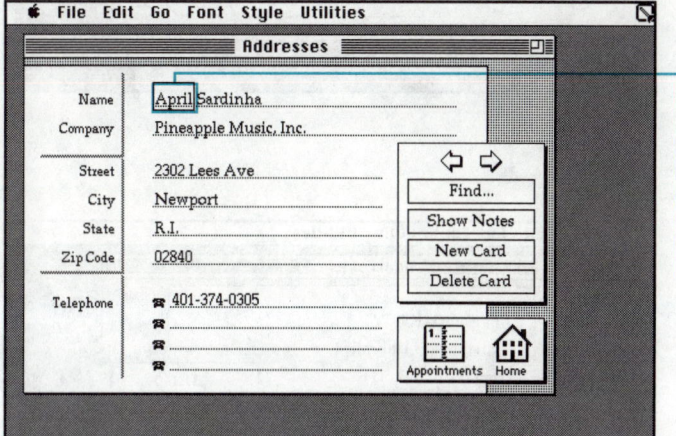

The card appears
with a box
around the
"found" text.

If you are unsure of the exact spelling of a name you want to locate, you can enter any part of the name in the Find dialog box, and HyperCard will look for the partial word. Or, for example, if you want to find all the cards that share a particular area code, follow these steps:

1. Click the Find button. Type the area code in the Find dialog box. For example, type 213.

2. Click OK.

63

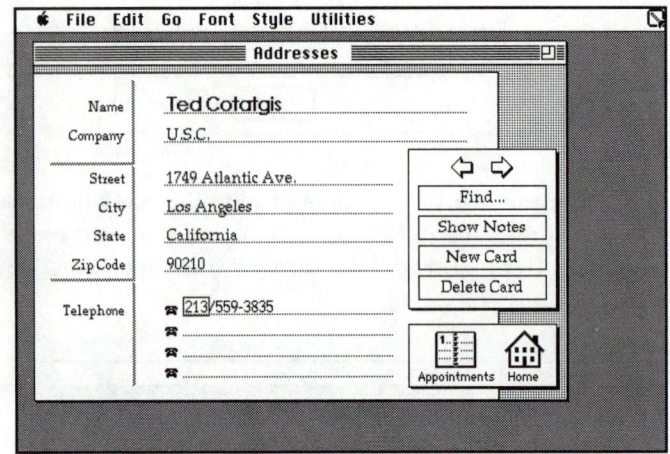

The first card
containing the
area code in the
Phone Number
field (or any other
field) appears.

3. Press Return .

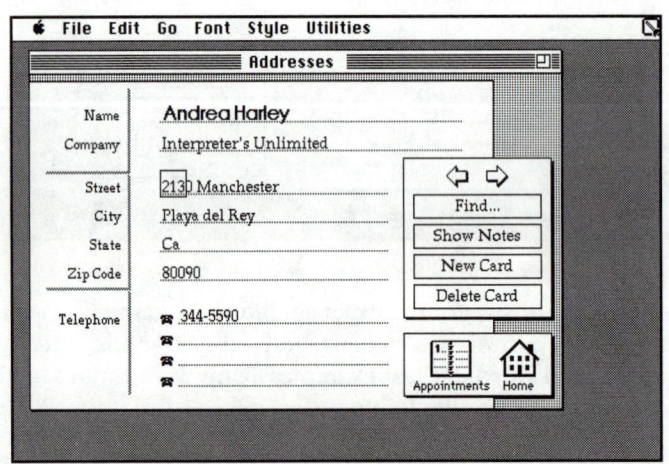

The next card that
contains the area
code in any of its
fields appears.

4. Press Return again.

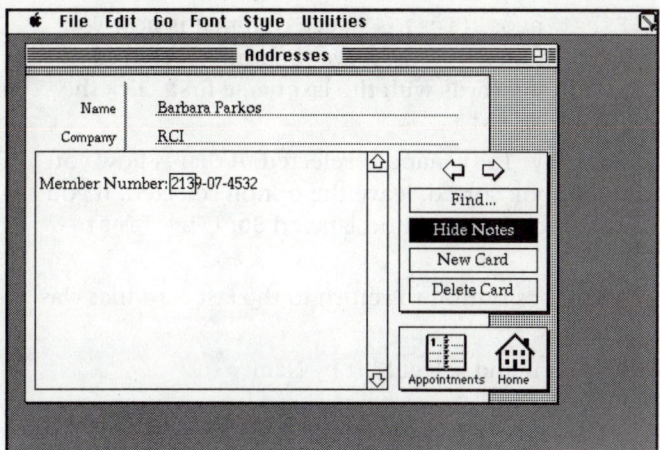

The next card that contains the area code in any of its fields appears.

3

Sorting a Stack

It is easy to use the Find button to search for a particular card in a stack, or even to flip through all the cards using the arrow buttons. As your stack grows, however, you may want to sort your cards either alphabetically or perhaps by company name. To sort your Address Book stack, follow these steps:

1. Pull down the Utilities menu and select Sort Preferences.

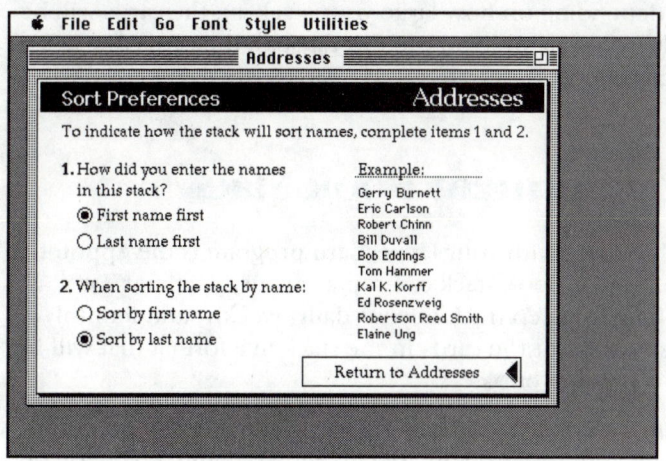

The Sort Preferences dialog box appears.

2. The button labeled `First name first` is selected. If that is how you entered the names on the Address cards, leave the option selected. If you entered the names on the cards with the last name first, click the button labeled `Last name first`.

3. The button labeled `Sort by last name` is selected. If that is how you would like your Address Book sorted, leave the option selected. If you want to sort by first name, click the button labeled `Sort by first name`.

4. Click the Return to Addresses button to return to the last card that was on your screen

5. Pull down the Utilities menu and select Sort by Name.

Here, Sort by Name is selected from the Utilities menu.

After a few moments (depending on how large your stack is), the cards will be arranged alphabetically by last name. You can flip through the cards one at a time to see the sorting sequence.

Using the Appointment Book Stack

Another handy stack that came with your HyperCard program is the Appointment Book. The Appointment Book stack can replace your "daytimer" or "executive organizer" book to keep track of your daily, weekly, and monthly appointments. You also can print the cards in the stack in a format that will let you insert them in your physical book.

To access the Appointment Book stack, click the Appointments icon in the lower right corner of the Address card you are currently viewing. If you are on the Home card of the Home stack, click the Appointments icon displayed.

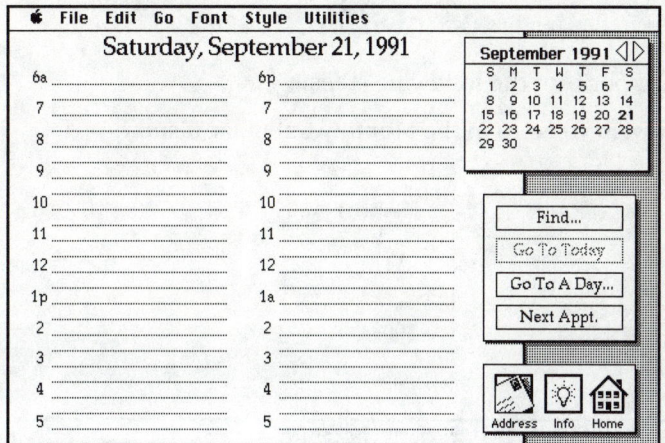

3

The first card of the Appointment Book stack appears. The card is for the current day.

Note: You may be asked if you would like to add a card for the current date. If so, click OK. A card for the current date will appear.

Once again, if you don't want to modify the original Appointments stack that came with your program, save a copy (as explained earlier in this chapter) before you begin this exercise.

Entering an Appointment for Today

To enter an appointment for the current day, click the field next to the desired time, and type the name of the activity. For example, type **Learn how to use HyperCard's Appointment stack**.

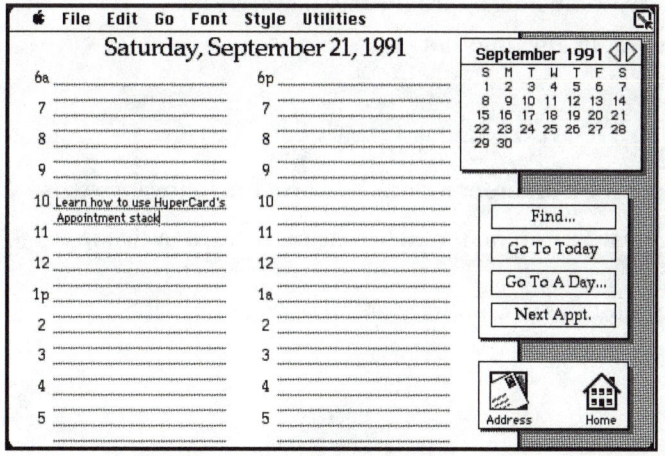

Your screen should look like this.

Entering an Appointment for a Different Day

To move to another day, perform the following steps:

1. Click the day you want to go to in the Monthly Calendar display.

3

For example, click
September 25.

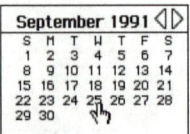

If HyperCard
does not contain
a card for that
day, the program
asks whether you
want to create a
new card for that
day.

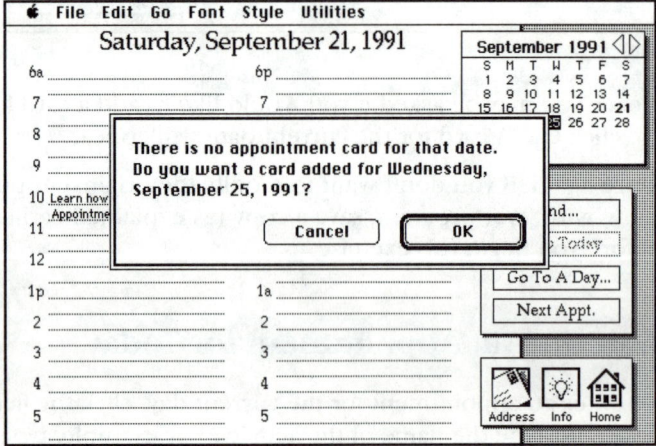

2. Click OK. After a few moments, a card for that day appears.
3. Type an appointment in any time slot.

Entering an Appointment for a Different Month

To enter an appointment for a different month, perform the following steps:

1. Click the Go To A Day button on the right side of the card. A dialog box appears.
2. Type the day you want to go to in the Month/Day/Year format.

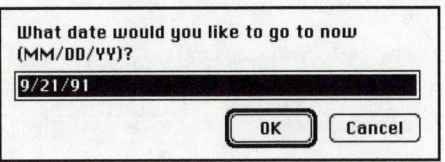

For example, type
9/21/91.

3

Note: You can also click the left- and right-arrow buttons on the Month calendar until the month you want is displayed, and then click the day you want to go to.

If a card for the day doesn't already exist, HyperCard will ask whether you want to create a new card.

Going to Today

From any card in the Appointment Book, click the Go To Today button. The card for the current day is displayed.

Finding Your Next Appointment

Click the Next Appointment button to see when your next appointment is scheduled. The card for that day is displayed.

Scheduling Weekly Appointments

Many times you may have an appointment that occurs on a weekly or monthly basis. You can use the Edit menu to copy and paste these reoccurring appointments. For an example, follow these steps:

1. Click the 7:00 time line and type in an appointment. For example, type **Writer's Group Meeting - Mary's house**

2. Select the line you just typed by dragging the cursor over the entire line.

3. Pull down the Edit menu and select Copy Text.

4. Now go to a new day. For example, click the day that is two weeks from today.

    (If you need to go to the next month, click the right-arrow button in the monthly calender display.)

5. Click the the 7:00 time slot.

6. Pull down the Edit menu and select Paste Text.

Rescheduling an Appointment

3

You also can use the Cut and Paste features when you need to reschedule an appointment. For example, if your meeting was canceled today and rescheduled for tomorrow, you would follow these steps:

1. Click the Go To Today button to go to the current day's card.

2. Select the appointment line you just entered for 7:00 ("Writer's Group Meeting - Mary's house").

3. Pull down the Edit menu and select Cut Text.

4. Click the next day in the monthly calender.

5. Click the 7:00 time slot.

6. Pull down the Edit menu and select Paste Text.

Going Home

When you have finished with the Appointment Book stack, click the Home button (house icon) to go Home. You can continue working with any of HyperCard's readymade stacks, or perhaps take a look at a stack you have acquired elsewhere.

Using Additional HyperCard Stacks

Now that you're comfortable with some of the HyperCard stacks that came with your program, you may want to see what other interesting HyperCard stacks are available. Many on-line services, such as CompuServe, GEnie, and America Online, have many HyperCard stacks for you to download. Often Macintosh software catalogs include a section specifically for HyperCard stacks. Also, Appendix B of this book will lead you to some other sources where you can acquire additional stacks. To start using a HyperCard stack that you acquire elsewhere, follow these steps:

1. Without leaving the HyperCard program, insert the diskette containing the new HyperCard stack into your floppy drive.

2. Pull down the File menu and select Open.

3. Click the Drive button for HyperCard to look at the disk in the floppy drive.

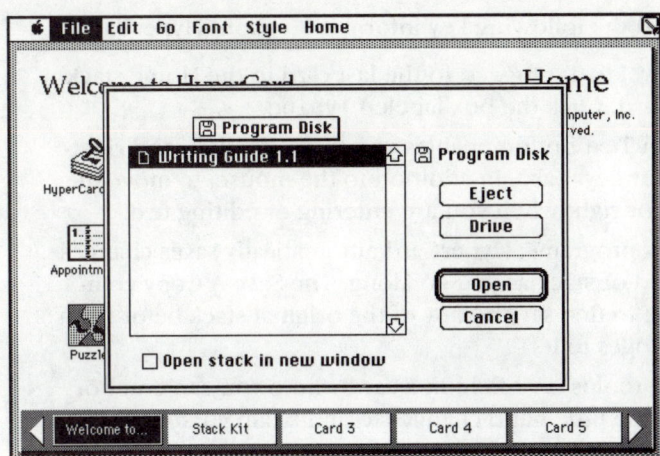

A list of all the HyperCard stacks that are on that diskette will be displayed.

3

4. Select the stack you want to use and click Open.

After you have opened the stack, the first thing you will want to do is save a copy onto your hard drive (if you have one). If you don't have a hard drive, then you still may want to save a copy of the original stack onto the diskette. Follow these steps:

1. With the first card of the new stack open, pull down the File menu and choose Save A Copy.

2. To save a copy of the stack onto your hard drive, click the Drive button. The name of your hard drive appears in the dialog box.

3. Enter a name for the stack, or accept the default name, Copy of... stack, and click Save.

Summary

This chapter showed you how to use the second level of HyperCard, which is called *Typing*. You learned how to add, delete, and edit cards in a stack, and how to change the appearance of text in a field, using different fonts and styles. You also learned how to use HyperCard's searching and sorting capabilities in a stack.

In this chapter, you also worked with both the Addresses stack and the Appointments stack that came with your HyperCard program. You learned how to open additional HyperCard stacks you may have acquired.

Specifically, you learned the following key information about HyperCard:

- To set the user level to Typing, go to the last card in the Home stack, the Preferences card. Click the box labeled Typing.

- The Arrow Keys in Text option enables you to use the left- and right-arrow keys on your keyboard, in addition to the mouse, to move the cursor to the left or right when you are entering or editing text.

- Unlike most other programs, HyperCard automatically saves changes you make to a card or stack as you go along. The Save A Copy command enables you to first save a copy of the original stack before you begin making changes to it.

- When the Browse tool is on a field in a card where you can enter or edit information, the little hand changes to an I-beam cursor.

- You can use the Font menu and the Style menu (which became available when you changed your user level from Browsing to Typing) to change the appearance of text in any field. First, select the text you want to change. Then, pull down either the Font or Style menu and select the font, size, and styles you want to use.

- To add a new card to a stack, select New Card from the Edit menu. Many stacks (including the Addresses stack) have a New Card button you can click to add a new card.

- You can use the standard Macintosh Cut, Copy, and Paste options (found in the Edit menu) to manipulate text in any field to and from other cards and stacks.

- To delete a card from a stack, select Delete Card from the Edit menu. Many stacks (including the Addresses stack) have a Delete Card button you can click to delete the card currently on the screen.

- The Find command in the Go menu enables you to search for specific text in a card or stack. After you type the text you want to look for in the Find dialog box, the card appears with a box around the "found" text.

- The Sort Preferences command in the Utilities menu enables you to sort a stack alphabetically, or by some other field you choose.

- The Appointments stack that came with the HyperCard program enables you to keep track of your daily, weekly, and monthly appointments.

- You can use additional HyperCard stacks by choosing Open from the File menu and selecting the drive or diskette where the stack is located. Select the stack you want to use and click Open.

After you have entered your information into the Address Book and Appointment Book stacks, you may want to print your cards and stacks. You also may want to create reports from the information you have entered. Move on to Chapter 4 to continue your work with both the Address Book stack and the Appointment Book stack, and learn how to print cards and stacks and create reports.

3

Printing Stacks and Reports

Now that you know how to get information into a HyperCard stack, the next thing you will learn is how to get the information out onto a printed page. You also will learn how to create different report templates for a stack and how to use the same templates for different stacks.

Before you begin the first exercise in this chapter, the Appointments stack should be open on your desktop.

Choosing a printer

Setting up the page

Printing cards, fields, and stacks

Printing reports

4

Key Terms in This Chapter

Dialog box
A box that appears on the screen, asking for information you must supply or options you must select before the program can proceed.

Page setup
A command in the File menu that brings up a dialog box of printing options, such as paper size and orientation. Depending on what kind of printer you have, the Page Setup dialog box will offer different options.

Marked cards
Cards that have been selected for meeting a particular criteria. Once certain cards have been marked, you can manipulate just those cards, such as viewing or printing the marked cards only.

Header
Additional information that can appear on the top of every printed page of the stack. The header might include the stack name, date, or time, or page numbers.

Report templates
Custom reports that display the field text in a stack in any way you like. After you create one report template, you can copy that template into any other stack and use it with that stack. You can create and save up to 16 report templates for each stack.

Report layout
The order and size of the fields in a report template.

Cells
Each square in a report template that represents one card in the stack. You can change the cell's position and/or size in a report template depending on how many cards of information you want to display on the page.

Choosing a Printer

Assuming you have a printer and it is correctly set up to work with your Macintosh, perform the following steps:

1. Move the mouse pointer onto the little apple to the left of the File menu.

2. Pull down the Apple menu and select Chooser.

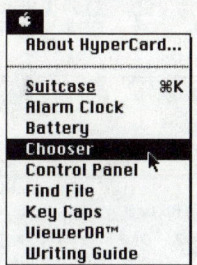

Here, Chooser is selected from the Apple menu.

4

A dialog box appears.

3. Select the icon (if there is more than one) that represents the printer you want to use.

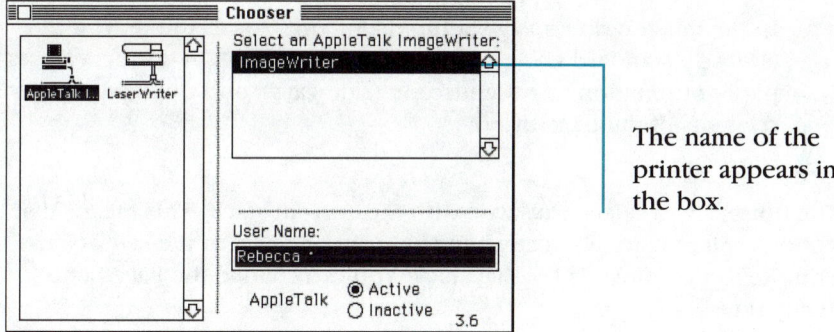

The name of the printer appears in the box.

4. Click in the upper left corner box (the close box) to close the window.

Setting Up the Page

After you have selected a printer to use, you need to select the appropriate Page Setup options. Follow these steps:

1. Pull down the File menu and select Page Setup. Depending on which printer you choose, one of the following Page Setup dialog boxes appears.

This is the Page
Setup dialog
box for the
ImageWriter.

```
AppleTalk ImageWriter                         v2.7    [ OK ]
Paper:  ● US Letter        ○ A4 Letter
        ○ US Legal         ○ International Fanfold  [ Cancel ]
        ○ Computer Paper
Orientation    Special Effects:  □ Tall Adjusted
   [🖨] [🖨]                      □ 50 % Reduction
                                 □ No Gaps Between Pages
```

4

This is the Page
Setup dialog
box for the
LaserWriter.

```
LaserWriter Page Setup                         5.2    [ OK ]
Paper: ● US Letter   ○ A4 Letter   ○ Tabloid
       ○ US Legal    ○ B5 Letter                      [ Cancel ]
       Reduce or [100] %       Printer Effects:       [ Options ]
       Enlarge:               ⊠ Font Substitution?
       Orientation            ⊠ Text Smoothing?       [ Help ]
          [🖨] [🖨]            ⊠ Graphics Smoothing?
                              ⊠ Faster Bitmap Printing?
```

2. Click the buttons for the desired paper size, orientation, and special effects.

   In the ImageWriter's Page Setup dialog box, for example, you can choose a standard US letter paper (which is 8 1/2-by-11 inches), set the paper orientation to be landscape (sideways), and perhaps reduce the contents of the page by 50%.

3. Click OK.

The options you select are saved with the current stack. This means that the options will remain in effect when you print any part of the stack or use the Print Report commands for that stack. You can change the Page Setup settings at any time.

Printing a Card

To print a particular card in a stack, you must first have the card open on your screen. You can print a card from any stack you want, but for the purpose of this exercise, you will use the Appointment Book stack and print the card for today's appointments.

To print the card currently displayed on your screen, follow these steps.

1. Hold down ⇧Shift on your keyboard.

2. Pull down the File menu and select Print Card. (Or, you can use the ⌘-P key combination on your keyboard.) A Print dialog box appears.

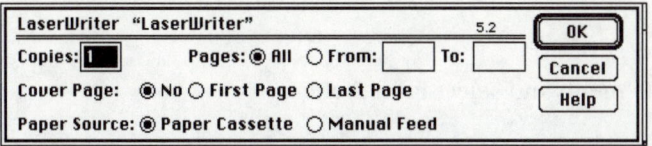

This is the Print
dialog box for the
ImageWriter.

This is the Print
dialog box for the
LaserWriter.

4

3. Enter the number of copies you want to print and the print quality.

   With an ImageWriter, you have three choices for Print Quality (Draft,
   Faster, and Best). Draft is not recommended for printing a card or
   stack. The difference between Faster and Best is not extreme. When
   you use Best, the printout is darker.

4. Select OK.

Note: If you do not want to change the number of copies and the print
quality, you do not need to hold down the Shift key before you choose Print
Card. The Print dialog box will not appear, and one copy of the card will
automatically print.

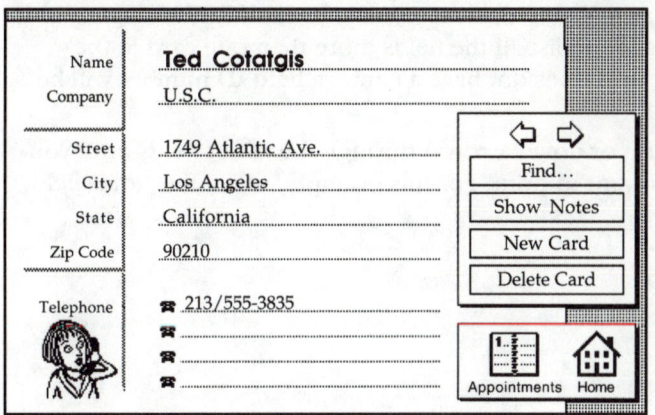

Here is the
finished card.

You can print the contents of just one field in a particular card. Printing one
field is very helpful, for example, if you added notes about a person (such as
contact history) in your Address Book and want a printed copy of that information. To print a field, follow these steps:

1. Click the Addresses button to go to the Address Book stack. Go to any card you like.

2. Click the Show Notes button and type some information in the Notes area. For example, type:

   9/29/91 Called to confirm balloon order and delivery date. He changed the order to: 10 blue, 70 red, and 150 yellow. Delivery date remains 11/26.

3. Click the Hide Notes button.

4. Pull down the File menu and select Print Field.

A dialog box
appears.

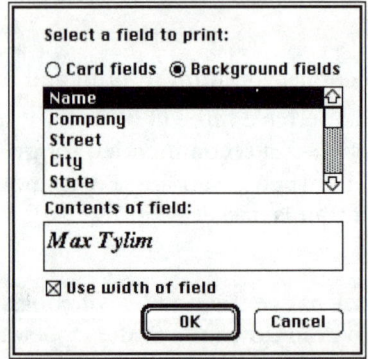

5. Click the button labeled Card fields to list all the fields that are unique to that particular card, if there are any. Click the button labeled Background fields to list all the fields more than one card in the stack share. (If a field does not have a name, a field ID number will be displayed.)

6. Scroll (click the up or down arrows) through the list of fields until you find the one you want to print. For this example, select the Notes field.

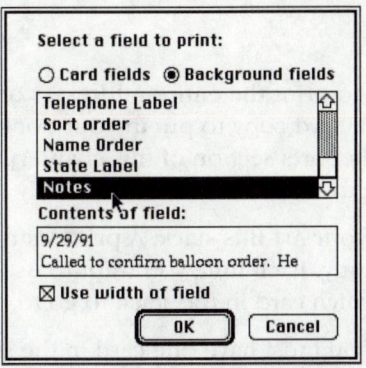

A portion of the
Notes field is
displayed in the
box labeled
`Contents of`
`field.`

4

You have two choices for printing the field information on the page.
You can either print the information exactly as it appears on the
card—meaning the same width of the field—or you can print the
information straight across the page. Currently, the Use Width of Field
button is selected (there is an X in the box). When this button is
selected, the information will print in the exact format as on the card.

7. Click the Use Width of Field button (to deselect it) if you want the
   information in the field to be printed across the page. Notice how the
   Contents of Field area now shows more text on the first line.

8. Click OK. The field contents for that card will print.

9. Close the Addresses stack by clicking the Home button or selecting
   Home from the Go menu to return to the Home stack.

9/29/91
Called to confirm balloon order. He changed the order to 10 blue, 70 red, 150 yellow. Delivery
date remains 11/26.

Here is a printout
of a field.

81

Printing a Stack

At this point, you may be anxious to print the entire Addresses or Appointments stack so that you will have a hard copy to put in your books. However, wait until you get to the Printing Reports section of this chapter; there are predefined templates you can use to handle the task effortlessly.

For now, you will print a copy of your Art Bits stack. A printout of your electronic art collection is very handy. Each time you want to use a drawing or image, you will know exactly which card in the stack to go to.

To print an entire stack of cards, you must have one card in the stack open on your screen. Follow these steps:

1. Pull down the File menu and select Open Stack.
2. Select Art Bits from the list of stacks and click Open. The Art Bits stack opens on your desktop.
3. Pull down the File menu and select Print Stack.

The Print Stack
dialog box
appears.

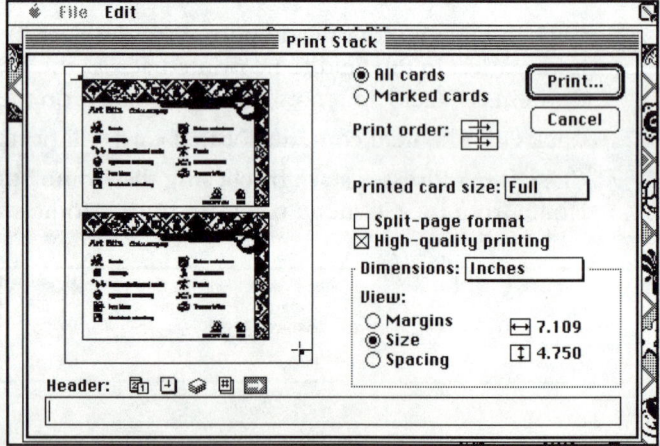

The diagram on the left displays the layout of what the printed page will look like. You can change the page margins, the size of the cards, and how much space there is between the cards. You also can define the number of cards printed per page, and the page format.

The bottom right corner of the dialog box is the View area. This is where you can see the current dimensions of the margins, size of the cards, and spacing between the cards. Click the appropriate button to view the dimensions of each option.

82

Here is a printout of a stack.

Printing All or Marked Cards

The Print Stack dialog box is initially set to print all the cards in the stack. If you want to print only some of the cards in the stack, you first have to mark which cards you want to print. This process will be discussed later in this chapter in the section "Marking Cards." For the purpose of this exercise, leave the All Cards option selected.

Specifying the Print Order

The Print Stack dialog box is initially set to print the cards in successive order from the left to the right of the page.

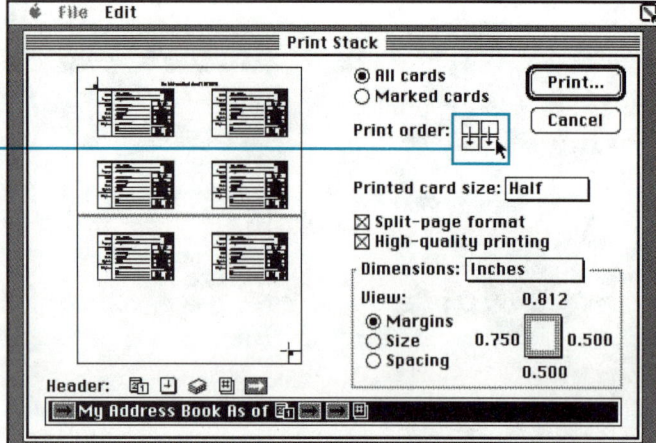

4

Click the boxes to change the print order from left/right to top/bottom.

Changing the Page Margins

Initially, the dimensions are set to inches. To change the dimensions, move the mouse pointer over the Dimensions box that is currently displaying Inches.

Keep the mouse button pressed to view the other choices, and move the mouse pointer to Centimeters, Millimeters, Inches, or Points. Release the mouse button.

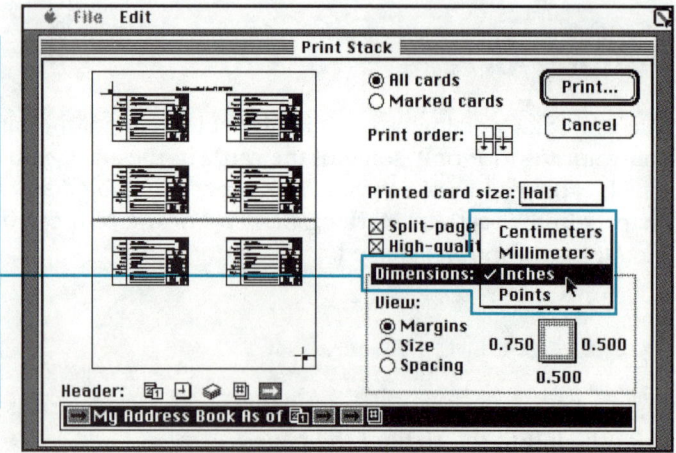

Look in the View area in the Print Stack dialog box to see the current page margins.

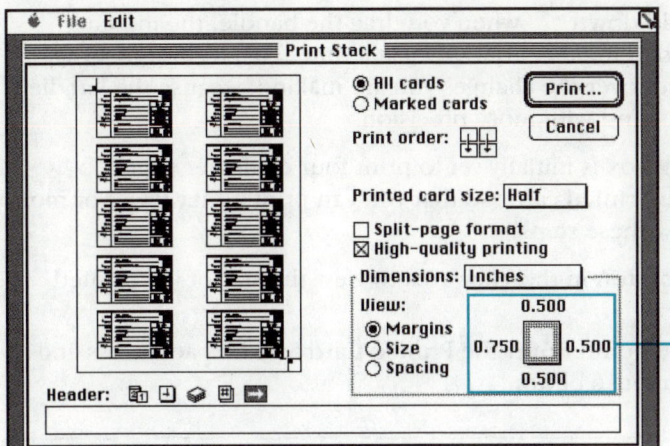

Depending on the size of the cards, the margins are set to approximately 3/4 of an inch on the left, and 1/2 inch on the top, bottom, and right side of the page.

4

To change the margins, follow these steps:

1. Move the mouse pointer to the upper left corner of the page display. Put the pointer on the small black square.

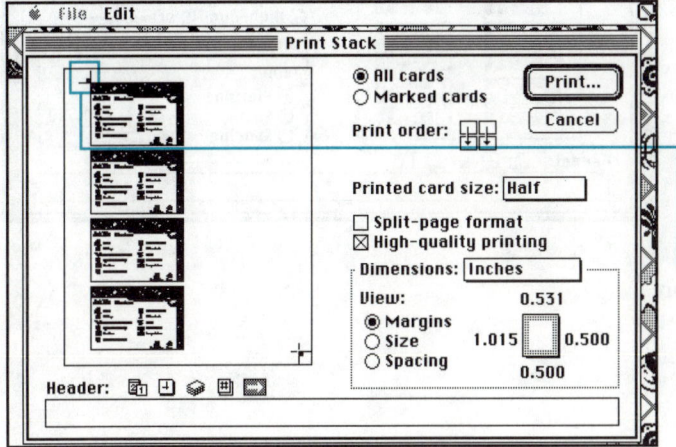

The black square is called the *handle*.

2. Keep the mouse button pressed and drag the handle to change the left and top margins.

3. Drag the lower right corner handle to change the right and bottom margins. Keep your eye on the View box to see the changes you are making in the dimensions.

Note: If you hold down ⬚ when you drag the handle, the margins will change in increments of one pixel at a time. This technique gives you more control over the changes you are making because the handle is moving slower and with more precision.

The Print Stack dialog box is initially set to print four cards per page. To change the size of the printed cards so that you can print either fewer or more cards per page, follow these steps:

1. Select the Size button in the View area to view the size of the printed card.

2. Move the mouse pointer over the Printed Card Size box and press and hold down the mouse button.

The options are
displayed.

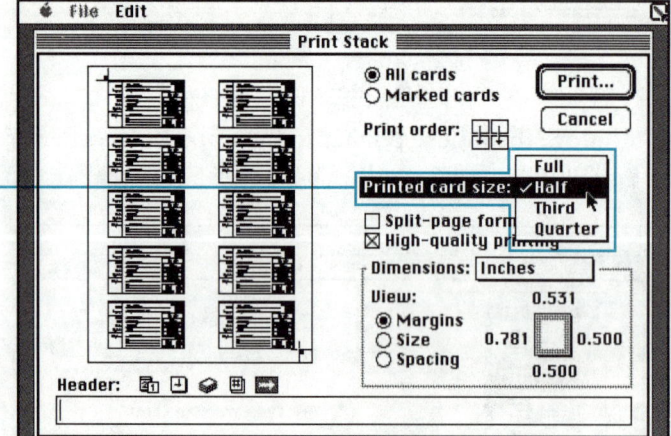

3. Select an option.

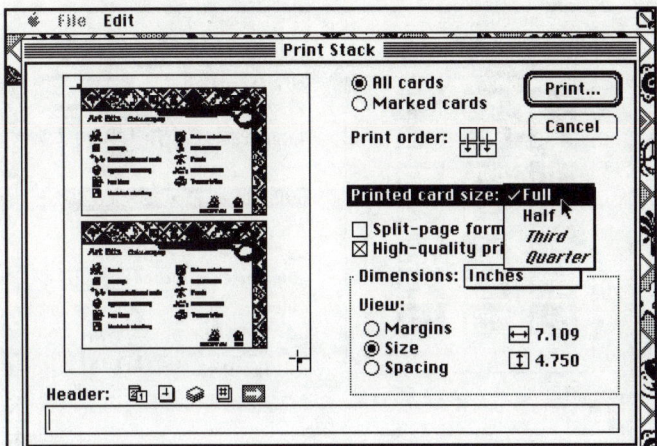

Select Full to print 2 cards per printed page.

4

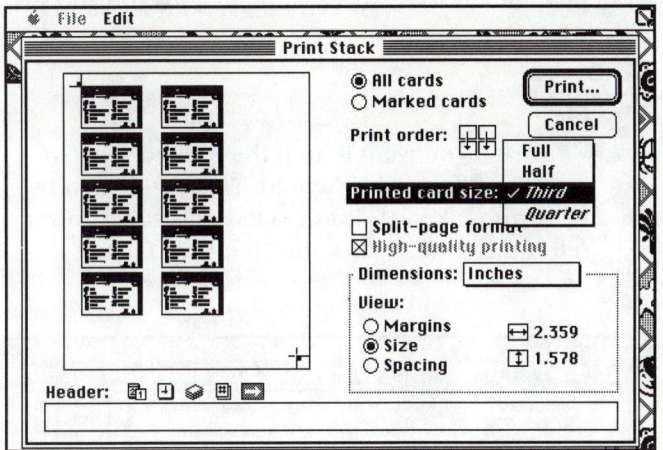

Select Third to print 10 cards per printed page.

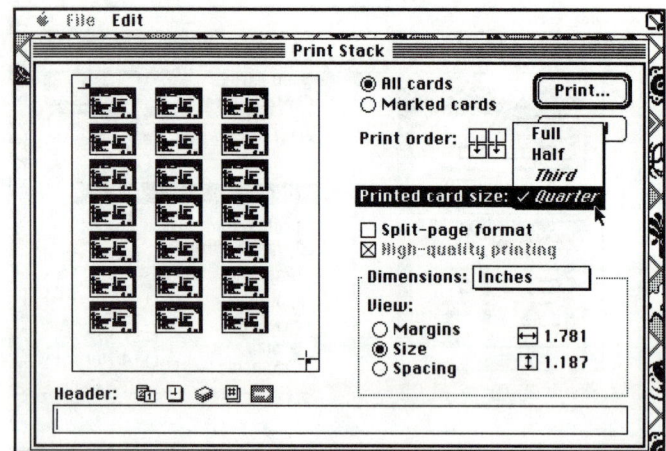

Select Quarter to print 21 cards per printed page.

4

Note: These figures vary depending on the card size and margins you choose.

Splitting the Page Format

You can select the split-page format if you want to fold the printed sheet in half; neither one of the cards will be affected by the fold. This option is very useful if you intend to insert the printed pages into a standard size organizer notebook, for example. To select this format, click the Split-Page Format button.

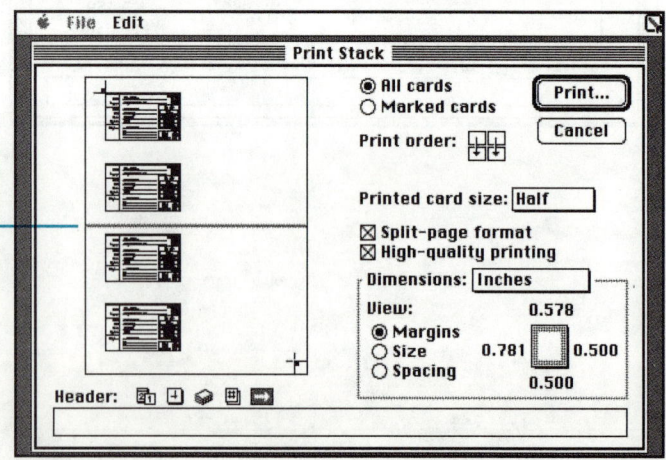

The dotted line that appears between the cards in the page display shows you the fold line.

88

Changing the Space between Cards

Click the Spacing button in the View area to view the initial setting of spaces between the cards. To change the spacing, follow these steps:

1. Move the mouse pointer onto any card in the page display EXCEPT the top left corner card. (Moving the top left card will change the page margins also.)

2. Keeping the mouse button pressed, drag the card either closer or farther from the other card.

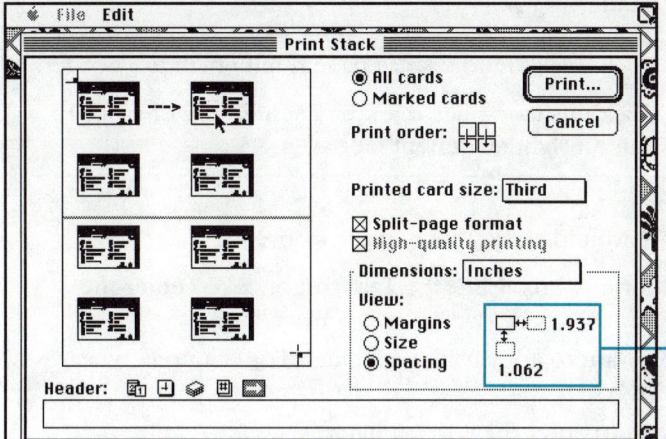

Note how the Spacing dimensions in the View box change as you move the card.

Note: If you set the spacing too wide and cause one of the cards to go off the page, drag the mouse pointer up on the page until the card reappears.

Adding a Header

You can add information to the top of every printed page of the stack. This information is called a *header*. The Header entry box is on the bottom of the Print Stack dialog box. You can add to a header the options in table 4.1.

**Table 4.1
Header Options in HyperCard**

Header Icon	Description
	Click this icon to display the current date in the header.
	Click this icon to display the time of printing in the header.
	Click this icon to display the name of the stack in the header.
	Click this icon to display page numbers in the header.
	Click this icon once to enter a center tab, or twice to enter a right alignment tab.

To add a header to the printed stack, follow these steps:

1. Click in the Header text box. Click the Tab icon once to center the text.

2. Type the text you want to appear in the header. For example, type **My Art Bit Collection As Of** .

3. Click the Date icon to enter the current date.

4. Click the Tab icon again to enter a right alignment tab.

5. Click the Page Number icon to enter the page number.

The Header box will look like this.

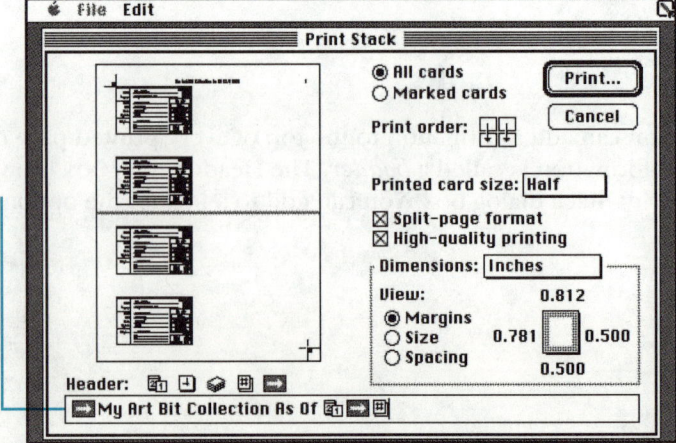

6. When you have selected all the options you want, click the Print button. A Print dialog box appears. Set the number of copies and print quality. Select the desired options, and press OK.

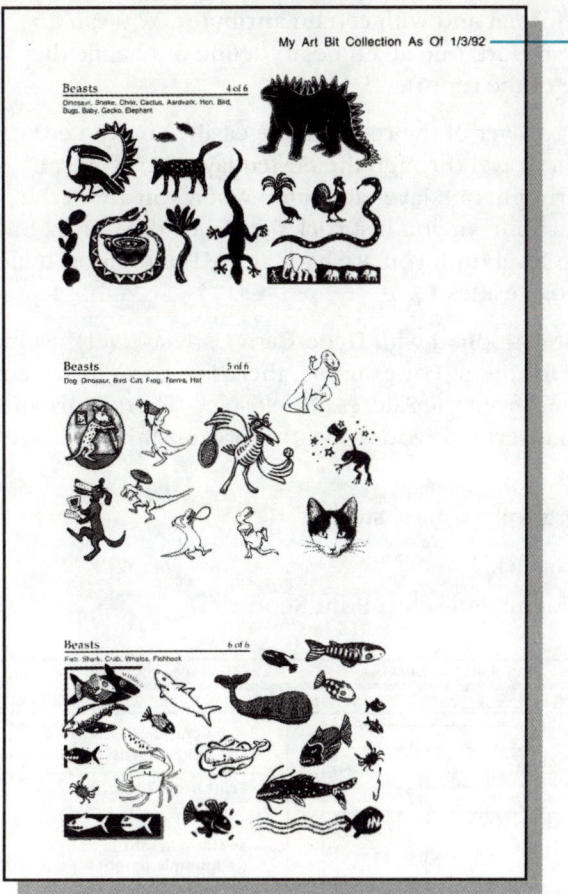

Here is a printout with a header.

Printing Reports

The capability to print reports is a new feature in HyperCard 2.0. The program enables you to create and print up to 16 different report templates for each stack. A report could mean a list of pertinent information from the stack, mailing labels, or a particular format display of the text in your cards. Reports can include any fields in your stack that contain text. Also, after you create a useful report template for any one stack, you can copy the report template to any other stack.

Report templates can be broken down into layers, or nested levels. The top layer is the report as a whole, consisting of cards displayed in a particular layout. The second layer is the cards themselves, consisting of fields organized in a certain manner. The third layer is the fields in the cards, consisting of text displayed in a particular format and with certain attributes. You can go through each layer of the report, one at a time, to define or change the information in that piece of the report.

4

You can get to each nested layer of the report quite easily. You can either use the Reports menu items to travel through the nested layers, or you can double-click your way through, one layer at a time. When you are in the deepest level (the field attributes), you just click the OK or the Cancel button to travel up through each level until you are back at the Print Report dialog box where the Print button resides.

Some of the stacks that are supplied with HyperCard also have very useful report templates created for them. For example, there is a predefined template to print mailing labels from the Address Book stack. There is also a daily appointment template to insert into your executive organizer book made from the Appointments stack.

To print a supplied report, follow these steps:

1. Open the Addresses stack.
2. Pull down the File menu and select Print Report.

A Print Report dialog box appears, and two new menus, Edit and Reports, appear at the top menu line.

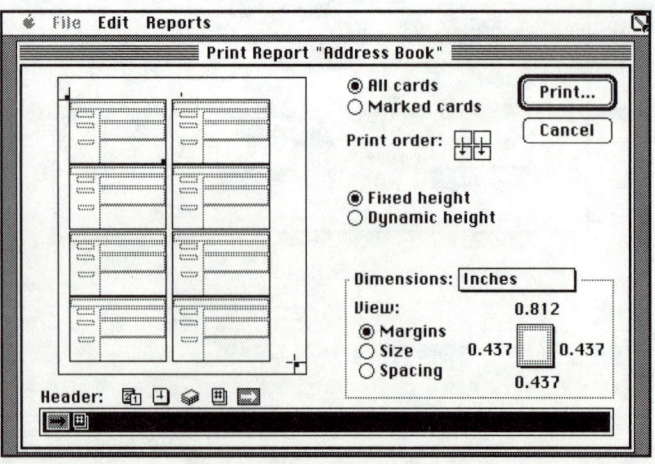

3. Pull down the Reports menu and select Name and Address List.

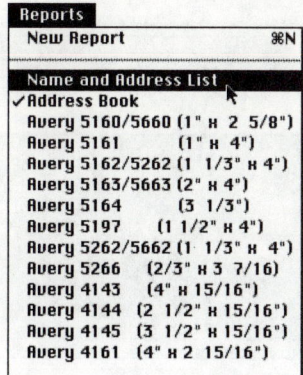

Here, Name and Address List is selected from the Reports menu.

4

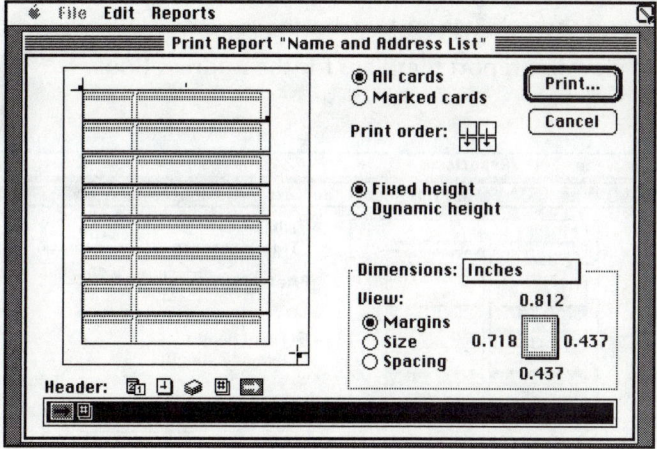

A Print Report dialog box appears, displaying the layout of the Name and Address List report.

4. Pull down the Edit menu and select Report Items.

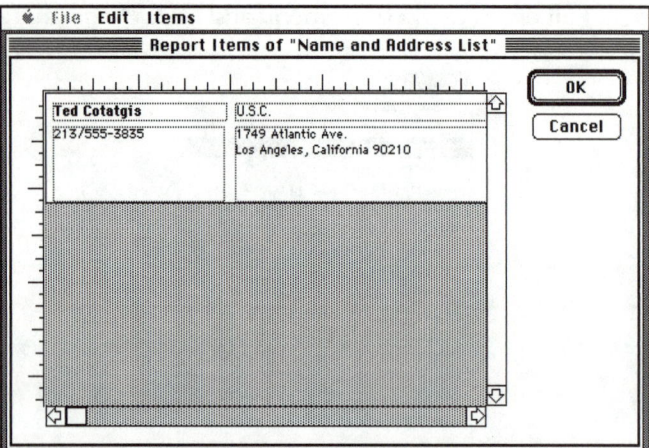

A close-up of the top left record space is displayed, illustrating the layout of the first card in your Addresses stack (or whatever card you were viewing).

5. If you are satisfied with the layout, click OK to return to the Print Report dialog box, and then click Print to print the report.

6. Repeat steps 3-5 to view the report template for the Address Book report.

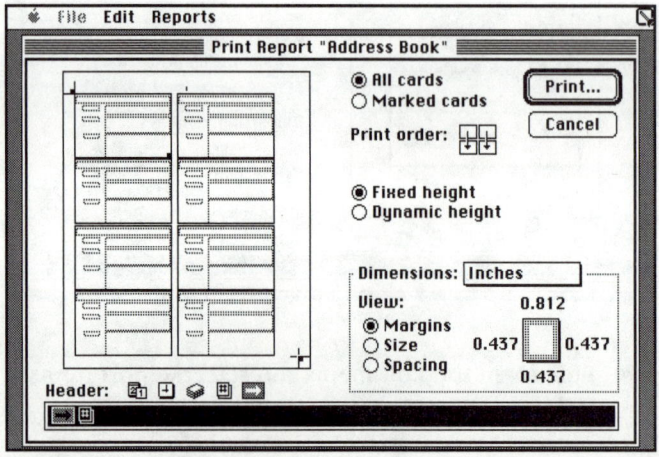

The template for the Address Book report is shown here.

If you want to change the field layout or attributes in any of the supplied reports, you can do so easily. The section in this chapter, "Creating New Reports," will take you through each level of a report and show how to add or modify the contents.

94

4

```
                              1
Roger Bloxberg                      Andrea Harley
  Address:  23801 Calabasas Road, St. 2050      Address:  2130 Manchester
           Calabasas  California 91302                   Playa del Rey Ca 80090
  Telephone: 818/992-3222                  Telephone: 344-5590


     Notes:  Mac Products:                 Notes:
            American English Writing Guide
            Instant Library of Quotations

Ted Cotatgis                        Shane Hopkins
  Address:  1749 Trojan Way                 Address:  5400 S. Abbey Lane
           Los Angeles California 90210               Portsmouth R.I. 02840
  Telephone: 555-3835                   Telephone: 494-0170


     Notes:                          Notes:
            9/21 Called to confirm meeting on 10/1.
            He assured me he would be there.

Pamela Cotatgis                     Jennifer Hopkins
  Address:  3151 Airway  Ave                Address:  802 Westerly Place
           Costa Mesa  CA 92626                      Newport Beach CA 90202
  Telephone: 714-540-4433                  Telephone: 714/851-1441


     Notes:                          Notes:

Gabriel Gold                        Alyssa Hopkins
  Address:  8802 Van Nuys Blvd.              Address:  1607 Calderwood
           Panorama City  Ca 91402                   Long Beach California 90809
  Telephone: 818-891-5655                  Telephone: 683-0789


     Notes:                          Notes:
```

Here is a portion of a printed report.

Printing Mailing Labels

To print mailing labels from all the cards in your Address Book stack, use the predefined template supplied for several different size labels. If you want to print labels only for a certain subset of cards, then you must first mark the cards you want to print.

Marking Cards

When you mark cards in a stack, you select cards that meet a particular criteria. For example, you might want to print address labels for people living within a particular ZIP code, or a contact list report of all people working for a particular company.

95

It is important to understand that each criteria you set will narrow the search. In other words, if you mark all cards that contain a particular company name and a particular ZIP code, then only those cards that match BOTH the company name criteria and the ZIP code criteria will be marked.

To mark cards in the Addresses stack, follow these steps:

1. Pull down the Utilities menu and select Mark Cards. If you are still in the Print Reports dialog box, select the Cancel button until you return to the Addresses stack.

4

A dialog box is displayed.

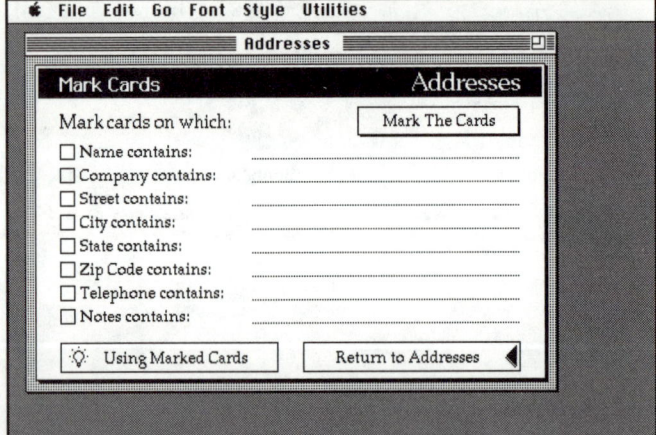

2. Select the appropriate boxes for the fields you want to use as criteria. Type in the specific text for which you want to look.

   For example, if you want to mark all the cards of people living in California, select the State contains box and type **Ca** in the field line.

   You can choose as many different criteria as you want.

   Note: If you type **Ca**, then all states beginning with *CA* will be marked. However, if you type **California**, then any cards with *Ca* as the state will be overlooked.

3. Click the Mark The Cards button in the upper right corner of the card.

A dialog box appears, asking whether you want to first unmark all cards.

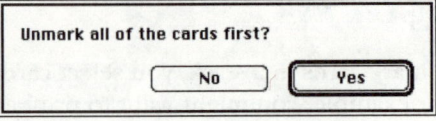

4. Click Yes.

   If you choose No, then whatever cards you previously had marked will remain marked. These marked cards will be added to the previously marked group of cards. If you choose Yes, then only the cards matching the current criteria will be marked.

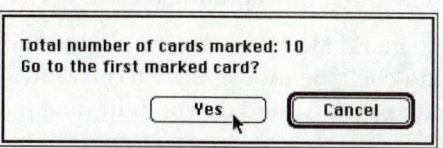

A dialog box appears, telling you how many cards were marked.

4

5. Click Yes to go to the first marked card.

Finding Marked Cards

When a card has been marked, the upper right corner appears turned down.

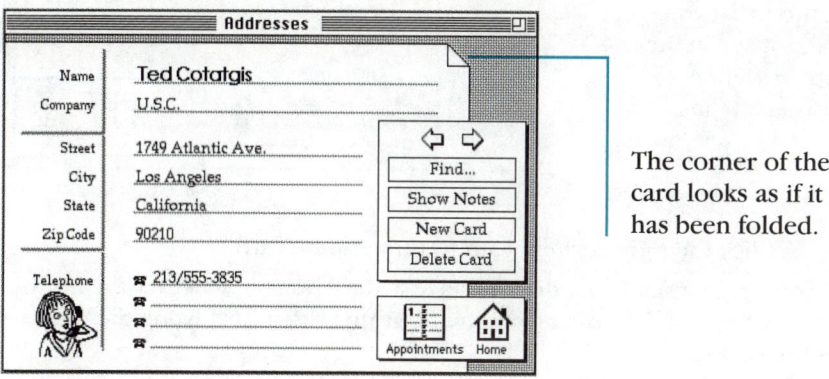

The corner of the card looks as if it has been folded.

To move quickly from one marked card to another, follow these steps:

1. Hold down ⇧Shift and click the right-arrow button to go to the next marked card in the stack.

2. Hold down ⇧Shift and click the left-arrow button to go to the previous marked card in the stack.

Marking or Unmarking Additional Cards

Sometime you may want to mark a particular card in a stack based on no criteria at all. Say, for example, that you marked all the cards for those people living in California so that you could print address labels. Then, you remember one other person for whom you also want to print out a label who doesn't live in California. You can still mark that one additional card.

1. Go to the card you want to mark. Move the Browse tool to the upper right corner of the card and click the mouse once to mark the card. The corner of the card will appear turned down, indicating the card is marked.

The card appears marked because in the Address Book stack there is a Mark Card button that you cannot see in the upper right corner of the card.

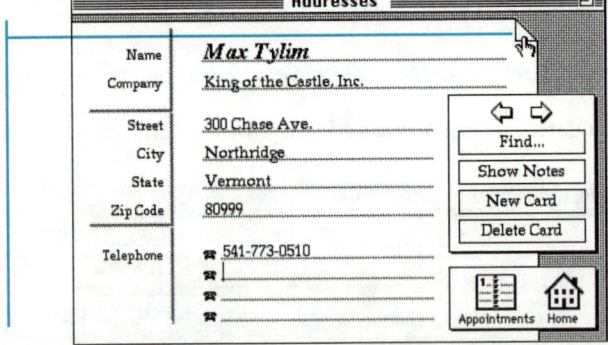

2. Click the right corner again to unmark the card.

If you are in a stack that doesn't have a Mark button, whether the button is invisible or not, you can always mark or unmark a card using the message box. Follow these steps:

1. Pull down the Go menu and select Message. (Or, use the key combination ⌘-M.)

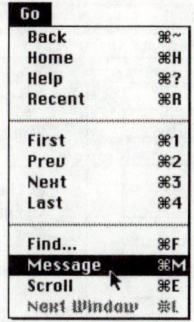

Here, Message is
selected from the
Go menu.

4

2. Type **mark this card** in the message box and press (Return) .

The message box
should look like
this.

Note: You will not see the card marked immediately, but if you move
to the next card and then go back to this one, you will see the card has
been marked.

3. Click the left corner close box of the message box.

You also can use the following mark/unmark commands in the message box:

- To unmark a card, type **unmark card**.
- To unmark all cards, type **unmark all cards**.
- To show marked cards, type **show marked cards**.
- To print marked cards, type **print marked cards**.

Printing Mailing Labels for Marked Cards

Now that you have marked the cards for which you want to print mailing
labels, all you have to do is use the predefined report template for printing
labels.

1. Insert the Avery label forms into your printer.

2. Pull down the File menu and select Print Report.

3. Pull down the Reports menu and select the correct Avery label dimen-
   sion report form. (The dimensions of your Avery labels should appear
   on the box they came in.)

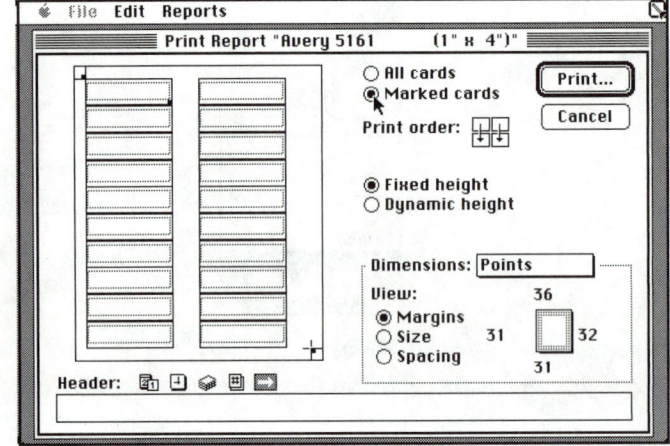

A Print Report
dialog box
appears, display-
ing the layout of
the labels.

4. Select the Marked Cards button.

5. Pull down the Edit menu and select Report Items. Or, as a shortcut,
   move the mouse pointer to the middle of one of the cells displayed
   and double-click the mouse.

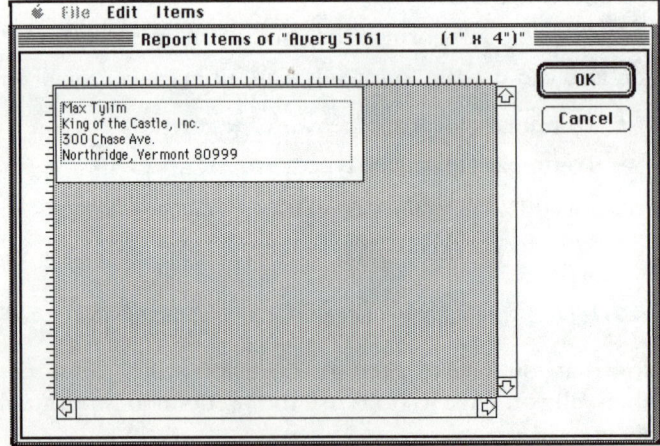

A close-up of the
top left record
space is dis-
played, illustrat-
ing the layout of
the text.

6. Click OK to accept the layout and bring you back to the Print Report
   dialog box.

7. Click Print to print the labels.

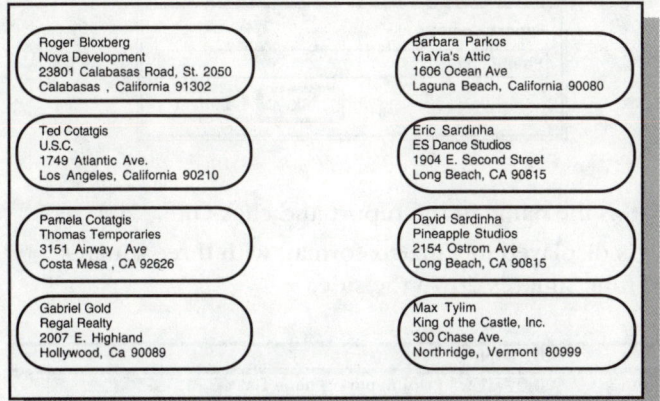

Here is a printout
of labels.

4

Creating New Reports

You also can create a new report template for a stack, using any of the text
fields the stack contains. You will see how easy it is to go to each nested level
and define each level as you go. After you have created the template, you can
copy it to any other stack you want.

To create a simple Phone List report from the Addresses stack, follow these
steps:

1. Pull down the File menu and select Print Report. The template for the
   last report you were using is displayed.

2. Pull down the Reports menu and select New Report.

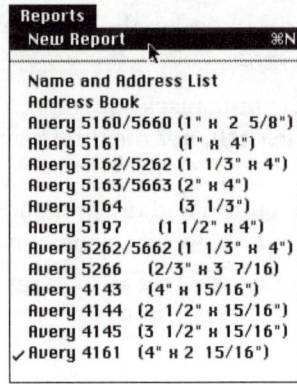

Here, New Report
is selected from
the Reports
menu.

A dialog box
appears.

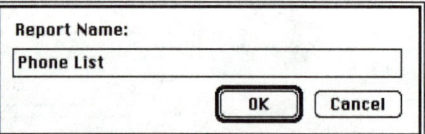

3. Type in **Phone List** as the name of the report and click OK.

A sample template is displayed in a matrix format, with three squares across the top and nine squares down the side.

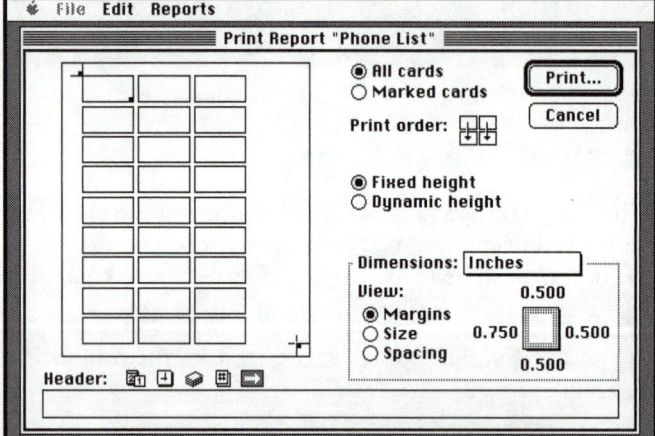

Each square is
called a *cell* and
represents one
card in the stack.

Designing a Report Layout

The first step in creating a new report is to design the page format, including the margins, size, and location of the cards. Follow these steps:

1. Move the mouse pointer onto the little black square, or the *handle*, in the bottom right corner of the first cell, *not* the little black square at the bottom right of the page.

2. Press and hold down the mouse button and drag the mouse to the right margin until only one cell is displayed horizontally across the page.

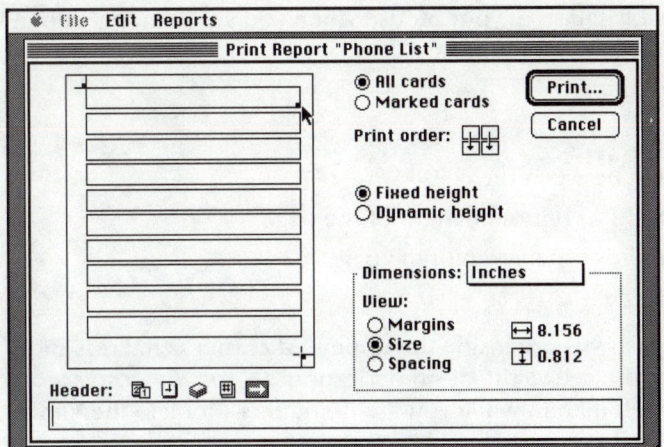

Your screen
should look like
this.

4

3. Select the bottom right corner of the cell again and drag the mouse up to the top margin as far as it will go until the maximum number of cell rows are displayed on the page.

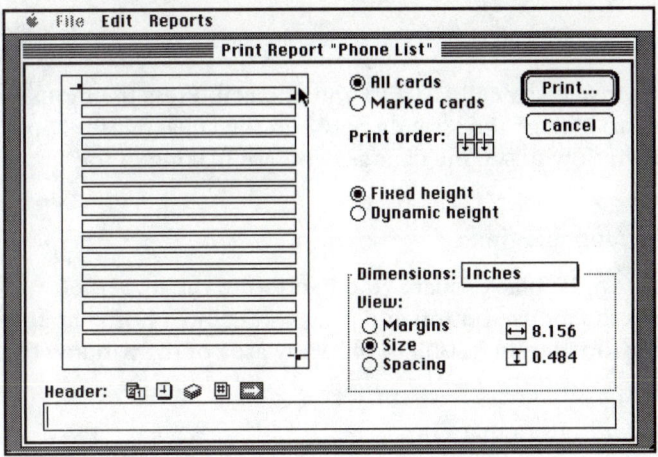

Your screen
should now look
like this.

Depending on the exact location of your mouse when you are working with the cells, you can do one of several things:

- Move the cell.
- Resize the cell.
- Change the spacing between the cells.
- Change the right and/or bottom margin of the page.
- Change the left and/or top margin of the page.

4

To move or position the cell:

Place the mouse pointer anywhere inside the upper left corner cell. Press the mouse button and drag the cell to the desired location. (**Note:** You also are changing the upper or left margin while you are doing this—look in the View area of the window.)

To resize the cell:

Place the mouse pointer on the black square (the handle) in the bottom right corner of the first cell. Press the mouse button and drag vertically or horizontally to resize the cell. (**Note:** Look in the View area of the window to see the cell's new dimensions.)

To change the spacing between cells:

Place the mouse pointer inside any cell EXCEPT the first cell. Press the mouse button and drag the cell to change the spacing between the cells. (**Note:** Look in the View area of the window to see the changes you are making in the spacing.)

To change the left and/or top margin:

Place the mouse pointer on the black square (the handle) in the upper left corner of the page. Press the mouse button and drag vertically or horizontally to change the left and/or top margin. (Look in the View area of the window to see the changes.)

To change the right and/or bottom margin:

Place the mouse pointer on the handle in the lower right corner of the page. Press the mouse button and drag vertically or horizontally to change the right and/or bottom margin. (Look in the View area of the window to see the changes.)

Selecting and Placing Fields in the Cells

The next step is to decide which text fields in the stack you want to include in the report and how you want to lay out the fields in the cells. Each cell reserves the space for information from one card in the stack. The information you display in each cell must come from a text field in the card. You can display as many fields in the cell as you can fit.

To identify the layout for the fields in this Phone List report, follow these steps:

1. Pull down the Edit menu and select Report Items. Or, as a shortcut, you can double-click inside any cell in your template to access the Report Items window.

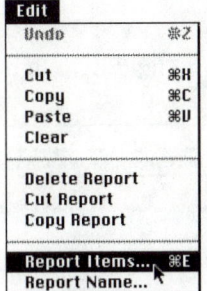

Here, Report Items is selected from the Edit menu.

A window appears, displaying an enlarged version of one cell in your template. Also, a new menu (Items) appears on the top menu line, replacing the Reports menu.

2. Pull down the Items menu and select New Item (or, use the key combination ⌘-N). A dotted rectangle appears in the upper left corner of the cell. This rectangle represents one text field.

3. Place the mouse pointer on any corner of the dotted rectangle. Pressing the mouse button, drag the mouse to resize the rectangle.

105

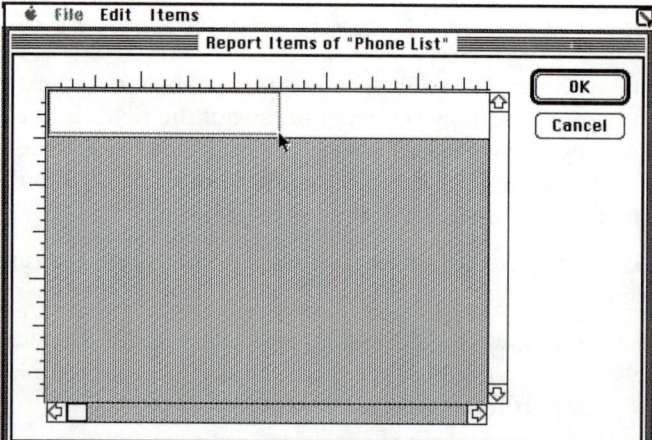

Enlarge the rectangle so that it covers about half of the entire cell space.

4. Repeat steps 2 and 3 to enter a second field item in the cell.

The second dotted rectangle appears in the middle of the first.

5. Place the mouse pointer inside the second dotted rectangle and, pressing the mouse button, drag the second item to the right of the first one.

6. Click the bottom right corner of the rectangle and, pressing the mouse button, drag the rectangle to enlarge it until it is about the same size as the first one.

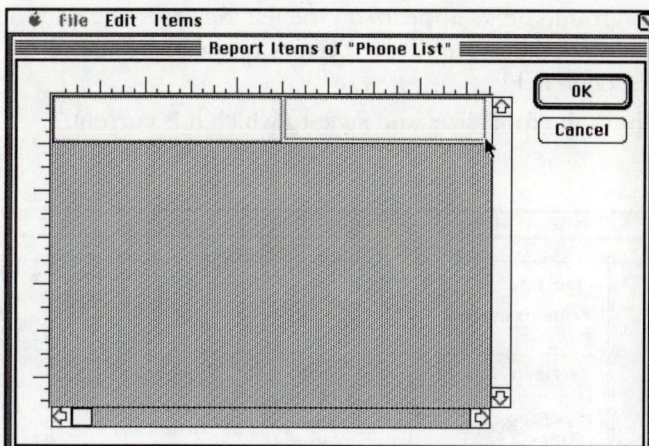

Your screen should look like this.

Identifying Field Contents

Now that you have designed the layout for the fields in the cell, the next step is to identify which fields you want displayed. To continue to the next level of the report, follow these steps:

1. Click inside the area designated for the first field. Then, pull down the Items menu and select Item Info. Or, as a shortcut, double-click inside the field area to access the Item Info dialog box.

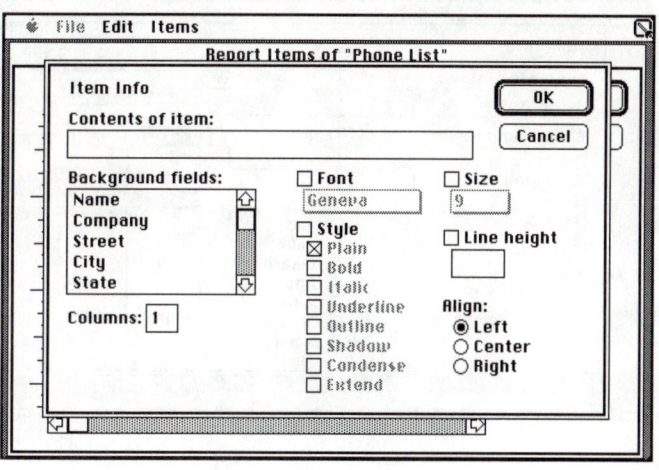

A dialog box appears.

107

2. A list of all the background fields appears on the left. Select Name and notice how the box labeled Contents of item is automatically filled in for you with the Name field.

3. The name will print in the font, size, and style to which it is currently set in the card.

4

However, you will notice that there are three "greyed out" menus in the dialog box for Font, Size, and Style.

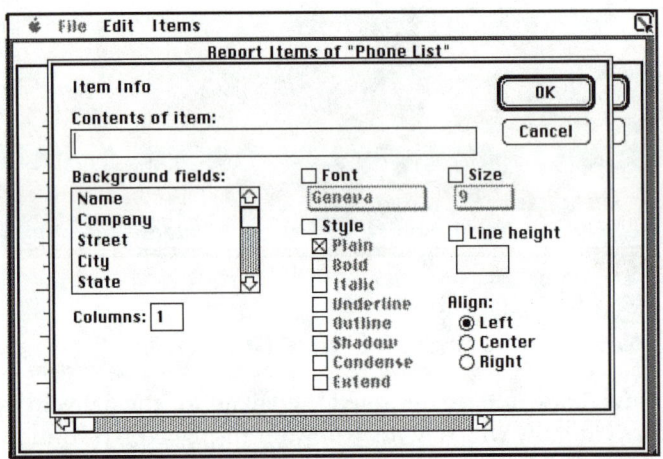

If you want to change any of the font properties, first click the Font checkbox, and then press and hold down the mouse button to reveal the fonts from which you can choose. Make your selection. The Size checkbox works in the same way. Then, select any of the Font styles listed.

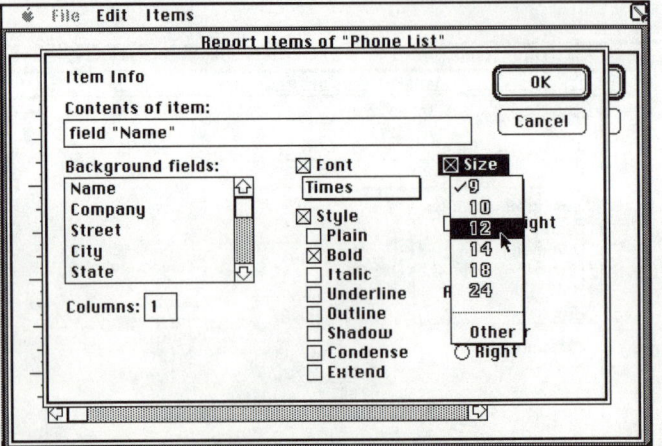

108

You also can change the line height and alignment, and the number of columns in which the text will print. The line height option refers to the spacing between the lines of text in the report. The alignment refers to how the text is displayed. If you want to override the line height and alignment of the original field, click the appropriate checkboxes to make your selections. The columns option is very handy if the field you are going to include in the report is a long text field. By setting the number of columns to 2 or more, the text will print in newspaper-style fashion.

4. After you have made your selections, click OK.

5. Move the mouse pointer inside the second field box and double-click to get to the Item Info dialog box again.

6. Position the mouse pointer onto the bottom arrow of the Background Fields window. Press and hold down the mouse button to scroll the list. Select Phone1.

7. Click OK. A display of the report appears.

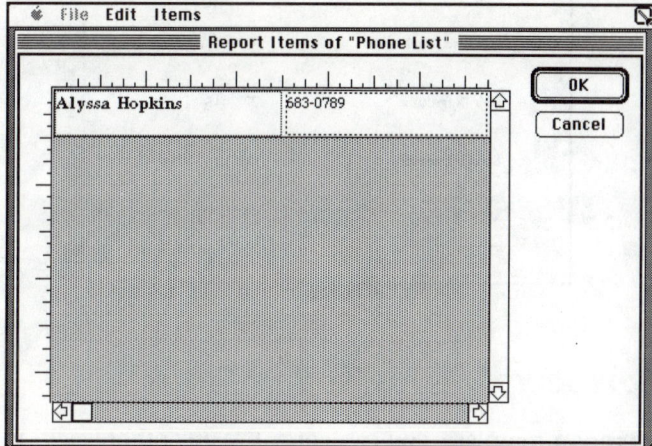

If you want to make additional changes to either field, double-click in the field and make your changes.

8. Click OK to return to the Print Report dialog box, and then click Print to print the report.

4

Roger Bloxberg	818/992-3222
Ted Cotatgis	555-3835
Pamela Cotatgis	714-540-4433
Gabriel Gold	818-891-5655
Andrea Harley	344-5590
Shane Hopkins	494-0170
Jennifer Hopkins	714/851-1441
Alyssa Hopkins	683-0789
Jack Kennedy	714-497-5665
Necia Mehling	374-0405
Barbara Parkos	433-9011
Eric Sardinha	376-4434
David Sardinha	(213) 430-7514
Max Tylim	773-0510

Here is the finished report.

Copying the Report Template to Another Stack

After you have created a report template, you can copy it to any other stack you want. Copying a report template is helpful if, for example, you maintain one Address stack for your personal friends and relatives and another for business contacts. The same reports would be useful for both stacks. To copy the report template to another stack, you first must be in the stack where the template you want to copy exists. Follow these steps:

1. Pull down the File menu and select Print Report.
2. Pull down the Reports menu and select the report template you want to copy. The report template appears.

3. Pull down the Edit menu and select Copy Report (or use the key combination ⌘-C).

4. Click the Cancel button to leave the Print Report dialog box.

5. Go to the stack into which you want to copy the report template.

6. Pull down the File menu and select Print Report.

7. Pull down the Edit menu and select Paste Report.

    From there you can make any modifications you like. Before you print the report, HyperCard will ask whether you want to save your changes.

Summary

This chapter showed you how to use HyperCard's printing and reporting capabilities. You learned how to choose a printer and set up the page for your printer, and how to print a card, a specific field in a card, or an entire stack. You also learned how to mark (and unmark) specific cards in a stack based on some criteria for sorting or printing.

This chapter also discussed Printing Reports, a new feature in HyperCard 2.0. You learned how to work with the Print Report dialog box and how to edit existing report templates and create new ones from scratch. You also learned how to copy report templates from one stack to another.

Specifically, you learned the following key information about HyperCard:

- To choose a printer, select Chooser from the Apple menu and select the printer you want to use.

- To set up the page for your selected printer, select Page Setup from the File menu, and then select the appropriate options.

- To print the card currently displayed on the screen, select Print Card from the File menu. If you hold down ⇧Shift while you select Print Card, the Print dialog box will appear.

- To print a specific field on the card, select Print Field from the File menu. Then, select from the dialog box the field (either the card field or the background field) you want to print.

- By deselecting the Use Width of Field option, you can display the information in the field across the page, rather than be restricted to the exact width of the field in the card.

■ To print a stack, select the Print Stack option in the File menu. The Print Stack dialog box appears, where you can change the page margins, size of the cards, and spacing between the cards. You also can define the number of cards printed per page, and the page format.

■ You can add a header to the top of every printed page of the stack. You can add several header options, including the current date, time, name of the stack, and page number.

■ To print a supplied report for a stack, such as an Address Book page or mailing labels, select Print Report from the File menu. A Print dialog box appears, displaying the supplied report's layout. Two new menus, Edit and Reports, also become available. Select the report you want to print from the Reports menu.

■ To mark one or more cards in a stack based on some criteria, select Mark Cards from the Utilities menu. Then, select the appropriate boxes in the dialog box for the fields you want to use as criteria. You also can mark or unmark cards by typing commands in the message box.

■ To move from one marked card to the next, hold down ⇧Shift and click the right- or left-arrow button.

■ You can create a new report template for a stack, using any of the text fields the stack contains. To create a new report, select New Report from the Reports menu. First, design the report layout, and then choose the specific fields you want to include in the report.

■ To copy a report template from one stack to another, choose Copy Report from the Edit menu, and then go to the stack into which you want to copy the report template. Select Print Report, and then select Paste Report. From there, you can make any modifications you like.

You can see that if you put a little thought into it, you can create plenty of useful reports from just about any HyperCard stack. The next chapter introduces you to the next level of HyperCard, called *Painting*, which gives you access to HyperCard's Painting tools. With these tools, you can add graphics to the cards in a stack.

4

Using HyperCard Graphics

Now that you're comfortable entering and editing text on a card, you're ready to move on to the next level of HyperCard, called *Painting*. Here's where your artistic abilities will emerge, although you certainly do not need to be an artist to have fun with HyperCard's graphic capabilities.

In HyperCard, as with other Macintosh "paint" programs, graphics are images made up of dots, where each dot is either black or white. The dots are sometimes referred to as *bits* or *pixels*. A HyperCard picture is sometimes referred to as a *bit-mapped image* because it is a collection of dots, or bits. You can place a Hyper-Card picture on a card or on a background so that the picture is shared by several cards.

This chapter will introduce you to each of the Painting tools and their basic functions, as well as a few special options and shortcuts. You also will learn how to import or export pictures from other graphics programs to and from your HyperCard stacks. And lastly, you will learn how to copy pictures from one card or stack to another and modify them as you wish.

But, like any other graphics program, the best way to learn HyperCard's graphic capabilities is simply to experiment and play with the tools and options available.

Setting the preference level to Painting

Using the Painting power keys

Using the Tools menu

Saving your work

Exporting pictures

Importing a MacPaint document

Customizing a card's appearance

5

Key Terms in This Chapter

Navigator palette	A floating window that provides buttons to replicate the functionality of the Go menu (except Scroll). You can show or hide the Navigator palette on any card you choose.
Painting	The third user level of HyperCard, which gives you access to HyperCard's Painting tools and graphics capabilities.
Bit-mapped image	A screen or printed graphic image consisting of dots, where each dot represents one or more bits of the image.
Pixel	Each single dot or picture element of the bit-mapped image.
General tools	The Browse tool, the Button tool, and the Field tool. At the Painting user level, you have access only to the Browse tool. When you change your user level to Authoring, you have access to the other two general tools.
Paint tools	There are 15 Painting tools available to use in the Tools menu. When you select any one of the Painting tools, the Browse tool (or the other general tools) is no longer functional.
Tear off palettes	To pull away a menu from the top menu bar and place it anywhere else on your screen. When you tear off a menu, the menu is referred to as a *palette*. You can tear off the Tools menu and the Patterns menu.
Export	To save the graphic on a card as a MacPaint document, so that you can use what you have created in a variety of other programs or documents.
Import	To retrieve a MacPaint document into a HyperCard card.

Setting the Preference Level to Painting

To move to the next level of HyperCard, you need to change the user preference level to Painting. Follow these steps:

1. With the Home card on your screen, pull down the Go menu and select Last (or press ⌘-④) to go to the Preferences card.

2. Click the button labeled `Painting`.

114

Note: The Power Keys option appears on this card. This option enables you to use special keyboard shortcuts with the Painting tools. With the Power Keys option selected, for example, you can press $\boxed{F}$ to fill a selected graphic. You probably won't need to use these keyboard shortcuts right away, but as you become more familiar with the Painting tools, you may want to speed up your work. You also can turn on the Power Keys option by selecting the option from the Options menu when you have a Painting tool selected. To learn more about the power keys, go to the Help stack, choose Find Topic, and type **Power Keys**.

3. Click the right-arrow button to return to the Home card.

After you change your user level to Painting, an additional menu, named Tools, appears on the top menu line. This menu contains several different items you will learn to use as you progress through this chapter.

5

Using the Tools Menu

The Tools menu consists of 3 general tools and 15 Paint tools. The three general tools include the Browse tool, the Button tool, and the Field tool. You already have worked with the Browse tool in the previous chapters. The Button tool and the Field tool are not functional until your user level is set to Authoring, which is covered in the next chapter.

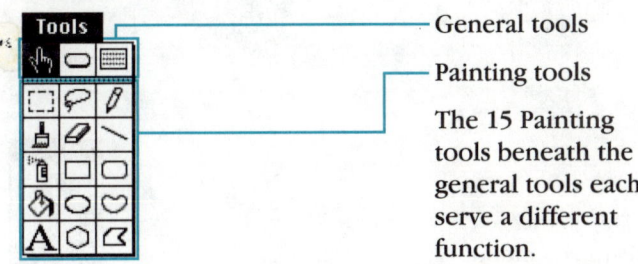

General tools

Painting tools

The 15 Painting tools beneath the general tools each serve a different function.

You will learn about each tool in this chapter and then have the opportunity to experiment with the tools. When you select any one of the Painting tools, three additional menus appear on the menu line: Paint, Options, and Patterns. These additional menus give you even more options to create, manipulate, and enhance graphic images.

5

This is the Paint
menu.

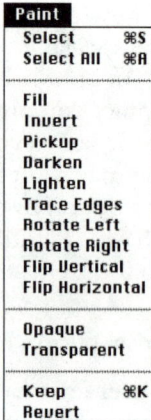

This is the
Options menu.

This is the
Patterns menu.

Note: When you select one of the Painting tools in the Tools menu, the Browse tool is no longer functional. If, for example, you are using a Painting tool and you click the right-arrow button to move to the next card in a stack, you would be unable to do so until you select the Browse tool from the Tools menu.

Using Tear-Off Palettes

There are two menus you use in conjunction with HyperCard graphics that you can "tear off" from the top menu line and put anywhere on the screen. These menus are the Tools menu and the Patterns menu.

When you tear off a menu, the menu is referred to as a *palette*. After you have torn off a menu, you can move the palette to any area on the screen that is convenient, and you do not have to continually pull down the menu to change tools or patterns. When you tear off a menu, you will find it much easier to use the "double-click" options on some of the menu items.

To tear off a menu, follow these steps:

1. Pull down the Tools menu and, keeping the mouse button pressed down, drag toward the middle of the screen to pull off the palette.

5

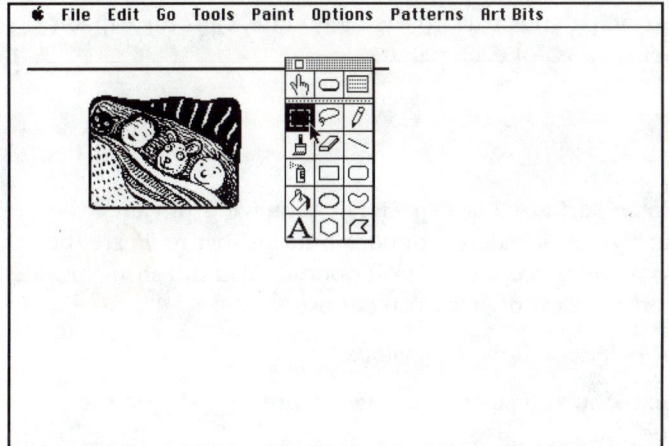

Here, the Tools menu has been torn off the top menu line.

2. To move the palette around your screen, position the mouse pointer onto the top line of the palette. Press and hold down the mouse button, and drag the mouse to move the palette. Moving a palette is identical to moving any Macintosh window.

After one of the tools in the Tools menu is selected, you also can tear off the Patterns menu in the same way.

117

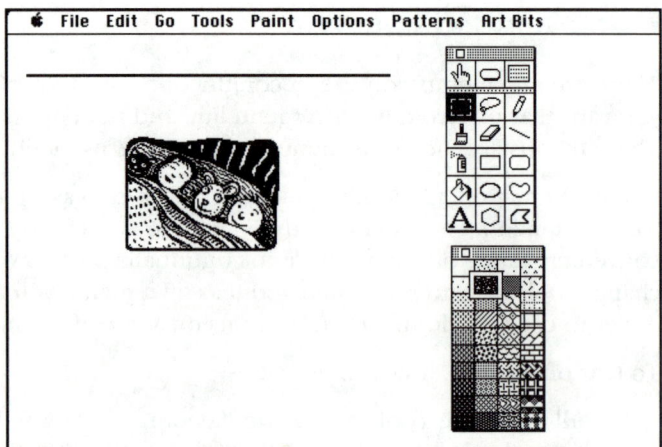

Here, the Patterns menu has been torn off and moved below the Tools menu.

5

3. To return the tear-off palettes back to the menu line, click the top left corner box (the close box) of each palette.

The Navigator Palette

Another new feature in HyperCard 2 is a special floating window called the *Navigator palette*. The Navigator palette contains buttons that replicate the functionality of the Go menu (except the Scroll option). You can show or hide the Navigator palette on any card or stack you choose.

To show the Navigator palette, follow these steps:

1. Pull down the Go menu and select Message, or press ⌘-Ⓜ. In the message box, type **NAV**.

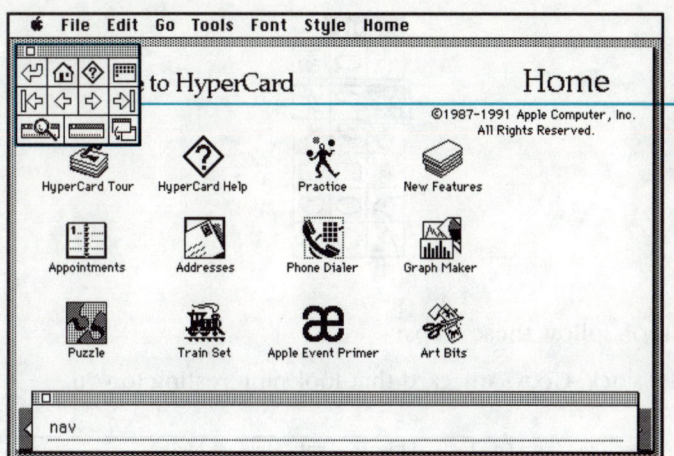

The Navigator palette appears.

5

2. You can move the Navigator palette anywhere on your screen. To hide the Navigator palette, click the close box of its window.

HyperCard stack authors can create their own custom navigator palettes, using some or all of the buttons that are shown on the Navigator palette. Some of the stacks that come with HyperCard have custom navigator palettes that will appear when you open the stack (or sometimes when you go to any card other than the first card in the stack).

For example, the Art Bits stack has a built-in custom Navigator palette that is automatically displayed on every card except the first card. It contains buttons to go to the previous card, the next card, or the first card (which is the Art Bits category card) in the stack. To hide the custom navigator palette in the Art Bits stack, click the palette's close box or choose Hide Palette from the Art Bits menu.

The Selection Tool

The Selection tool is used to select pictures or parts of pictures to move, copy, or delete. The Selection tool works best with rectangular images because along with the picture, the tool also selects a rectangular background around the image.

When you use the Selection tool in combination with the Shift key, the Option key, or the ⌘ key, you are given more options to make your work easier or to create special effects.

This is the
Selection tool.

To use the Selection tool, follow these steps:

1. Open the Art Bits stack. Go to any card that looks interesting to you.

For this example,
click the Beasts
button.

Note: If you do not want the custom Navigator palette to remain on the screen, pull down the Art Bits menu and select Hide Palette, or click the close box of the palette's window.

2. Pull down the Tools menu and select the Selection tool. The mouse pointer turns into a dotted-line cross.

3. Position the mouse pointer at the upper left corner of any picture on the card. Pressing and holding down the mouse button, drag the mouse down and to the right to enclose the picture. Release the mouse.

The moving rectangle around the picture and background indicates that the picture is currently selected.

5

Now you can move, delete, cut, or copy the image. First, you will copy the selected image onto a new card so that you can experiment with all the Selection tool options.

Copying a Picture

After you have selected a picture with the Selection tool, you can copy the picture. When you copy a picture, the original stays where it is; you can put the new copy anywhere you choose without affecting the original.

To copy a picture, follow these steps:

1. With the picture still selected (enclosed in the moving rectangle), pull down the Edit menu and select Copy Picture. Or, use the key combination ⌘-C.

2. Pull down the Edit menu and select New Card.

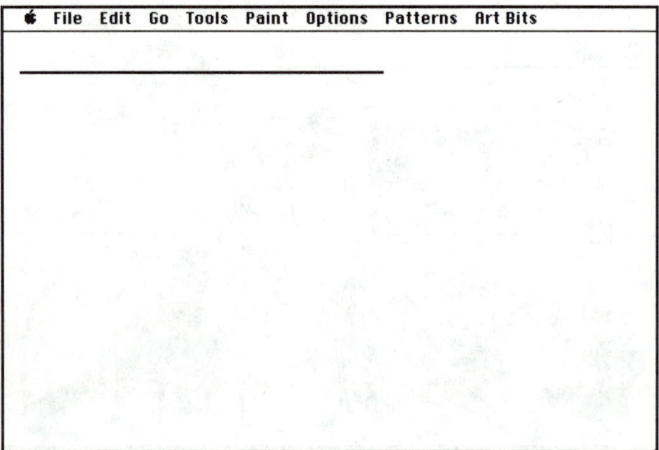

A blank card appears, containing only the background graphics on it.

5

3. Pull down the Edit menu and select Paste Picture, or press ⌘-V.

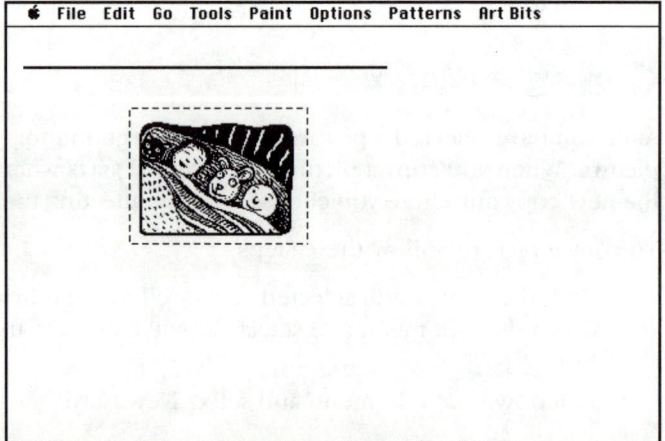

The picture you copied appears on the new card.

Moving a Picture

After you have selected a picture with the Selection tool, you can move the picture. When you move a picture, unlike when you copy it, the picture moves to the new location and disappears from the original location.

With the picture selected (enclosed in the moving rectangle), position the mouse pointer in the center of the picture. Pressing and holding down the mouse button, drag the mouse in any direction to move the selected picture anywhere on the screen.

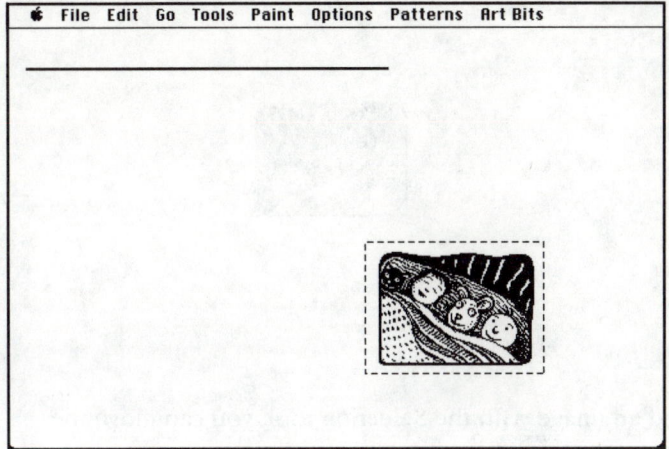

Here, the picture
is moved down
and to the right.

The picture will remain selected and able to be moved until you click the mouse outside the dotted selection area.

Clearing or Deleting a Picture

To clear, or delete, a picture after you have selected it with the Selection tool, follow this procedure:

1. Select the picture with the Selection tool. Then, either pull down the Edit menu and select Clear Picture, or press [Del].

2. If you change your mind after you have cleared or deleted a picture, you can immediately undo the operation by selecting Undo from the Edit menu (or press [⌘]-[Z]). However, you must undo the operation *immediately* after you delete the image.

Note: The difference between Clear/Delete and Cut Picture is an important one to understand. When you clear, or delete, a picture, it is gone forever—unless you immediately undo the operation. When you cut a picture, you put it into a temporary storage area to paste it in at a later time (or until you cut or copy another picture into the storage buffer).

Tightening a Selection

When you select a picture with the Selection tool, you may want to force the rectangular area around the picture to be as small as possible. To "hug" the image, use the Selection tool as described earlier, but before you release the mouse button, hold down [⌘].

When you release
the mouse
button, the
rectangular,
selected area is
tightened to the
smallest rectangle
in which the
picture will fit.

Restricting a Move

After you have selected an image with the Selection tool, you can move the image in any direction on the card. Sometimes, however, you may want to restrict your movements to a vertical or a horizontal motion. Restricting movement is especially helpful when trying to line up several images, for example.

To restrict your movement in a vertical or a horizontal motion, hold down `⇧Shift` before you move the selected image.

Cloning an Image

After you have selected an image with the Selection tool, you can clone, or duplicate, the selected image or area. Cloning is especially useful when you want to make multiple copies of a graphic, and it is much quicker than the conventional copy/paste method.

To clone a selected image, hold down `Option` before you move the selected image. An exact duplicate of the image will remain in the original position.

Here, an image is
duplicated.

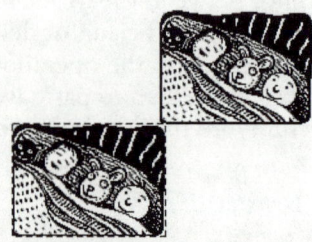

A combination of the Option and Shift keys enables you to clone an image while restricting the movement of its copy.

124

Stretching and Shrinking Images

After you have selected an image with the Selection tool, you can stretch or shrink the image in any direction. You can create some interesting effects by using (or combining) both the stretching and shrinking techniques.

To stretch or shrink the image in the direction you choose, hold down ⌨ while you drag any of the selection's four corners.

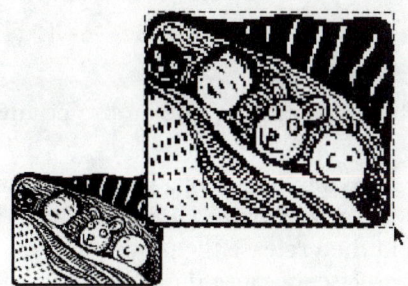

Here, the image is being stretched.

5

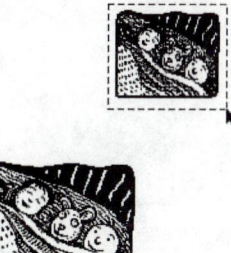

Here, the same image is being shrunk. If you want to resize the picture but keep its proportions intact, hold down both ⇧Shift and ⌨ while resizing the image.

The Lasso

The Lasso is another tool used to select graphic images. It works much the same way as the Selection tool with one major distinction. When you "lasso" an image, you capture the graphic only, without the rectangular area in the background. The Lasso is a handy tool to use when you want to work with nonrectangular images. It might take you a little time to get used to working with the lasso, but once you get the hang of it, you will probably use this tool more often than the rectangular Selection tool when copying graphics from one card or stack to another.

This is the Lasso tool.

To use the Lasso, follow these steps:

5

1. Select the Lasso tool from the Tools palette. The mouse pointer turns into a small lasso.

2. Position the mouse pointer onto any corner of a picture on the card. Pressing and holding down the mouse button, drag the mouse in a circle around the picture, and then release the mouse button. You don't need to be extremely precise, because the lasso hoop will connect itself to the starting point with a straight line when you release the mouse.

Here, the Lasso tool surrounds the image.

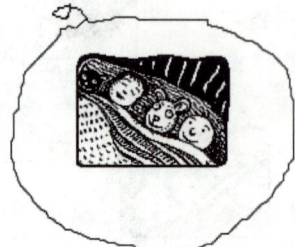

The outer pixels of the image appear to be jumping, indicating that the image is selected. Now you can move, delete, cut, or copy the image in the same ways as explained earlier in the chapter.

Note: If you select an image with the rectangular Selection tool and hold down (Option) before you release the mouse, the rectangular Selection tool will turn into the Lasso tool and will select the image only.

When you use the Lasso tool in combination with (⇧Shift), (Option), or (⌘), you are given more options. You can restrict a move vertically or horizontally; clone, or duplicate, an image; or make multiple copies of an image.

Restricting a Move

After you have selected an image with the Lasso tool, you can move the image in any direction on the card. Sometimes, however, you may want to restrict your movements to a vertical or a horizontal motion. Restricting movement is especially helpful when trying to line up several images, for example.

To restrict your movement in a vertical or horizontal motion, hold down ⇧Shift before you move the lassoed image.

This process works exactly the same way as with the rectangular Selection tool.

Cloning an Image

After you have selected an image with the Lasso tool, you can clone, or duplicate, the selected image or area. Cloning is especially useful when you want to make multiple copies of a graphic, and it is much quicker than the conventional copy/paste method.

To duplicate the image as you move the mouse away from the original image, hold down Option before you move the lassoed image.

This process works exactly the same as with the rectangular Selection tool.

Making Multiple Copy Images

When an image is selected with the Lasso tool, you can create a multiple copy image of the selection. By holding down both ⌘ and Option before moving a lassoed image, a trail of image copies will be left behind the original image.

Hold down both ⌘ and Option before you move the lassoed image.

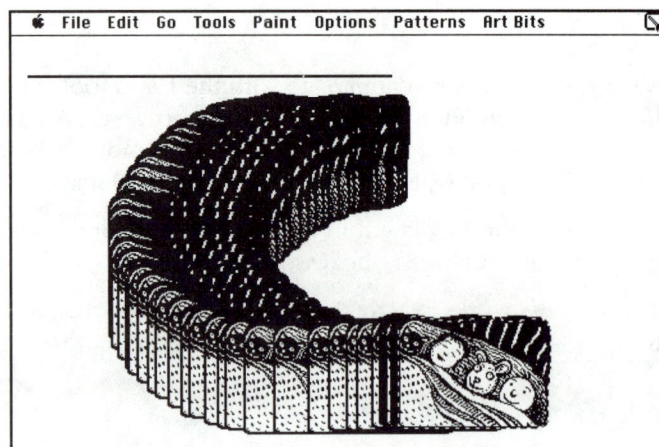

This process leaves behind a trail of the same image as you move the mouse.

Stretching and Shrinking an Image

After you have selected an image with the Lasso tool, you can stretch or shrink the image in any direction. You can create some interesting effects by using (or combining) both the stretching and shrinking techniques.

To stretch or shrink the image in the direction you choose, hold down ⌘ while you drag any of the four corners in the lassoed image. (Or, use ⌘ in combination with ⇧Shift to keep the image's proportions intact.)

This process works exactly the same way as with the Selection tool.

The Pencil Tool

You will probably use the Pencil tool often when you are working with HyperCard graphics. With the Pencil tool, you can draw freehand lines and shapes the same way you would with a regular pencil. Each time you click the mouse with the Pencil tool selected, you create one pixel (either white or black) on the screen. Using the Pencil tool in combination with the FatBits option enables you to create precise graphic images. (Before continuing your work with the various tools, pull off both the Tools menu and the Patterns menu, and place them on the right side of the card. Also, clear the image that is currently on the card.)

1. Select the Pencil tool from the Tools palette. The mouse pointer turns into a pencil.

128

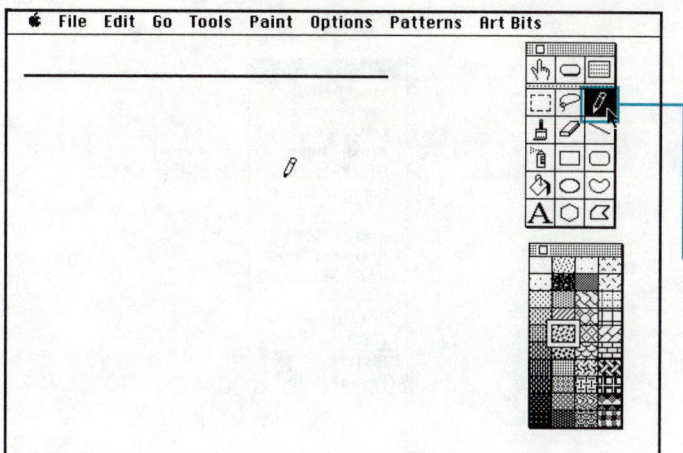

This is the Pencil tool.

5

2. Position the mouse pointer anywhere on the empty card. Pressing and holding down the mouse button, drag the mouse in any direction.

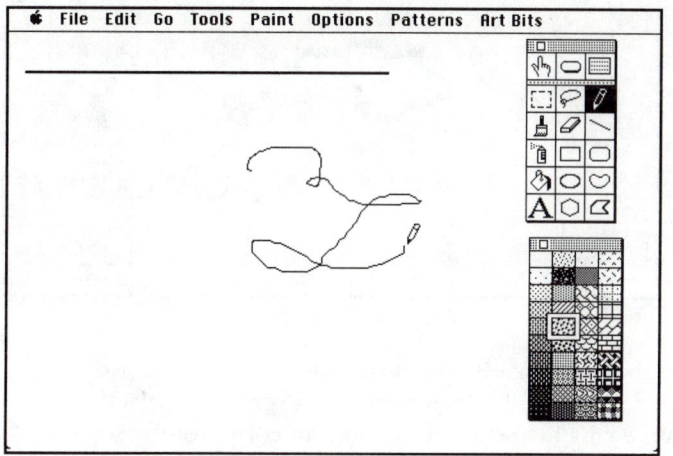

You can draw freehand lines and shapes the same way as you would with a regular pencil.

The Pencil tool is often used in conjunction with the FatBits option, which is on the Options menu. The FatBits option magnifies the graphic with which you are working so that it shows each pixel (dot) the picture is made of. You then can use the pencil to draw or remove one pixel at a time and precisely modify graphic images. To use FatBits, follow these steps:

1. Pull down the Options menu and select FatBits.

129

Here, FatBits is
selected from the
Options menu.

5

An enlarged
version of the
shape you drew
with the pencil
appears, showing
the line as a series
of black dots, or
pixels. The minia-
turized screen in
the bottom left
corner shows
the area of the
shape you are
looking at.

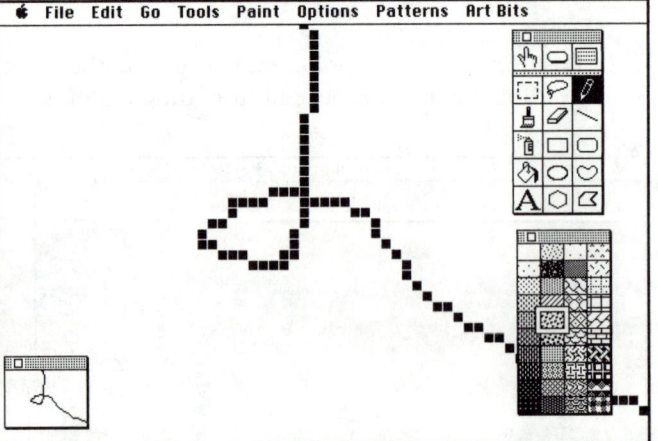

2. Click any one of the black pixels, and it will turn into a white pixel.
   Click a white pixel, and it will turn black. Click every other black
   square. Look in the small window in the bottom corner of the screen
   to see the changes you are making.

3. To move the image up or down the page, press Option . The pencil
   turns into a small hand. Hold down the mouse button and drag the
   hand up or down to view a different area of the page. Every time you
   move the image in any direction, the small screen in the lower left
   corner shows in full view the area on which you are working.

4. Click anywhere in the small window to deselect FatBits and return to
   the graphic's full image.

130

Note: You also can double-click the Pencil tool to get in and out of FatBits. Or, you can first position the pencil onto the area on which you want to work, hold down ⌨, and click the mouse button to go into FatBits.

The Brush Tool

The Brush tool works the same way as the Pencil tool. With the brush, however, you decide which pattern the brush will apply, as well as specify the size and shape of the brush.

To use the Brush tool, follow these steps:

1. Select the Brush tool from the Tools palette. The mouse pointer turns into a small black dot.

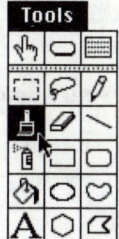

This is the Brush tool.

2. Select any pattern in the Pattern palette by clicking its square.

Here, a pattern is selected.

3. Pull down the Options menu and select Brush Shape.

A dialog box appears, displaying several different brush shape sizes. The one with the box around it is currently selected.

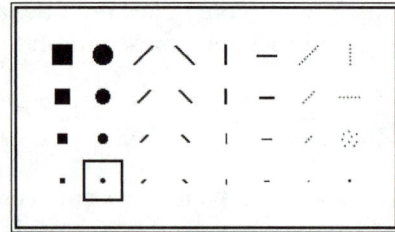

Note: As a shortcut, you can double-click the Brush tool, and the Brush Shape dialog box appears.

4. Select one of the shapes by clicking it.

5. Position the mouse pointer onto any area in the card, and press and hold down the mouse button. Drag the mouse in any direction to paint with the brush.

6. Hold down ⇧Shift to restrict the brush's movements to be horizontal or vertical.

The Eraser Tool

The Eraser tool is the simplest tool to use and the one you will use more than any other, especially at first. As you might guess, the Eraser tool erases any graphic image on the card layer. To use the Eraser tool, follow these steps:

1. Select the Eraser from the Tools palette.

This is the Eraser tool.

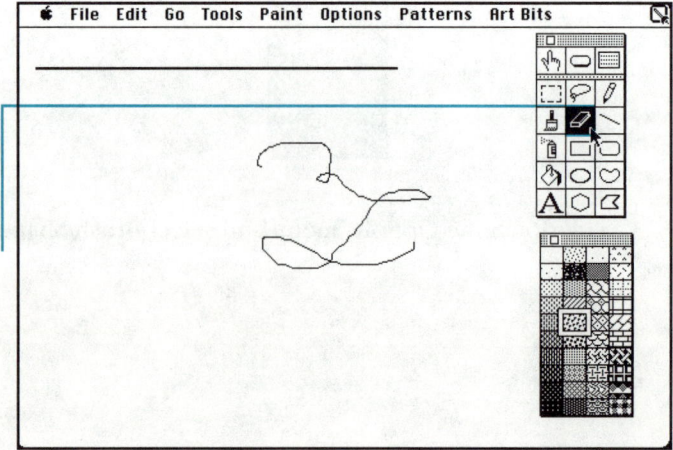

2. Position the mouse pointer onto the graphic you want to erase. Every time you click the mouse, a white pixel replaces the black pixel from the card's graphic. (The Eraser tool will not erase the background graphics.)

You also can keep the mouse button pressed down and drag the mouse to erase a wider area on the screen.

3. Hold down ⬆Shift while you are using the Eraser tool if you want the movement restricted vertically or horizontally. This technique is useful if you need to erase a horizontal or vertical lined shape.

4. Hold down ⌘ while using the Eraser tool to replace the black pixels on the screen with white ones (whether the graphic resides on the card layer or background layer). Although the tool appears to be erasing the background graphics, it is not. It is simply covering the black pixels on the screen with white ones. To make the background graphic reappear, use the Eraser tool without the Option key. This technique erases the white pixels you placed over the background graphic.

5. To erase the entire graphics layer of the card, double-click the Eraser tool. After you have done this, you always can choose Undo from the Edit menu (or press ⌘-Z) to immediately bring back the graphics layer.

The Line Tool

The Line tool is used primarily to create either vertical or horizontal lined objects, other than the shape objects that already appear on the Tools menu. You can change both the thickness of the Line tool and the pattern of the "ink." To use the Line tool, perform the following steps:

1. Select the Line tool from the Tools palette. A cross cursor appears.

133

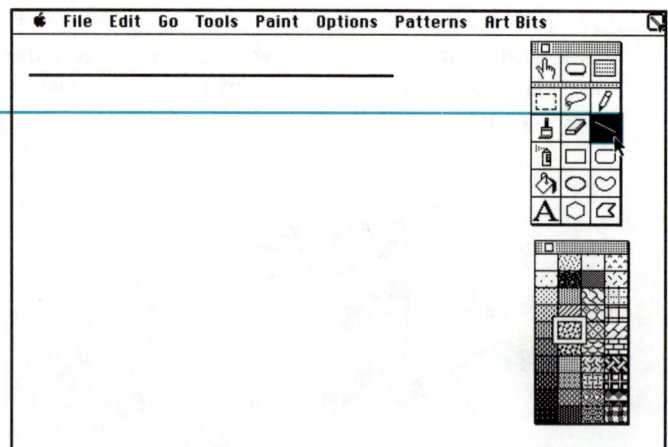

This is the Line
tool.

2. Position the mouse pointer anywhere in the drawing area. Pressing
   and holding down the mouse button, drag the cross cursor in any
   direction to draw a straight line.

3. Pull down the Options menu and select Line Size.

A dialog box
appears, display-
ing several
different line-size
options.

   Note: As a shortcut, you also can double-click the Line tool to access
   the Line Size dialog box.

4. Select one of the line sizes to change the thickness of the Line tool.

5. Select a pattern from the Patterns palette. Then, hold down Option
   while you use the Line tool; the line you draw appears in whatever
   pattern you selected. To restrict lines vertically, horizontally, or in
   15-degree increments, hold down Shift as you draw.

The Spray Tool

The Spray tool works the same way as a can of spray paint. The paint sprays
out of the can in pulses rather than a straight stream. Slowly dragging the
spray will give you a different effect than dragging the can quickly across the
screen.

134

1. Select the Spray tool from the Tools palette. The mouse pointer turns into a circular object in the selected pattern.

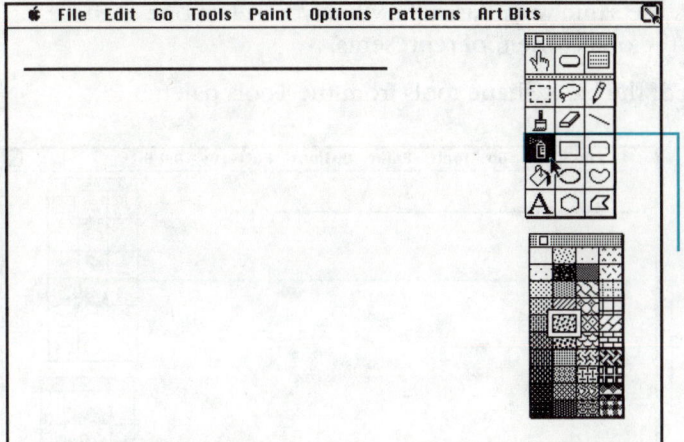

This is the Spray tool.

5

2. Position the "nozzle" anywhere in the drawing area. Keeping the mouse button pressed down, drag the nozzle in any direction.

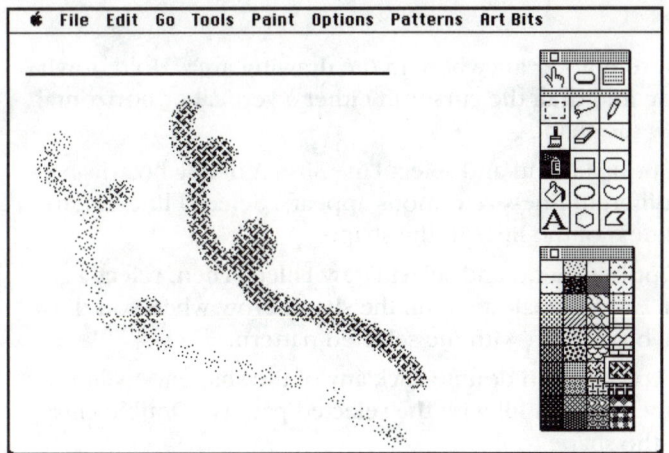

Paint sprays across the screen.

3. Select a pattern from the Patterns palette to change the spray pattern.

4. Hold down ⊞ while using the Spray tool to spray white paint in the selected pattern.

The Basic Shape Tools

The shape tools in the Tools palette—Rectangle, Rounded Rectangle, Oval, and Curve—all work the same way. Basically, when you select one of these tools, you can draw the object the tool represents.

1. Select any one of the basic shape tools from the Tools palette.

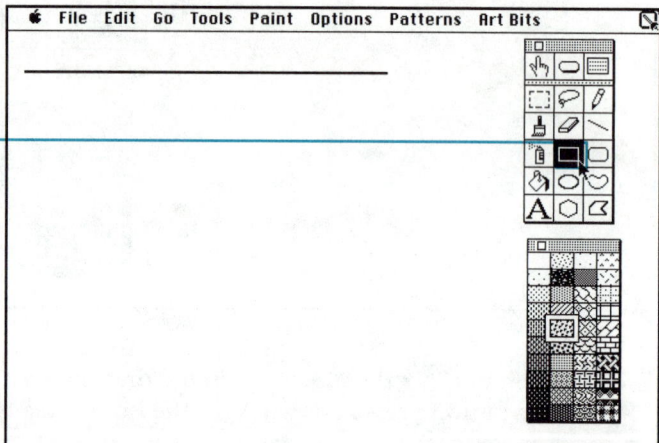

Here, the Rect-
angle shape tool
is selected.

2. Position the mouse pointer anywhere in the drawing area. Hold down the mouse button and drag the cursor in either a vertical or horizontal direction to draw the shape.

3. Pull down the Options menu and select Line Size. A dialog box displaying several different line-size options appears. Select a line-size to change the thickness of the lines in the shape.

4. Pull down the Options menu and select Draw Filled. Then, select a pattern from the Patterns palette to fill the shape. Now when you draw the shape, it will be filled in with the selected pattern.

   Note: As a shortcut, you can double-click any of the shape tools in the palette. The shape tool will fill with the selected pattern. Double-click again to "unfill" the shape tool.

5. Hold down (Option) if you want to draw the shape without the usual black border lines around it. If Draw Filled is not selected, the Option key will cause the rectangle to be outlined in the current pattern.

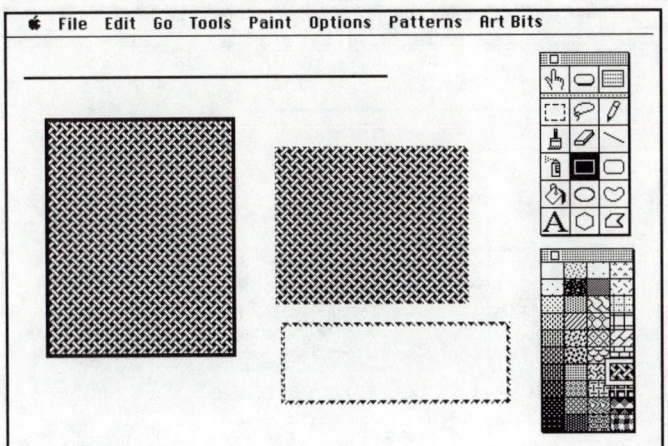

If the shape is not filled, the outline will appear in the selected pattern.

5

6. Press and hold down ⇧Shift while using the Oval tool to draw a perfect circle, or the Rectangle tool to draw a perfect square.

7. After you have drawn the shape, keep the mouse button pressed down. Hold down ⌘ to move the shape anywhere on the screen.

8. Pull down the Options menu and the Paint menu. Select various options to experiment with, such as Rotate, Slant, and Darken. Options in the Paint menu are not available until you select a shape to work with. If the options appear greyed out, select a shape with either the Selection tool or the Lasso tool; the Paint options then become available.

The last four options on the Options menu let you rotate, slant, distort, and show an image in perspective.

This image is
rotated with the
Rotate option
from the Options
menu.

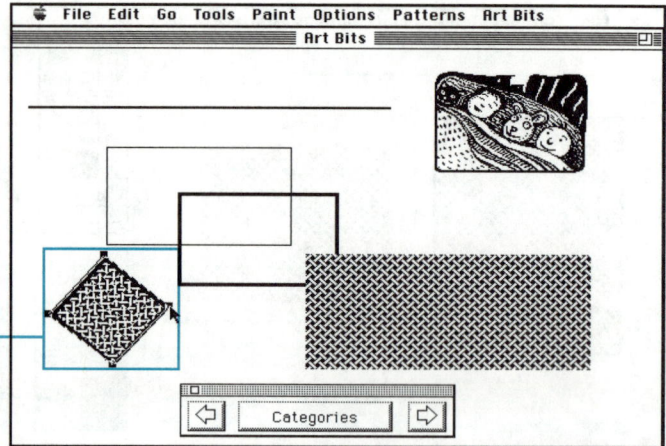

This image is
distorted with the
Distort option
from the Options
menu.

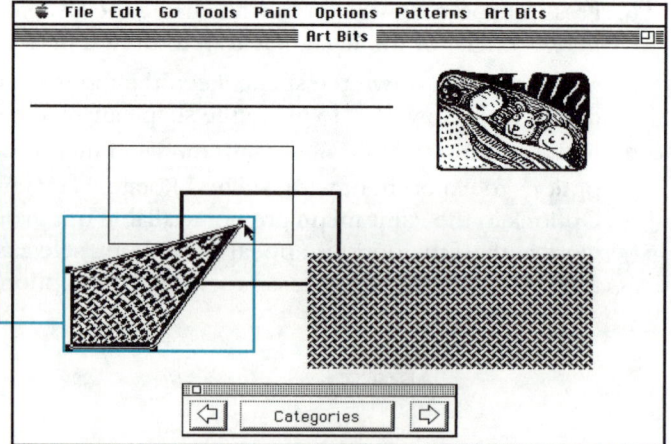

138

The options on the Paint menu let you manipulate the image further.

5

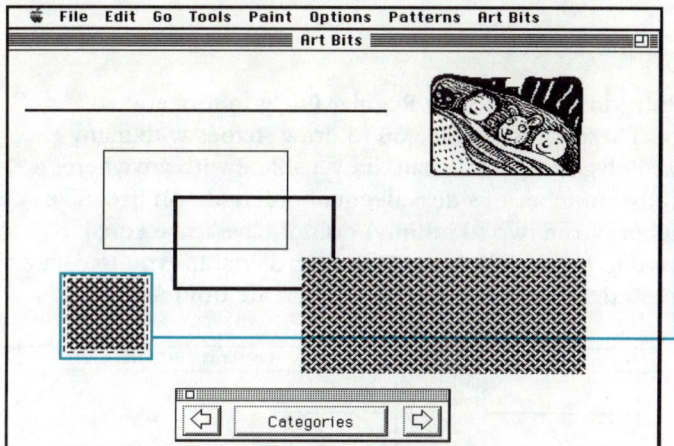

This image is inverted with the Invert option on the Paint menu.

139

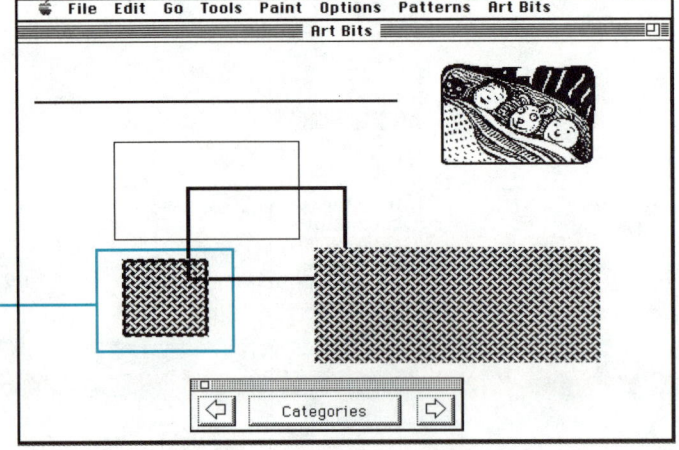

This image is
made transparent
with the Trans-
parent option on
the Paint menu.

5

The Polygon Shape Tools

HyperCard has two Polygon shape tools: a Regular Polygon tool and an
Irregular Polygon tool. These tools enable you to draw shapes with many
sides. With the regular Polygon tool, you can draw a shape with anywhere
from three to an infinitive number of sides, all equal in length. An irregular
polygon's sides (anywhere from two to infinity) do not have to be equal in
length, but they do have to be straight lines. HyperCard enables you to rotate
and size polygons as you draw them so that you can create unique images.

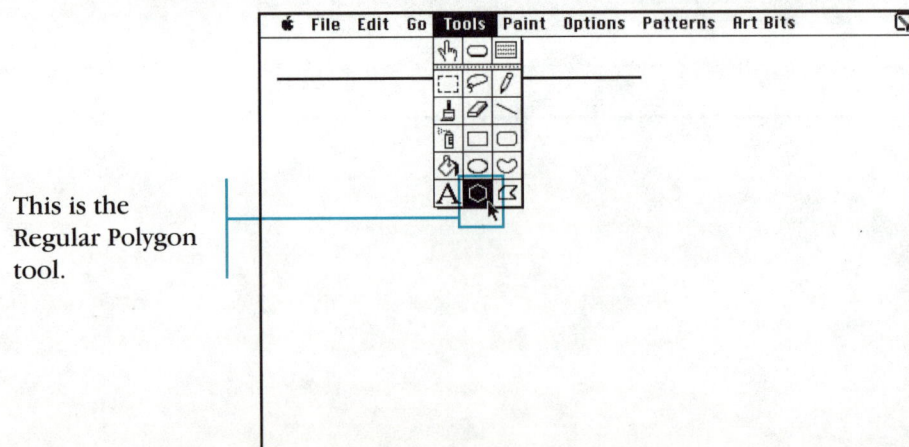

This is the
Regular Polygon
tool.

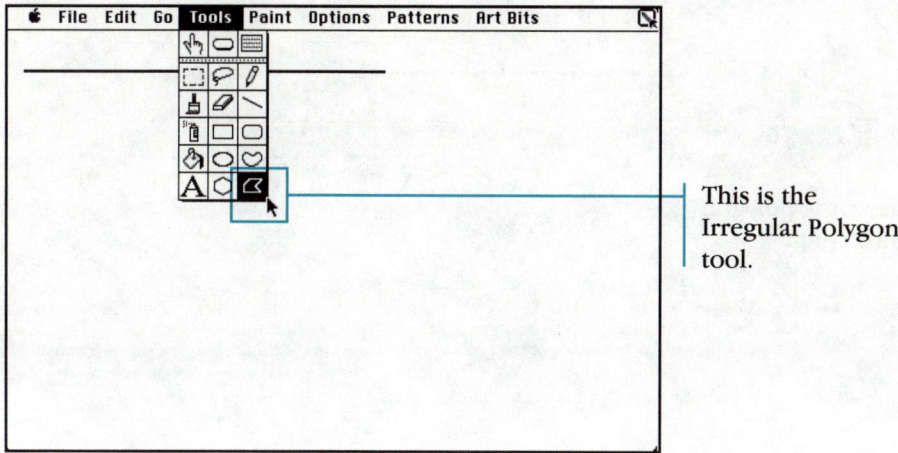

This is the
Irregular Polygon
tool.

5

The Regular Polygon Tool

To use the Regular Polygon tool, perform the following steps:

1. Select the Polygon tool from the Tools palette.

2. Pull down the Options menu and select Polygon Sides.

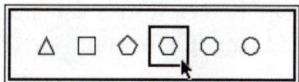

A dialog box
appears, display-
ing various
polygon shapes.

Note: As a shortcut, you can double-click the Regular Polygon tool in
the palette to access the Polygon Sides dialog box.

3. Select a polygon shape by clicking it.

4. Click anywhere in the drawing area. Keeping the mouse button
pressed down, drag the cross-cursor in any direction to draw the
polygon you selected. Move the mouse to the right or left to rotate
the polygon.

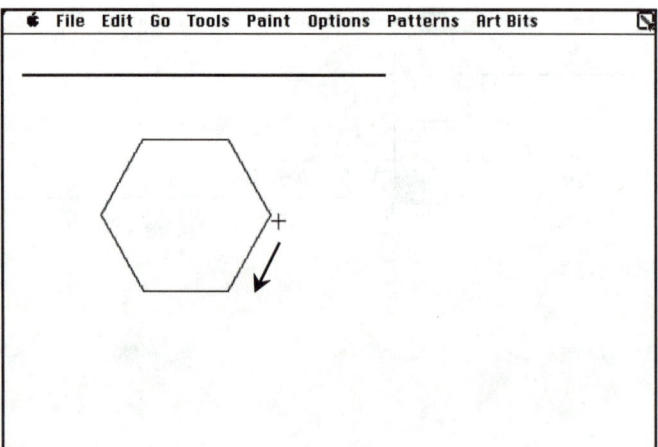

Here, the polygon is rotating.

5

5. Pull down the Options menu and select Line Size. A dialog box appears, displaying several different line-size options. Select any one of the line sizes to change the thickness of the lines in the polygon.

6. Pull down the Options menu and select Draw Filled. Then, select a pattern from the Patterns palette to fill the polygon. When you draw the polygon, it will be filled in with the selected pattern.

7. Hold down ⌈Option⌉ if you want to draw the polygon outlined in the selected pattern. Or, if the Draw Filled option is selected, the polygon will be drawn without the usual black line outline.

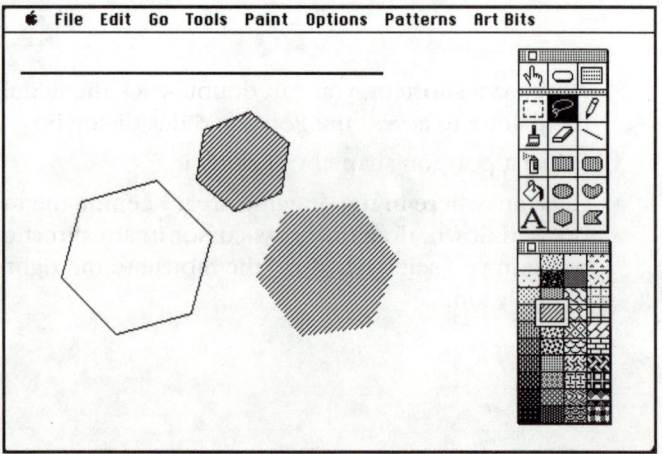

Here, regular polygons are drawn both with and without the Draw Filled and Option key enhancement.

142

8. After you have drawn the shape, keep the mouse button down. Hold down 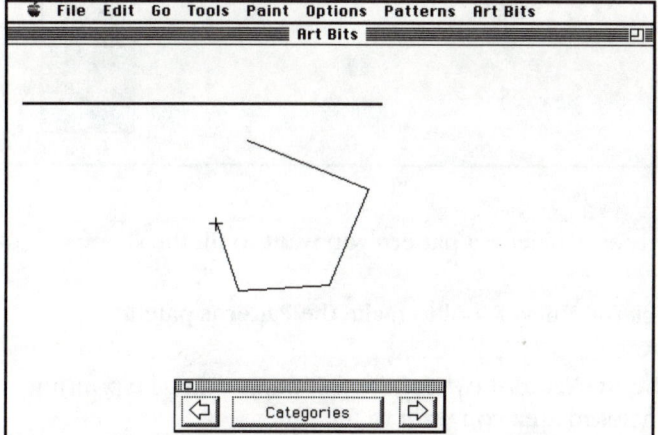 to move the shape anywhere on the screen.

The Irregular Polygon Tool

The Irregular Polygon tool works exactly the same way as the Regular Polygon tool, with one major distinction. The irregular polygon is drawn one line at a time, so you have to close the polygon yourself. To use the Irregular Polygon tool, follow these steps:

1. Select the Irregular Polygon tool.

2. Click anywhere in the drawing area. Keeping the mouse button pressed down, drag the mouse in any direction to draw one line of the polygon. Click the mouse.

3. Drag the mouse in another direction to draw the second line of the polygon. Click the mouse.

The polygon looks something like this.

4. Draw as many lines as you want. To connect the lines, drag to the connecting point, and double-click the mouse.

All the other options you can use with the Regular Polygon tool are available with the Irregular Polygon tool.

The Bucket Tool

The Bucket tool is used to fill enclosed areas of any type with whatever pattern you select in the Patterns palette. To use the Bucket tool, follow these steps:

1. Select the Bucket tool from the Tools palette.

This is the Bucket tool.

2. Select from the Patterns palette a pattern you want to fill the shape with.

   Note: Double-click the Bucket tool to make the Patterns palette appear or disappear.

3. Place the tip of the Bucket tool (where the paint appears to be pouring out) inside the enclosed area you want to fill.

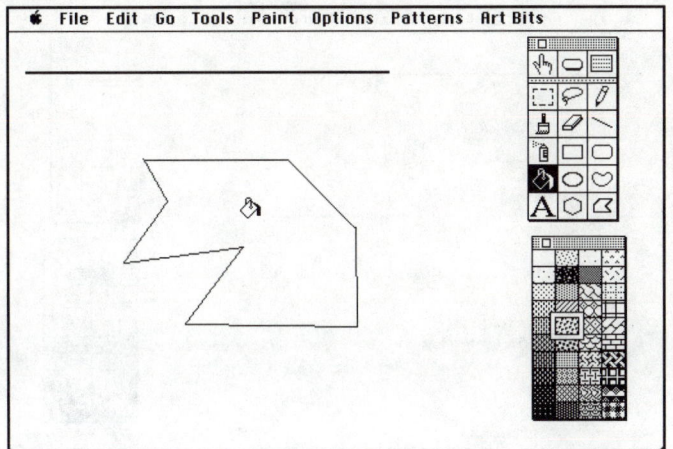

Your screen should look something like this.

5

4. Click the mouse once. The enclosed area will fill with the selected pattern.

    If you accidently fill the entire page with the selected pattern, you did not close the shape entirely, and the bucket of paint "spilled" onto your page. If the page fills with the pattern, immediately pull down the Edit menu and select Undo, or press ⌘-Z.

5. If a shape is not completely closed, use the Pencil tool (and FatBits) to close the shape, then try again.

The Text Tool

You can enter text on a card using the Text tool. However, there are some drawbacks you should be aware of. First of all, when you use the Text tool, you are actually painting text on the screen. The text is a bit-mapped image and works the same way as graphics. You cannot edit painted text the same way you edit regular text, nor can you use the Find option to search for painted text. In some cases, however, because you can treat text drawn with the Text tool as a graphic image (for example, you can rotate, slant, or invert the text), painted text may be exactly what you need. To use the Text tool, follow these steps:

1. Select the Text tool from the Tools palette. The mouse pointer turns into an I-beam cursor.

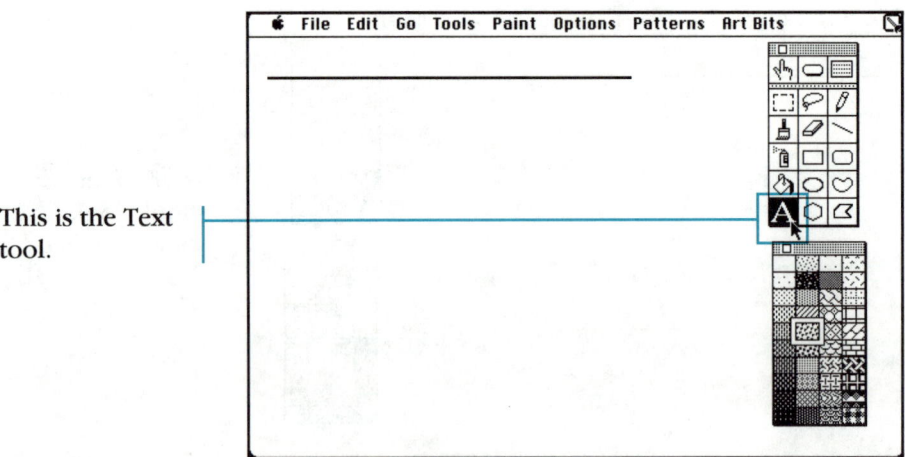

This is the Text
tool.

5

2. Click anywhere in the drawing area.

3. Pull down the Edit menu and select Text Style, or press ⌘-T.

The Paint Text
Style dialog box
appears.

Note: You also can double-click the Text tool to access the Paint Text
Style dialog box.

Choose whatever font type, size, and style you want. Each time you
make a selection, a sample of the text style is displayed in the box in
the lower right corner. Click OK.

4. Type the text in the area. You can use the backspace key to delete a character only until you click outside the text area. Then, you must use the Eraser tool to erase the text you want to delete. To replace text, paint new text in a different area, and do your best to line up new text with the old.

Saving Your Work

When you work with the graphics tools, HyperCard automatically saves your work when you change cards or stacks, switch to or from the background of a card, or click one of the general tools, such as the Browse tool, the Button tool, or the Field tool.

When you are working with HyperCard graphics, an additional save option is available. If you are creating extensive art work on a card and you want to be sure that the current work is saved, pull down the Paint menu and select Keep to save your changes, or press ⌘-K.

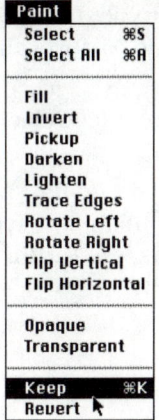

The Keep option is selected from the Paint menu.

If you decide to undo your changes and go back to the last saved version, select Revert from the Paint menu to undo your changes.

Exporting Pictures

HyperCard also gives you the option to save the graphics on a card as a MacPaint document so that you can use your graphics in a variety of other programs or documents. To export graphics, follow these steps:

1. Pull down the File menu and select Export Paint.

A dialog box
appears.

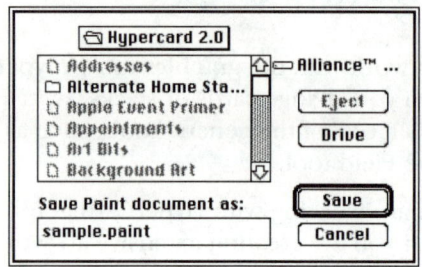

Note: If the Export Paint option does not appear on the File menu, you have not selected one of the graphics tools. Select a tool in the Tools menu, and then the Import and Export Paint options appear in the menu.

2. Type a name for the document. Select the folder or disk you want to save the graphic in. Click Save.

The image of the current card is saved into the specified document in MacPaint format. Any other window that may have been on your screen (the palettes, the message box, the FatBits window, etc.) will not be saved as part of the document.

Importing a MacPaint Document

In addition to exporting a card's graphics as a MacPaint file, you also can import a MacPaint document into a HyperCard card. To import a graphic, follow these steps:

1. Pull down the File menu and select Import Paint.

148

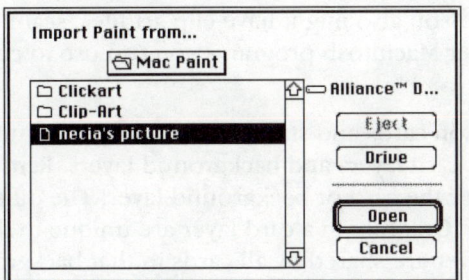

A dialog box
appears.

Note: If the Import Paint option does not appear in the menu, you
have not selected one of the graphics tools. Select a tool in the Tools
menu, and then the Import Paint and Export Paint options appear in
the menu.

2. Select the document you want to import from the current folder or
   disk, or change folders or disks to find the MacPaint document. When
   you select the document you want to import, click Open.

   The MacPaint document appears on the card as a graphic image. You
   can use any of the graphics tools to modify it.

   Note: You also can bring in graphics from just about any other Macintosh application by using Copy and Paste.

Customizing a Card's Appearance

Now that you have had some time experimenting with HyperCard graphics
tools, you can use what you have learned in a "real" scenario. First, you will
copy a graphic image from one stack to another, and then modify the image in
the new stack. You then will learn how to work with graphic images both in
the card layer and the background layer.

Copying a Graphic into Another Stack

One of HyperCard's most distinguished characteristics is the capability to
personalize any HyperCard stack—those stacks that came with the program as
well as those you purchased separately. In terms of graphics, personalizing a
stack could mean anything from adding a picture to a single card, to changing
the entire look of a stack. You can use the Art Bits stack supplied with Hyper-

149

Card for personalizing stacks. You also might have clip art files, scanned images, or graphics from other Macintosh programs you can use to customize a stack's appearance.

When working with graphics on cards and stacks, it is important to understand the difference between card layers and background layers. Remember, you can put graphics on either the card or background layer. The difference is apparent in the next exercise. Graphics in a card layer are unique to that card. Graphics on a background layer are shared by all cards in that background.

To copy a graphic into another stack, follow these steps:

1. Go to the fourth card of the People category in the Art Bits stack.

This is the fourth card of the People category.

2. Select the Selection tool from the Tools menu.

3. Move the mouse pointer to the third graphic in the last row, which is a picture of a woman on the phone.

4. Drag the cross-hair cursor down and to the right to enclose the image. Before you release the mouse button, hold down Option.

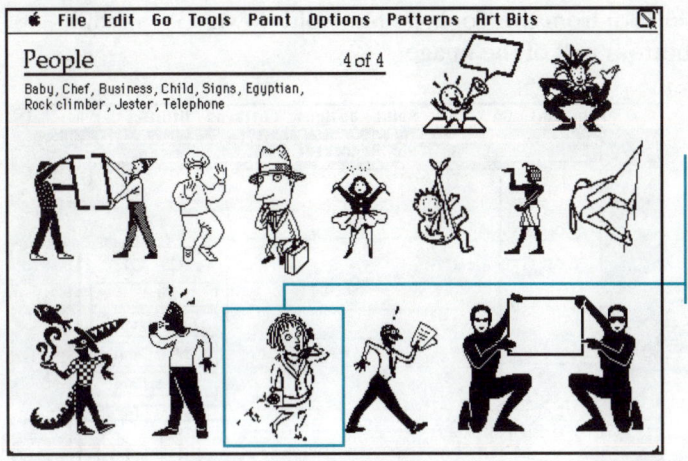

Baby, Chef, Business, Child, Signs, Egyptian,
Rock climber, Jester, Telephone

The Selection tool
turns into the
Lasso tool and
selects the image
only.

5. With the image selected, pull down the Edit menu and select Copy (or press ⌘-C) to copy the picture.

6. Pull down the File menu and select Open Stack (or press ⌘-O) to open a stack. Choose the Addresses stack, and go to any card in the stack you choose.

7. Pull down the Edit menu and select Paste (or press ⌘-V) to paste the picture in the stack.

8. Move the picture to the area on the card next to the Telephone area.

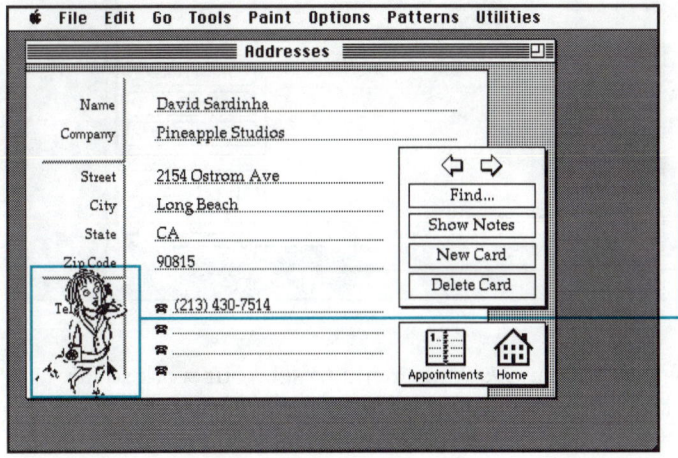

Here, the image is
moved next to the
Telephone area.

9. Select the Eraser tool from the Tools menu. Hold down ⌖Shift while you erase the bottom half of the image.

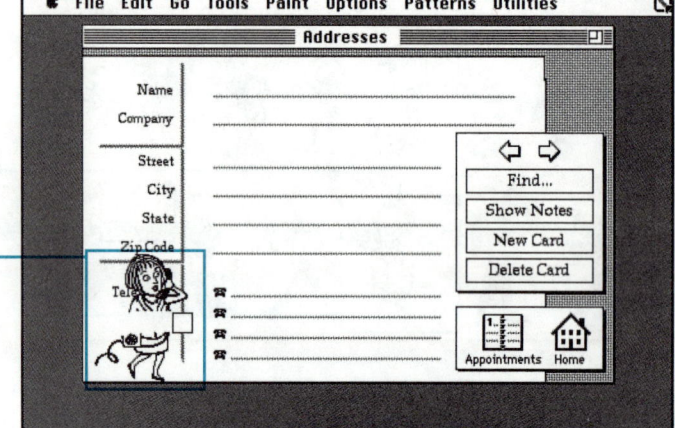

Here, the bottom half of the image is being erased.

5

10. Select the picture again with the Selection tool and move the picture to the square below the Telephone line.

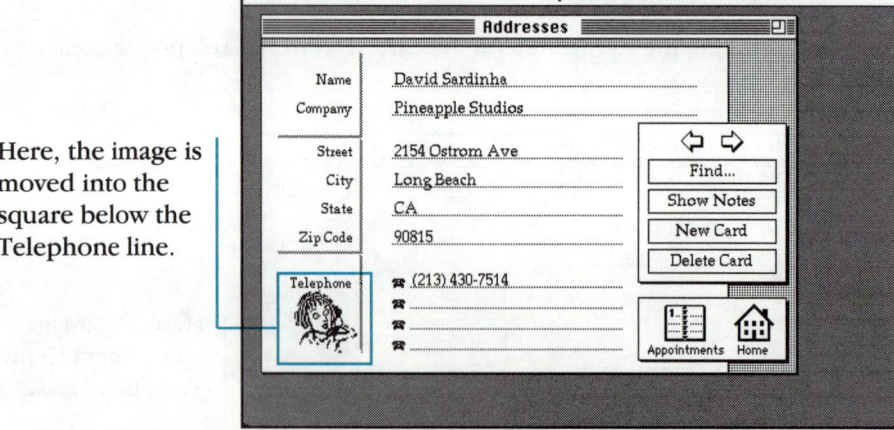

Here, the image is moved into the square below the Telephone line.

11. Select the Browse tool from the Tools menu to see your work so far. Then, click the right-arrow button to go to the next card.

You will notice that the next card does not have the picture in the Telephone area that you just pasted into the previous card. You pasted the graphic into the card layer and not the background layer, so the picture will appear only on that one card.

Copying a Graphic into the Background Layer

To copy a graphic into the background layer of a card, follow these steps:

1. Pull down the Go menu and select Back to go back to the card you were just working on (or click the left-arrow button to go to the previous card).

2. Select the Selection tool from the Tools menu, and select the picture again.

3. Pull down the Edit menu and select Cut Picture (or press ⌘-X) to cut the graphic out of the card layer.

4. Pull down the Edit menu and select Background (or press ⌘-B).

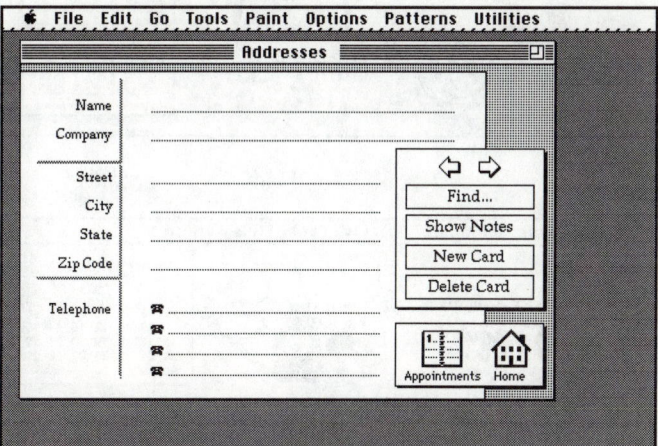

Notice the diagonal lines across the top menu line that distinguish the background layer of the card.

5. Pull down the Edit menu and select Paste (or press ⌘-V) to paste the picture onto the background layer of the card.

6. Pull down the Edit menu and select Background (or press ⌘-B) to get out of the background layer and back to the card layer.

7. Select the Browse tool from the Tools menu and go to the next card, or any other card in the stack. You will see the picture appears on all the cards in this background.

5

153

Sometimes you may want to copy a picture into the background layer of a stack so that the picture appears on all cards in the stack. Or, you may want pictures or graphics to appear on one or more cards in particular. If you are a teacher, you might want to make a daily agenda using different graphics to represent activities for each day. You could put pictures in the background layer of those activities that remain the same every day, and in the card layer those that change. Just remember what layer you are in: the card or the background layer of the stack.

Here are the graphics that appear in the card layer.

Here are the graphics that appear in the background layer.

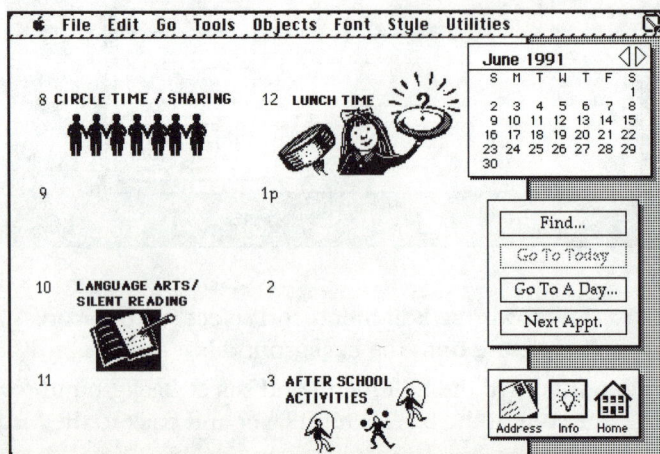

Moving On

This chapter showed you how to use the third level of HyperCard, called *Painting*. You learned how to use each of HyperCard's Painting tools as well as several of the options on the two new menus, Paint and Options. You also learned how to import and export pictures to and from MacPaint or other Macintosh graphic programs. And lastly, you learned how to copy pictures from one card or stack to another and customize a stack's appearance.

Specifically, you learned the following key information about HyperCard:

5

- HyperCard graphics are often referred to as *bit-mapped images* because the graphics are made up of dots, where each dot represents one or more bits of the image.

- To set the user level to Painting, go to the last card in the Home stack, which is the Preferences card, and click the button labeled Painting.

- The Tools menu consists of 3 general tools (Browse, Button, and Field) and 15 Painting tools. At the Painting user level, you can use the Browse general tool and each of the 15 Painting tools.

- When you select any one of the Painting tools, 3 additional menus appear: Paint, Options, and Patterns.

- In HyperCard, you can tear off the Tools menu and the Patterns menu from the top menu line and place the menus anywhere on the screen. When you tear off a menu, the menu is referred to as a *palette*.

- You can display the Navigator palette on any card or stack by typing the command **Nav** into the message box. The Navigator palette contains buttons to replicate the functionality of the Go menu (except the Scroll option).

- You can use both the Selection tool and the Lasso tool to select images you want to move, delete, copy, or manipulate in some way.

- When you use the Painting tools in combination with the Shift, Option, or ⌘ keys, you have more options to manipulate graphics. For example, you can restrict movement and stretch, shrink, duplicate, or make multiple copies of a selected image.

- You can use the FatBits option in conjunction with the Pencil tool to magnify a graphic so that it shows each pixel the graphic is made of.

- When working with graphics in HyperCard, your work is automatically saved when you change cards or stacks, switch to or from the background of a card, or click one of the general tools. You also can save your work by selecting Keep from the Paint menu or by pressing ⌘-K.

■ To import or export a MacPaint picture, select Import Paint or Export Paint from the File menu. If the options don't appear on the File menu, select one of the graphic tools, then the options will appear.

■ To copy a selected graphic image from one card or stack to another, choose Copy Picture from the Edit menu, and then choose Paste Picture.

■ Graphics in a card layer are unique to that card. Graphics on a background layer are shared by all cards in that background.

Now that you have a handle on both the text and the graphic capabilities of HyperCard, the only things left to master are fields and buttons. In the next chapter, you will move on to the next level of HyperCard, called *Authoring*. As a HyperCard author, you can change not only the look of a card or stack but also its purpose and function.

5

Customizing a Stack

In this chapter, you will explore the Authoring level, which is by far the most exciting level. At the Authoring level, you have access to the two most important tools of HyperCard: the Button tool and the Field tool.

While the graphics tools enabled you to personalize a stack's *appearance*, the Button and Field tools enable you, as a HyperCard author, to change a stack's purpose and function by adding or modifying buttons and fields. You also will now be able to establish direct links between cards and stacks, so that clicking a button on one card will take you to a specific card in another stack. Then, after you have done what you need to do, you can click a button to take you right back to where you were initially.

You can use several different kinds of buttons and fields. And, as with graphics, buttons and fields can reside in the card layer or in the background layer. Sometimes you may have a button or field in just one card in a stack, or you may have a button or field in all of the cards in the stack.

In this chapter, you will learn how to create and modify buttons and fields, and how to link cards and stacks together. You first will create a new stack by copying a template from those supplied with HyperCard. You then will use both the Field and the Button tool to customize the stack for your particular needs (at least, in terms of this exercise).

6

Key Terms in This Chapter

Authoring	The fourth user level of HyperCard, which gives you access to HyperCard's Button and Field tools and capabilities.
Stack Templates	A stack that came with your HyperCard program. The stack contains several different samples of stacks to create.
Button tool	One of the three general tools in the Tools menu. The Button tool is used to create, modify, and delete buttons from a card or stack.
Field tool	One of the three general tools in the Tools menu. The Field tool is used to create, modify, and delete fields from a card or stack.
Readymade Buttons stack	A stack that came with your HyperCard program. The stack contains several different buttons you can copy into your stacks.
Readymade Fields stack	A stack that came with your HyperCard program. The stack contains several different fields you can copy into your stacks.
Background layer	The background area of the card. This layer may contain fields, buttons, or graphics that are shared by more than one card. When you are in the background layer of a card, diagonal lines appear on the top menu line.
Card layer	The foreground area of the card. This layer may contain fields, buttons, or graphics that are unique to that particular card.
Link	When a button on one stack takes you to another stack, the two stacks have an established (one-way) link. To establish a circular link, a button takes you back to the original stack.

> *Visual effects*
>
> When a button is activated, before the action of the button begins, the card might display a noticeable change, such as opening from the center, or from the top to bottom, etc. There are 23 different effects you can choose from, and each one has four speeds.

Setting the Preference Level to Authoring

To use the Authoring level of HyperCard, you need to change the user preference. To change the user preference, follow these steps:

1. With the Home card on your screen, click the right-arrow button (or press ⌘-4) to go to the Preferences card.

2. Click the Authoring button.

6

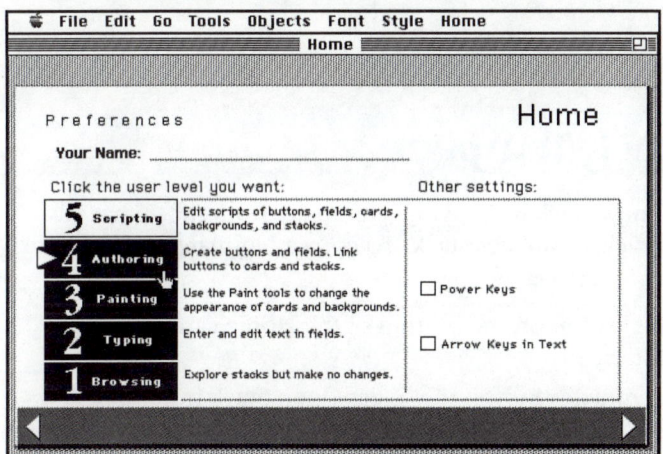

Here, the user level is set to Authoring.

3. Click the right-arrow button to go back to the Home card.

When you change your user level to Authoring, an additional menu, named Objects, appears on the top menu line after the Tools menu.

The Objects menu contains several different options you can use as a Hyper-Card author.

Also, you now can use the two general tools in the Tools menu that were previously unavailable: the Button tool and the Field tool.

Button tool Field tool

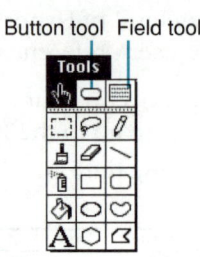

Using the Stack Template

First, you will create a new stack by copying a template from those that have been supplied in the Stack Templates stack. To copy a template, follow these steps:

1. Click the Stack Kit button on the bottom of the Home card. You will go to the Stack Kit card.

2. Click the Stack Templates button (or select Open Stack from the File menu, and then select Stack Templates).

160

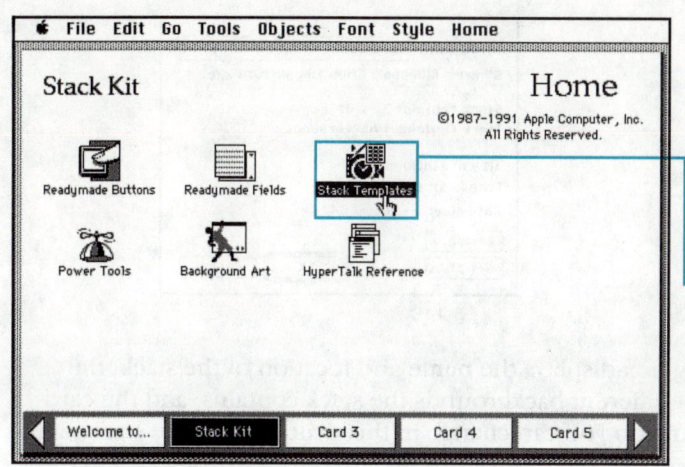

The Stack Templates button is selected.

3. Click the Invoice button to access the card for an invoice template.

   The invoice template card is displayed.

4. Click the Create Stack button on the Custom Navigator palette.

5. Click the Save button to accept the name *Invoice* for your stack (or name the stack something different, if you prefer). After a few moments, your stack is created, and you are on the first card. Click OK.

You have now created your Invoice stack. You can modify it as you wish.

What's in a Stack?

Every stack is made up of one or more cards, at least one background, one or more buttons or fields, and perhaps graphics in the background or card layer. Sometimes you may not be able to tell where the buttons and fields are on a card, and if the fields, buttons, or graphics are on the card layer or the background layer. As a HyperCard author, you can use the Objects menu to get information about the stack, cards, or background.

Stack Info

To get information about the current stack, pull down the Objects menu and select Stack Info.

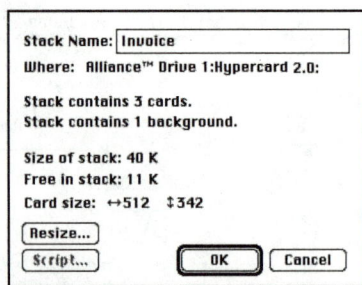

The Stack Info
dialog box
appears.

The Stack Info dialog box displays the name and location of the stack, the
number of cards and different backgrounds the stack contains, and the card
size. The only information you can change in this dialog box is the stack name
and card size.

Card Size

The capability to change the card size is new in HyperCard 2.0. Remember
that the size of the card is the same for all cards in the stack, regardless of how
many backgrounds or different appearances the cards may have. Also, usually
a card size is determined before the stack is fully created, so that the fields,
buttons, and graphics placed on the card fit nicely within the card size. If the
card's elements are already on the card when you change its size, they might
look out of place if you later modify the card's size.

To change the card size, follow these steps:

1. Click the button labeled `Resize`.

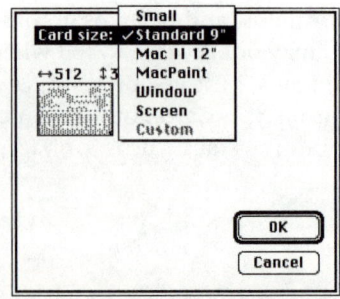

A dialog box
appears, showing
the current card
size.

2. Position the mouse pointer on the Card Size button. Press and hold
    down the mouse button to reveal the choices.

The choices you have are listed in table 6.1. Depending on how much memory your Macintosh has, you may not have all the options available to you.

Table 6.1
Card Size Options

Option	Description
Small 416x240	Smaller than 9-inch Macintosh screen.
Standard 9" 512x342	Screen of standard size Mac Plus or Mac SE, SE30.
Mac II 12" 640x480	Size of typical Mac II family monitor.
MacPaint 576x720	Size of MacPaint document; prints to an area of 8" by 10".
Window	Sets the card size to the current stack's window.
Screen	Fills the entire screen (removing the window's title bar from view); size depends on your current monitor size, up to 1280 x 1280, and available memory.
Custom	Any size you drag the window to be that doesn't conform to any of the other settings.

3. Highlight the choice you want and click OK.

Card Info

Just as the Stack Info dialog box provides important information about the stack in which you are working, the Card Info dialog box gives you information about the particular card on your screen. To access the Card Info dialog box, pull down the Objects menu and select Card Info.

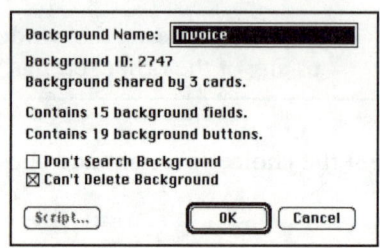

The Card Info
dialog box
appears.

For every card in a stack, HyperCard assigns a unique card identification number. This number is stated in the Card Info dialog box. The dialog box also tells you the number of fields and buttons on the card. You can assign the card a name, search or delete protection, and mark a card for printing or reports.

6

Background Info

Not only can you get information about stacks and cards, but you also can get information about the background layer of a stack. To get background information, pull down the Objects menu and select Bkgnd Info.

The Background
Info dialog box
appears.

HyperCard assigns a unique background identification number to each background. This number is stated in the dialog box. You also can assign the background a name, and search or delete protection. The Background Info dialog box gives you the number of background fields and buttons, and the number of cards that share that particular background.

Now that you have all this information about the stack you just created, you can start customizing the stack.

Viewing Buttons and Fields

Just about every card or stack in HyperCard has at least one button and, usually, at least one field. Buttons cause an action to occur when you press them. Fields are places where you type text. Fields and buttons might not look anything like you would expect.

When you place buttons and fields on a card, you have several options. The appearance and purpose of buttons and fields is up to you, the HyperCard author.

In this stack, buttons are arranged in a hierarchical order. One button on this card links you to another card.

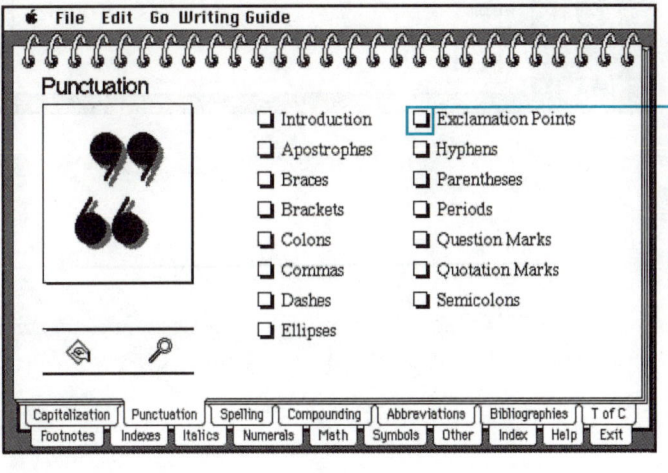

That card contains several other buttons.

165

One button leads to yet another card.

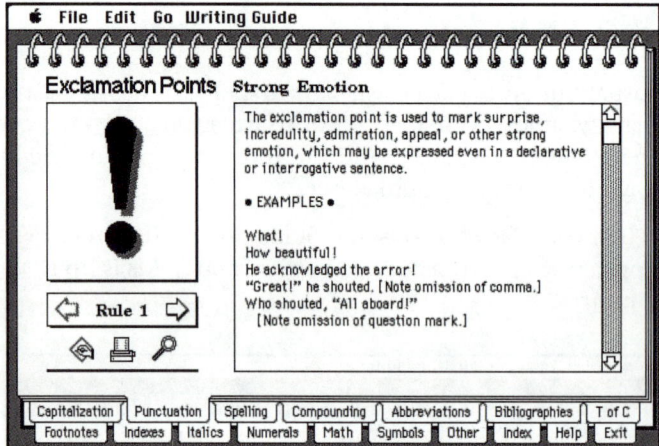

In this stack, fields appear and function similar to buttons. One field on this card takes you to another card.

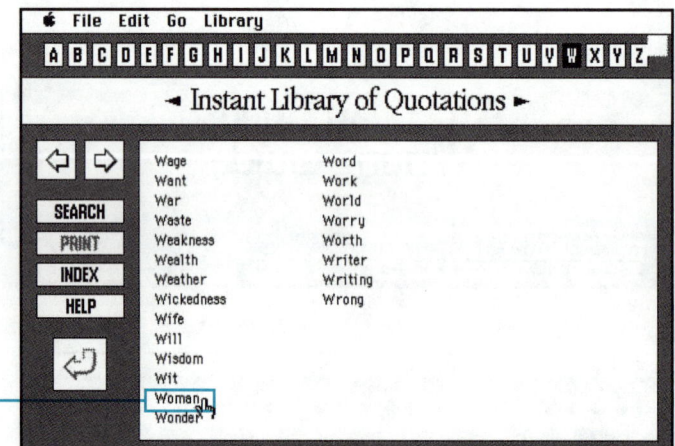

6

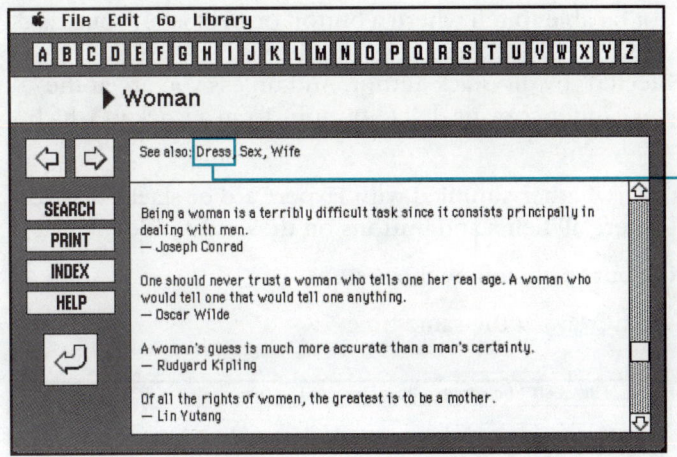

That card contains other fields that are related.

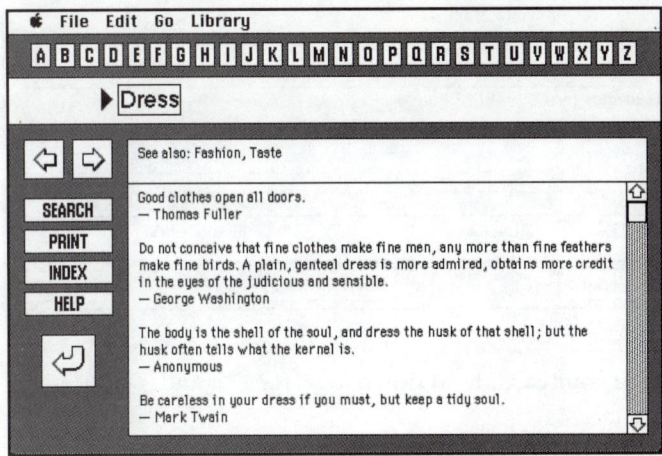

One field leads to yet another card.

6

Sometimes you may not be able to tell where a button or field is on your card or stack. With some stacks, the Tools menu may not be visible because it has been "locked" or "protected" by the stack author. And unless you are at the Scripting user level, you cannot copy or delete buttons from a stack in which they have been protected.

However, with any stack (whether supplied with HyperCard or stacks that you acquire), you can tell where all fields and buttons on the card reside.

To view the buttons in your stack, follow these steps:

1. Hold down ⌘ and Option at the same time.

6

The buttons in the card are outlined with shaded rectangles.

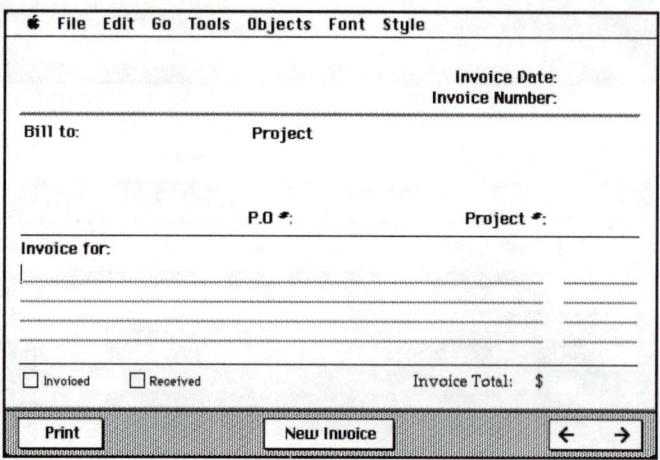

2. To view the fields in your card, hold down ⇧Shift, ⌘, and Option at the same time.

168

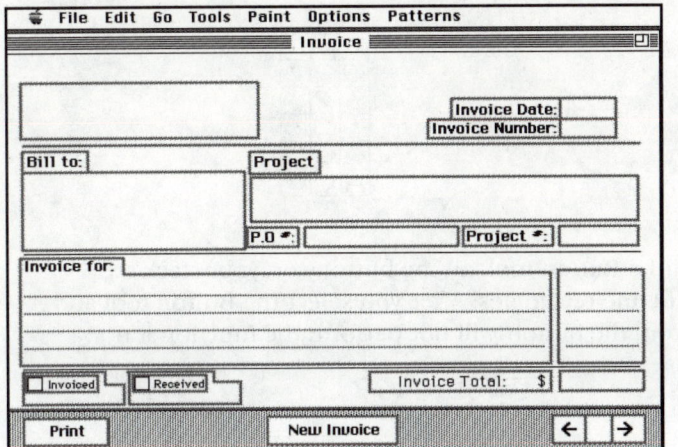

The fields in the card are outlined with shaded rectangles, along with the buttons.

The thick gray rectangles indicate that the buttons or fields reside in the background layer. The dotted rectangles mean they are in the card layer.

Using the Button Tool

With the Button tool, found in the Tools menu, you can decide what the buttons on your card or stack will look like, the visual effect the buttons will have when they are activated, and most importantly, what the buttons will do. Buttons can move to the next or previous card, print a card or stack, play a sound, search for text, bring up an additional field to use with that card, or link you to another card or stack, just to name a few examples.

The Button tool is not accessible until you are at the Authoring user level. To use the Button tool, follow these steps:

1. Pull down the Tools menu and select the Button tool.

169

Here, the Button tool is selected from the Tools menu.

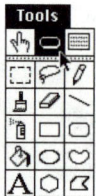

After you select the Button tool, all the buttons on your stack are enclosed in solid line rectangles. After you select the Button tool and you click a button, the button will not perform the function it normally does.

Instead, the button itself becomes selected so that you can modify its appearance or function.

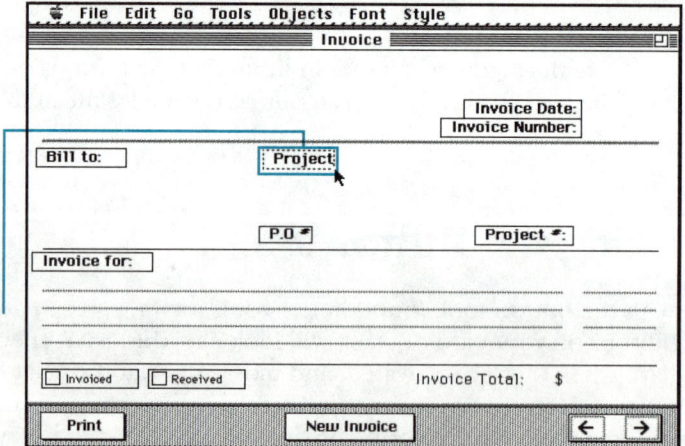

2. Pull down the Edit menu and select Background (or press ⌘-Ⓑ) to see which buttons reside in the background of the card. Note how when you are in Background mode, diagonal lines appear across the top menu bar. In this particular stack, all the buttons reside in the background and appear on all the cards in the stack.

Button Info

Whenever a button is created (either from scratch or copied from another button), HyperCard automatically gives it a unique button number and a default style and attributes. You can change any of these attributes from within the Button Info dialog box.

To select a particular button to work with, click anywhere inside the rectangle surrounding the button. The solid-lined rectangle becomes a moving line, and the button looks like a graphic selected with the Selection tool.

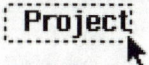

Here is a selected button.

To change a button's attributes, follow these steps:

1. With the button selected, pull down the Objects menu and select Button Info.

   Note: If the Button Info option is grayed out, you do not have a button selected on the card.

   You also can access the Button Info dialog box by double-clicking a selected button.

The Button Info dialog box appears.

2. You will learn about each option in the Button Info dialog box as you go through the following exercise. For now, click Cancel to go back to the Invoice card.

Moving and Resizing Buttons

When a button on a card is selected, the button not only looks like a graphic selected with the Selection tool, but the button is also moved and resized in the same way.

171

Moving a Button

To move a button, follow these steps:

1. Position the mouse pointer anywhere within the Invoice Date button and click the mouse once to select the button.

2. Hold the mouse button down and drag the selected button to just below the top menu bar.

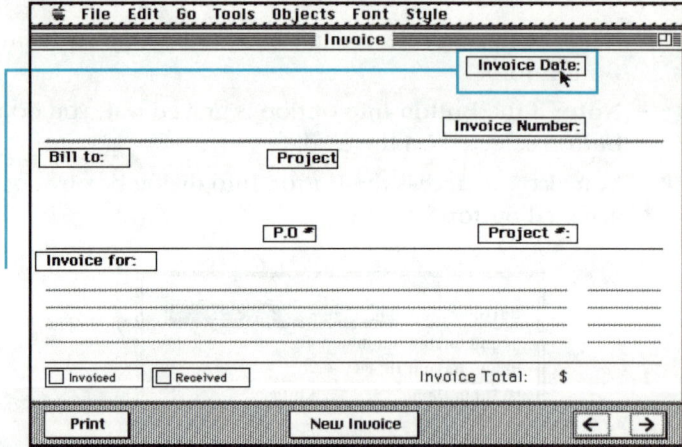

Here, the button is placed below the top menu bar.

Hold down ⚹Shift to restrict your movement to a vertical motion. The button will remain selected until you click the mouse outside of the dotted selection area.

3. Move the Invoice Number button to directly below the Date button.

4. Move the P.O. # button (that is currently near the center of the card) directly below the Invoice Number button.

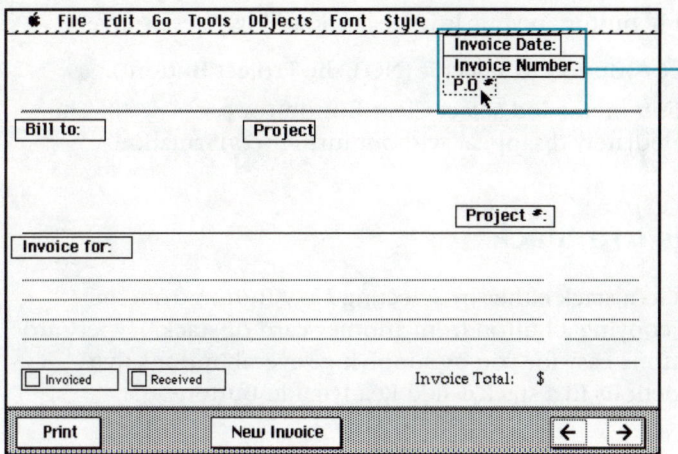

The three buttons should be lined up by their left margins, and they should be as close to each other as possible.

5. Move the Print and New Invoice buttons to the right, closer to the left- and right-arrow buttons to make room for more buttons later.

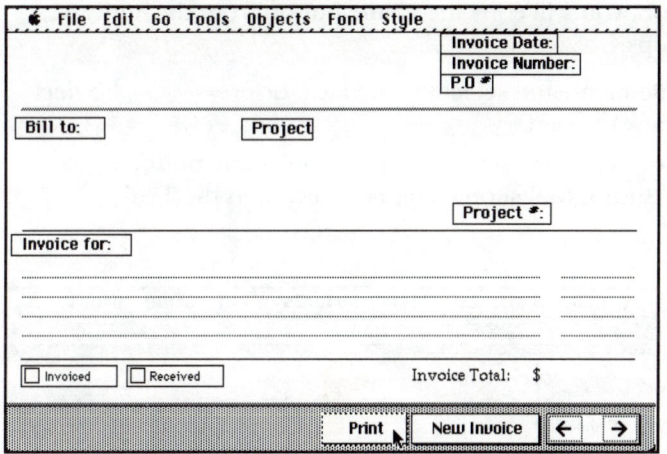

Here, the buttons have been moved to their new location.

Clearing, Deleting, and Cutting Buttons

After you clear or delete a button, you *cannot undo* the operation. So, if you're not sure that you want to delete the button, use the Cut Button option in the Edit menu rather than Clear or Delete. Also, remember that if you delete a button that resides in the background layer of the stack, you will delete that button from all the cards that share that particular background in the stack.

To delete the Project # button in your Invoice stack, follow these steps:

1. Click the Project # Button to select it (NOT the Project Button!).

2. Pull down the Edit menu and select Clear Button (or press ⌴Del⌴). The button will immediately disappear without further confirmation.

Adding Buttons to a Stack

You can add buttons to a stack either by selecting New Button from the Objects menu, or by copying a button from another card or stack. HyperCard has made adding buttons easy for you by supplying several buttons that perform standard functions in a stack called Readymade Buttons.

Copying Buttons from Another Stack

Because it's generally a good idea for all HyperCard stacks to have a button that takes you Home, the first button you add to your Invoice stack will do just that. To add this button, you will copy the Home button from the Addresses stack. Follow these steps:

1. Pull down the File menu and select Open Stack, or press ⌴⌘⌴-⌴O⌴. Select the Addresses stack to open.

2. In the first card of the Addresses stack, select the Home button by clicking it. (The Button tool should still be selected in the Tools menu.)

Here, the Home button on the Addresses stack is selected.

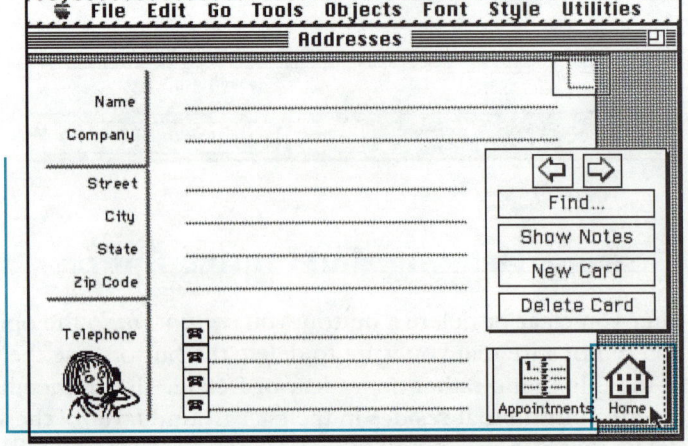

3. Pull down the Edit menu and select Copy Button, or press ⌘-Ⓒ.

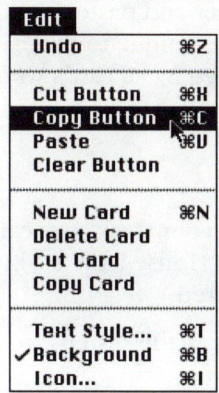

Here, the Copy Button option is selected from the Edit menu.

Note: If the Copy Button option is grayed out in the menu, the Button tool is not selected in the Tools menu.

4. Pull down the Go menu and select Back to go back to the Invoice stack in which you were working.

5. Pull down the Edit menu and select Paste Button, or press ⌘-Ⓥ.

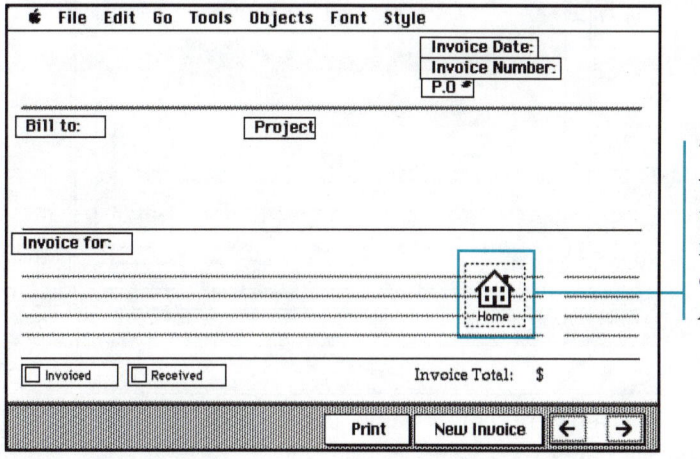

The Home button will be pasted in the exact location from where it was copied in the Addresses stack.

Note: If you were not in the background layer when you pasted this button, pull down the Edit menu and select Cut Button, then press ⌘-B to go to the background layer and paste the button back in. (Any buttons pasted onto a card are unique to that card. Any buttons pasted onto a background are shared by all cards within that stack.)

Modifying Button Attributes

Now that you have copied a button into your stack, you can change any of its attributes. In this stack, for example, the House icon is a bit too large, and the button name does not need to be displayed.

With the Home button still selected, follow these steps to change the button's icon and to hide the button name:

1. Double-click the Home button to access the Button Info dialog box.
2. Click the Show Name checkbox to deselect it.
3. Click the Icon button.

A dialog box appears, displaying a visual list of icon choices.

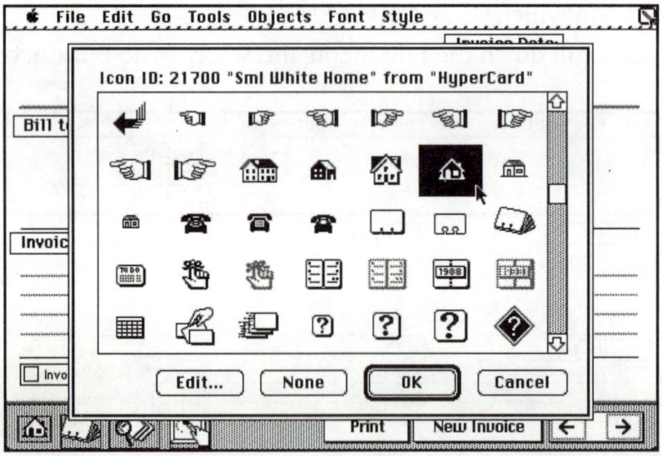

4. Select an icon displayed here. For example, choose a smaller house icon, and then click OK.

6

176

Resizing Buttons

The button size is represented by the square that encloses it, not the size of the icon that represents the button. Now that you have changed the icon, the button appears to be too large. To resize the button, follow these steps:

1. Position the mouse pointer on the bottom right corner of the selected button. Pressing and holding down the mouse button, drag the mouse up to shrink the rectangle.

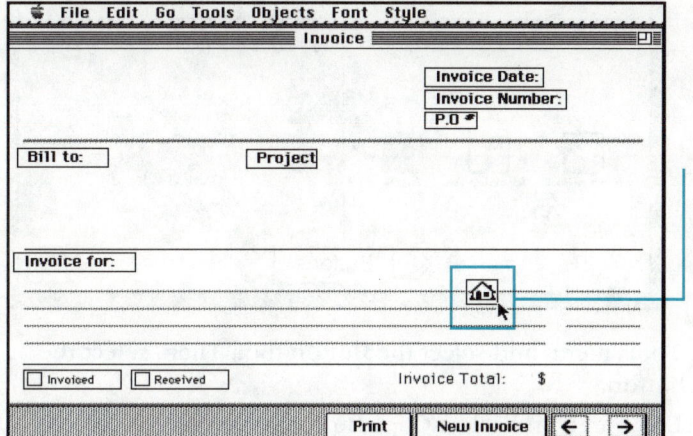

Here, the button is being resized to fit the icon that represents it.

6

2. Move the new Home button to the bottom left corner of the card.

Using the Readymade Buttons Stack

Now you will go through similar steps to add two more buttons to this stack: one button to go to the Addresses stack and one to perform a search function. You can copy both buttons from the Readymade Buttons stack provided with HyperCard. To copy the buttons, follow these steps:

1. Pull down the File menu and select Open Stack, or press ⌘-O. Select the Readymade Buttons stack to open.

   Note: If you don't see anything on the card, you probably are in the background layer. Press ⌘-B to go to the card layer. You also may have to select the Browse tool from the Tools menu.

177

2. In the first card of the Readymade Buttons stack, click Open Stacks to take you to the Open Stacks card. There, you will see a button to take you to the Addresses stack as well as to the Appointment book and Puzzle stack.

This is the Open Stacks card in the Readymade Buttons stack. You can copy any of these buttons into your stack to take you to the stack they represent.

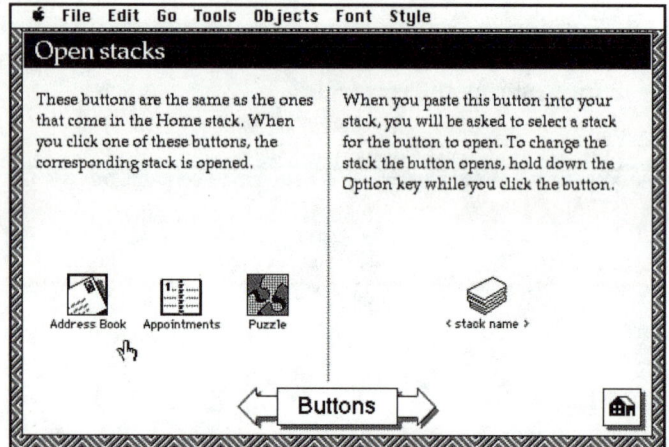

3. Pull down the Tools menu and select the Button tool. Then, select the Address Book button.

4. Pull down the Edit menu and select Copy Button, or press ⌘-C.

5. Pull down the Go menu and select Back two times to go back to your Invoice stack. (You also can select Recent and click the Invoice card.)

6. Press ⌘-B to go to the background layer. Then, pull down the Edit menu and select Paste Button, or press ⌘-V.

The Address Book button is copied into your Invoice stack.

178

Note: If you were not in the background layer when you pasted this button in, pull down the Edit menu and select Cut Button, then press ⊞-Ⓑ to go to the background layer and paste the button back in.

7. Go through the same steps as you did with the Home button to change the Address Book button icon to a smaller one, hide the icon name, and make the button smaller. When you have finished, move the new Address button next to the Home button.

Here, the Address Book button has a new icon and is placed next to the Home button.

Remember, if you're not in the background layer when you paste a button into your stack, cut the button out of the card stack, go to the background layer, and paste the button back in.

8. Now copy the Find button from the Readymade Button stack into your Invoice stack. (The Find button is on the Do Various Things card in the Readymade Buttons stack.) Place the button next to the Address Stack button.

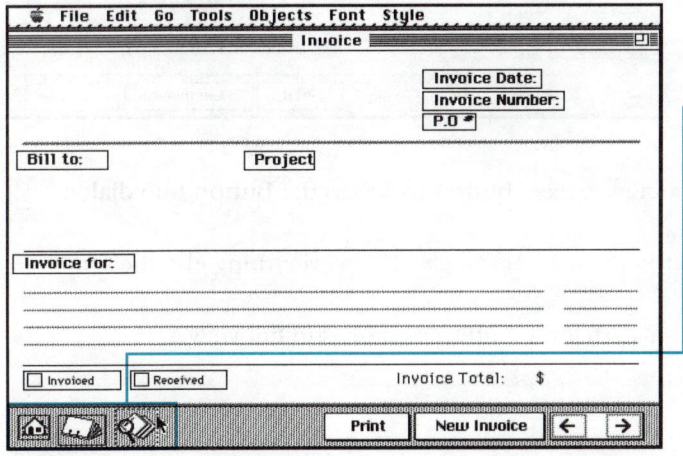

You have added three new buttons to this stack: one to go Home, one to go to the Address stack, and one to search for text.

Cloning a Button

If you want to copy a button from one stack to another, use the conventional copy/paste method described previously in this chapter. If, however, you want to copy a button onto the same card, you can use the same duplicating method you used for duplicating graphics.

To duplicate a button, follow these steps:

1. Select the Project button.

2. While pressing Option, press and hold down the mouse button. Drag the mouse away from the Project button to duplicate it.

Also hold down ⇧Shift to restrict your movements to a vertical motion.

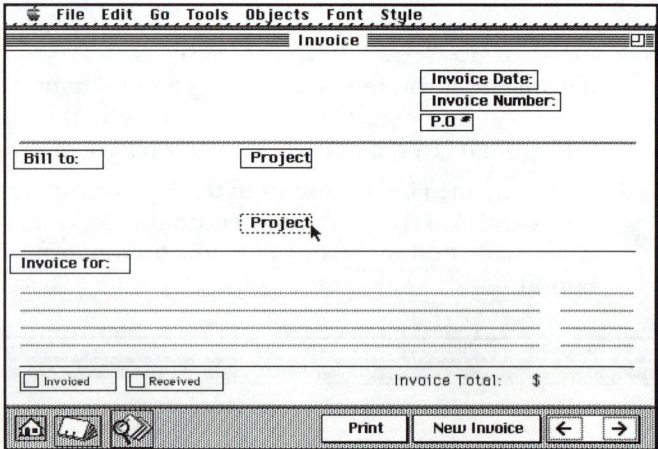

3. Double-click the new Project button to access the Button Info dialog box.

4. Change the button name to *Manager:*. Keep everything else the same, and click OK.

5. Resize the button so that the button's name is in full view.

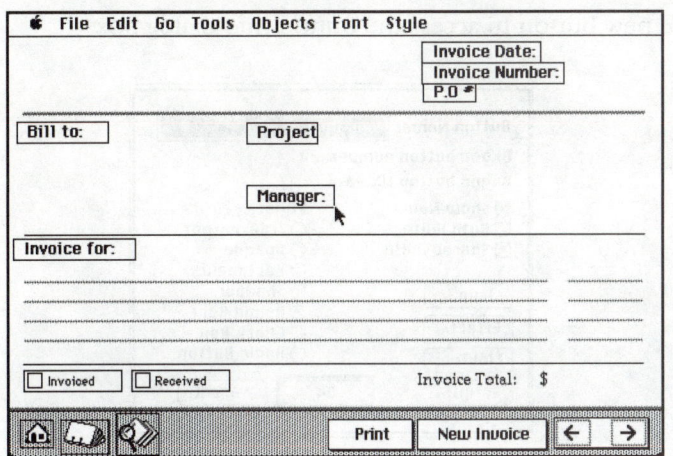

Here is the
copied button
with a new name.

Creating a New Button

Although you can use several supplied buttons in the Readymade Buttons
stack and others, you may want to create a button from scratch. In this example, you will create a new button that will take you to a specific card in the
Art Bits stack so that you can personalize each invoice with an applicable
picture.

To create a new button, follow these steps:

1. Pull down the Objects menu and select New Button. (Again, be sure
    you are in the background layer.)

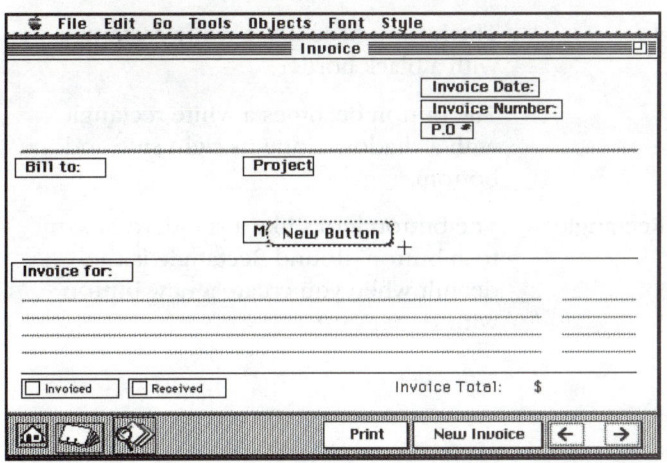

A button, labeled
New Button,
appears in the
middle of your
card.

181

2. Double-click the new button to access the Button Info dialog box.

The default style for a new button is Round Rectangle.

6

3. Select a button style. You can choose between seven different styles. See table 6.2 for information about each style.

Table 6.2
Button Styles

Button	Style	Description
Transparent	Transparent	The button becomes transparent. Usually a transparent button would not have the button name displayed.
Opaque	Opaque	The button becomes a white (borderless) rectangle.
Rectangle Button	Rectangle	The button becomes a white rectangle with a black border.
Shadow Button	Shadow	The button becomes a white rectangle with a shadow along its right side and bottom.
Round Rect. Button	Round Rectangle	The button looks like a standard Macintosh button. Round Rectangle is the default when you create a new button with HyperCard.

Button	Style	Description
⊠	Check Box	The button becomes a small square with an opaque interior. It will function like a standard Macintosh checkbox. When you click it, an X appears in the box.
◉	Radio Button	The button becomes a small circle with an opaque interior. It will function like a standard Macintosh radio button. When you click, a dark circle appears in the center.

Because you will add an icon to your button, select Transparent for the style.

4. Name the button *Add Picture*.

5. Click the Show Name checkbox to deselect the option.

6. Click the Auto Hilite checkbox to select the option. This option will cause the icon to darken when you click your button to activate it.

7. Click the Icon button.

   A dialog box appears, displaying a visual list of icon choices. Select an icon for your button.

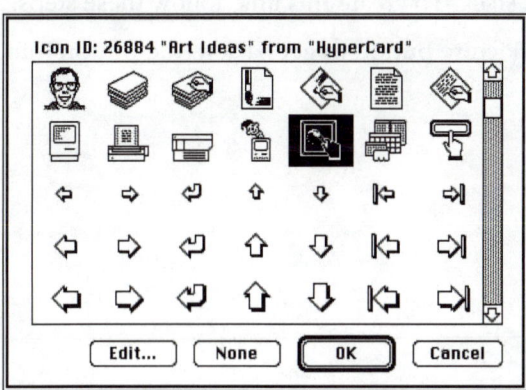

Because this button is going to take you to a card in the Art Bits stack, select an icon that is representative of Art Bits.

8. Click OK to select the icon.

9. Resize the button so that you can see the entire icon.

Linking Buttons to Stacks and Cards

Now that you know how to create a button, take a look at the most powerful function (and certainly one of the most useful) a HyperCard button can perform: establishing links between cards and/or stacks.

You can establish a link that takes you to a specific card in the same stack, or to the first card in another stack, or to a specific card in another stack.

You can set up one way links or circular links. Most links are one way. A one way link will take you to another card or stack; after you get there, you have to find your own way back to where you started. A circular link will take you back to where you started. To establish a circular link, put a button in each stack to link you back to the previous stack.

The Invoice stack with which you are working already has several established links. For example, the left- and right-arrow buttons link you to the next or previous invoice; the Home button you copied from the Addresses stack links you to the Home card, and the Addresses stack you copied from the Readymade Buttons stack links you to the Addresses stack.

In this example, you will link the Add Picture button you just created to a specific card in the Art Bits stack. To create this link, follow these steps:

1. Double-click the Add Picture button to get back to the Button Info dialog box.

2. Click the Link To button.

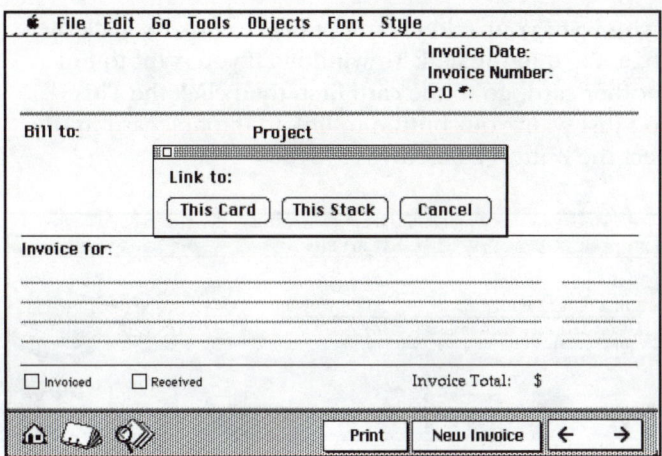

The Link To window appears in the middle of the card, prompting you to go to whatever card or stack you want the button to link to.

6

3. Because you want your button to link to a specific card in the Art Bits stack, press ⌘-Ⓞ to open a stack, and choose Art Bits.

   The Art Bits stack opens.

4. If you are still in the background layer, press ⌘-Ⓑ to leave the background layer or select Background from the Edit menu. Now you can see the card layer graphics in the Art Bits stack. Click the Small Treasures button.

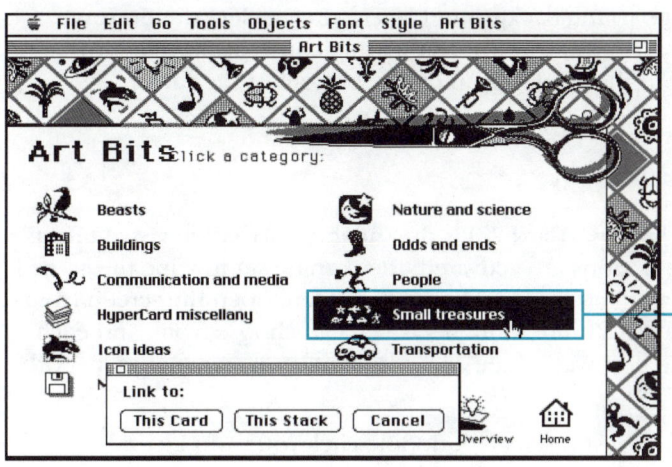

Here, the Small Treasures button on the Art Bits stack is selected.

185

5. If this is the card you want your Add Picture button to link to, click the button labeled `This Card` in the Link To window. If you want to link your button to another card, go to the card first, then click the This Card button. If you just want your button to link to the first card in the Art Bits stack, select the button labeled `This Stack`.

Click This Card to establish a direct link to the card on the screen. Click This Stack to link to the first card in the stack.

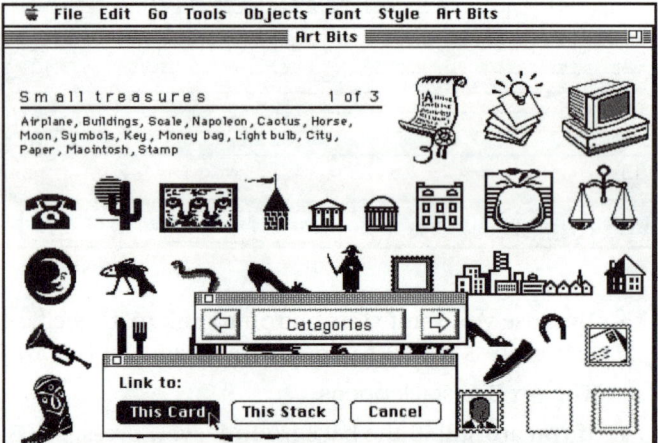

HyperCard establishes the link and then takes you back to the Invoice stack where you were working.

6. Press ⌘-B to go to the background layer. Then, select the Button tool again and resize your button so that the icon is displayed. Move the button next to the Find button on the bottom of the card.

Using Visual Effects

Another new feature in HyperCard 2.0 is the capability to assign visual effects to buttons. When the buttons are activated, they can be set to wipe the screen vertically or horizontally, scroll up or down the screen, open the screen from the center, etc. There are 23 different effects you can choose from, and each one has 4 speeds. The best way to see each visual effect is to experiment with each one.

1. With the Button tool still selected, double-click your Add Picture button to display the Button Info dialog box again.

2. Click the Effect button. A dialog box appears with a list of all the effects from which you can choose. Scroll down the list and click any one. The name of the effect appears in the box above the list. Then, choose a speed, and click OK.

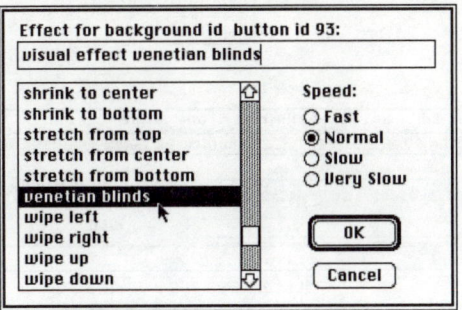

For one example, select venetian blinds.

3. Hold down ⇧Shift and click the Browse tool in the Tools menu. (Holding down ⇧Shift when you choose the Browse tool automatically takes you out of the background layer.)

4. Click the Add Picture button to see the visual effect you chose. The Small Treasures card will open like horizontal blinds on your screen.

5. Select Back from the Go menu to go back to the Invoice stack where you were working. Try out a few other effects.

Using the Field Tool

Fields are a very important part of a HyperCard stack because they hold the majority of a stack's information. Fields can reside either in the background or on the card layer, but usually fields reside in the background so that they appear on all cards. As with buttons, you can assign styles to fields, and you can assign various fonts and styles to the text in fields. You, the HyperCard author, have several options when working with the fields in a card or stack.

To work with the fields in your Invoice stack, follow these steps:

1. Pull down the Tools menu and select the Field tool. All the fields in the stack are outlined in solid-lined rectangles.

187

Here, the Field tool is selected from the Tools menu.

6

All the fields in the card are outlined in solid-lined rectangles.

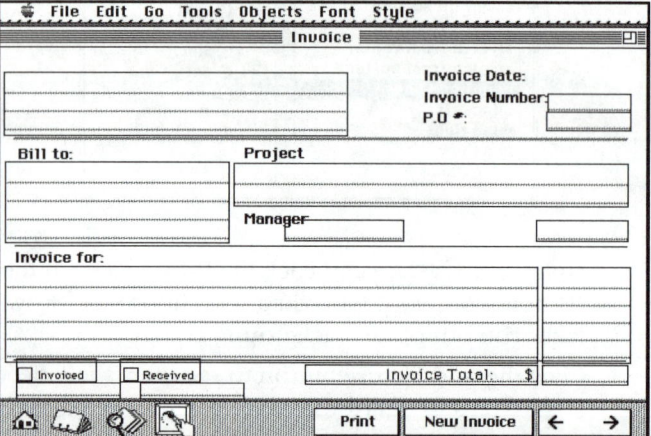

2. Pull down the Edit menu and select Background (or press ⌘-B) to see which fields reside on the background of the card. In this particular stack, all the fields reside in the background and appear on all the cards in the stack.

Field Info

When you create a field, HyperCard automatically gives the field a number that corresponds to its placement order in the card. And, as with buttons, you also can give the field a name and special attributes.

To modify a field, you first must select the field. Then, you can view and change the field's attributes in the Field Information dialog box.

To view the Field Info dialog box, follow these steps:

1. Click the field next to the Invoice Number button. A moving rectangle encloses the field, meaning that it is selected.

2. Pull down the Objects menu and select Field Info.

188

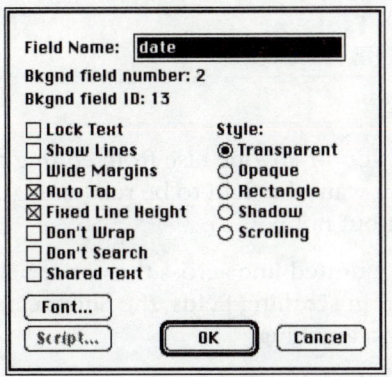

The Field Info
dialog box
appears.

You can choose from five different styles for your field and eight different attributes. You will use some of these styles and attributes as you progress through this exercise.

Using Field Styles and Attributes

The styles for fields are similar to those for buttons. Field styles are described in table 6.3. Field attributes are described in table 6.4.

Table 6.3
Field Styles

Style	Description
Transparent	The default style when a new field is created. A transparent field has no outline around it and looks invisible. You can place a picture under a transparent field.
Opaque	A white rectangle with no border around it.
Rectangle	The most common style for text fields. An opaque rectangle with a thin black border around it.
Shadow	An opaque rectangle with a shadow on the bottom and right border, giving the field depth.
Scrolling	Works exactly like a scroll bar. You can enter an unlimited amount of text, and the field will automatically scroll down to accommodate it. To view text that is not visible, hold down the mouse button on either the top or bottom arrow of the scroll bar.

6

189

Table 6.4
Field Attributes

Attribute	Description
Lock Text	Prevents you or anyone else from editing text. Use when you want the field to be read only (users can read text but not edit it).
Show Lines	Displays a dotted line across the entire field width. However, in scrolling fields, the Show Lines option doesn't do anything.
Wide Margins	Increases the left and right margin of the field by approximately one character, and the top margin by about one-half line.
Auto Tab	Enables the Return key to act like the Tab key when the cursor is on the last visible line in a text field. The Return key advances the cursor to the next field in the field order.
Fixed Line Height	Maintains an even line height, no matter which font size or style is chosen for specific characters, words, or lines in the text field. The Fixed Line Height option is automatically turned on when you choose Show Lines for a text field.
Don't Wrap	Turns off automatic word wrapping when text comes to the end of a line. User must press Return to go to the next line.
Don't Search	Prevents text from being searched when you use the Find command to look for a specific text. When you use the Find command to search for specific text, the text in a Don't Search field will be ignored.
Shared Text	Causes the text in the field to appear on every card in the stack. An option for background fields only. When you turn on Shared Text, the field is locked during normal browsing. You can only edit the text in a Shared Text field when you are in the background layer. When you turn on Shared Text, the Don't Search option is automatically turned on also.

6

Moving and Resizing Fields

When a field is selected, you can move and resize it in the same way that you move and resize a button.

Moving a Field

To move a field, follow these steps:

1. Position the mouse pointer at the center of the Date field, which is next to the Invoice Number button. Holding down the mouse button and ⇧Shift (to restrict movement), move the field up next to the Invoice Date line.

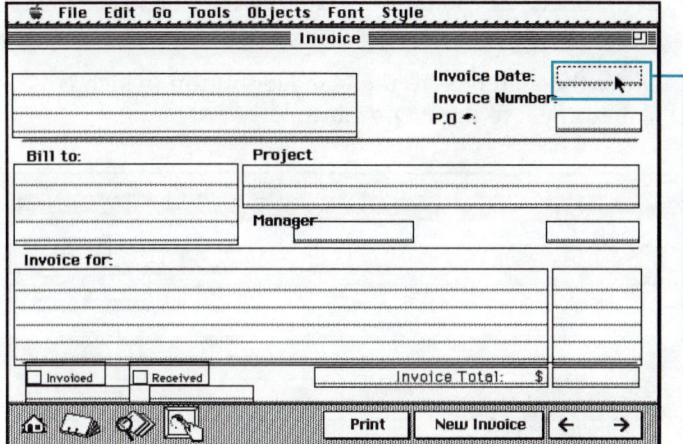

6

Here, the Date field is moved next to the Invoice Date button.

2. Repeat step 1 above to move the field positioned next to the button for P.O.# next to the Invoice Number button. Don't worry if the field and button overlap; you will resize the field in a moment.

191

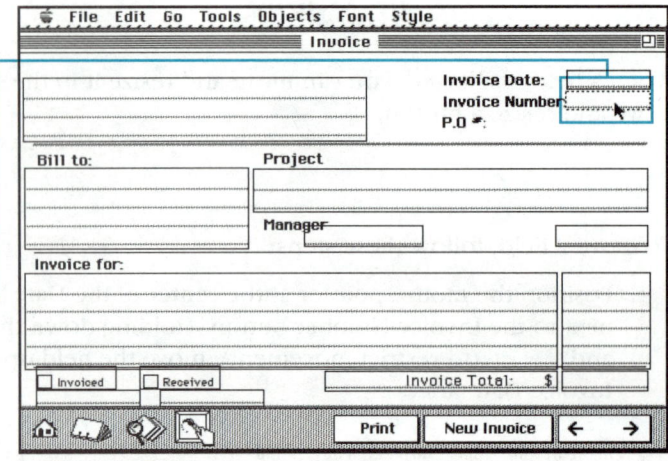

Here, the Invoice Number field is moved next to the Invoice Number button.

3. Repeat step 1 to move the field next to the Manager button (which is actually the P.O.# field) next to the P.O.# button.

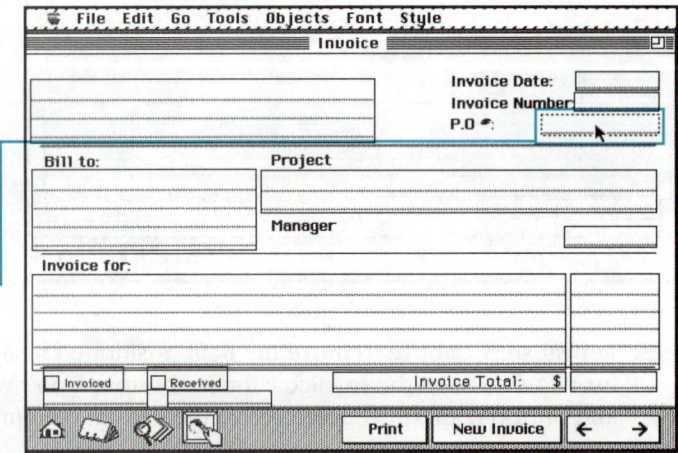

Here, the P.O.# field is moved next to the P.O.# button.

Resizing a Field

Resize fields the same way that you resize buttons and graphics. To resize a field, follow these steps:

1. Click inside the Invoice Number field to select it.

2. Position the mouse pointer on the lower left corner of the field. Keeping the mouse button pressed down, drag the mouse closer to the right margin to resize the field.

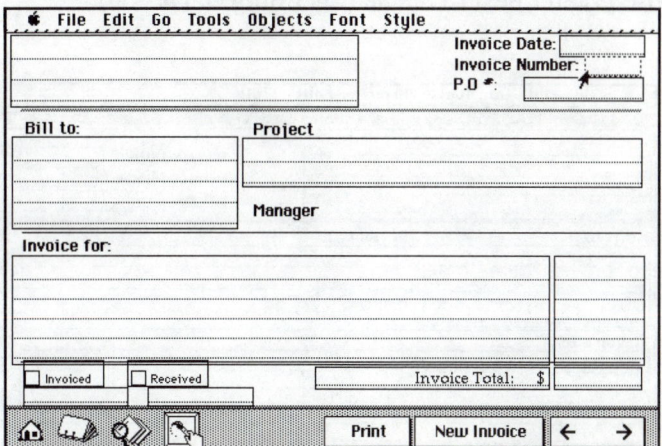

Here, the Invoice Number field is being made smaller.

Clearing, Deleting, and Cutting Fields

You also can clear, delete, or cut a field the same way you did with buttons. Remember, once you clear or delete a field, you cannot undo the operation. If you're not positive that you want to delete the field, use the Cut Field option in the Edit menu rather than Clear or Delete.

1. Select the field to the far right of the Manager button, which used to be the Project Number field.
2. Pull down the Edit menu and select Clear Field, or press Del.

Adding a New Field

You can add a field to a card or stack either by copying or duplicating an existing field or by creating a new field from scratch.

To copy a field, select the field, and then select Copy Field from the Edit menu. Paste the field wherever you want.

To duplicate a field, hold down Option and drag the field you want to duplicate.

To add a new field to the stack, first be sure that you are in the background layer (if you want the new field to be shared by all cards in the background), and then follow these steps:

1. Position the mouse pointer next to the Manager button. Press and hold down 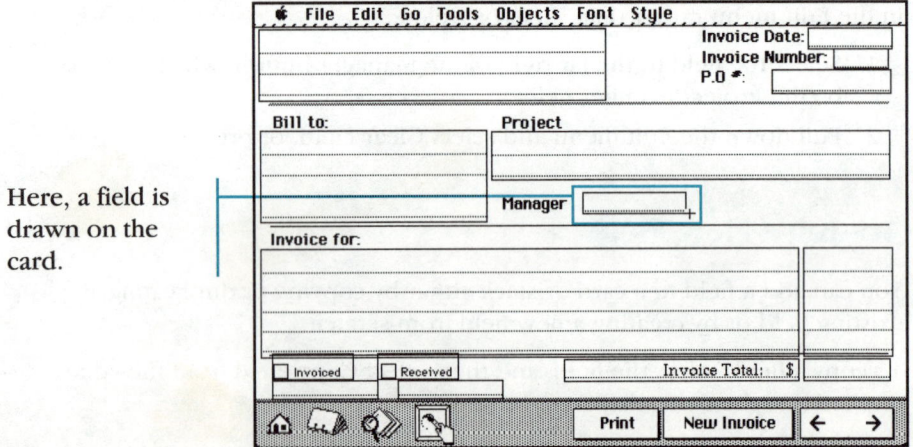.

The mouse pointer turns into a cross.

2. Holding down the mouse button, drag the cursor down and to the right to draw a rectangle.

Here, a field is drawn on the card.

Note: You also can add a field by selecting New Field from the Objects menu, but the default size is much larger than what is needed for this stack.

3. With the new field still selected, double-click it to access the Field Info dialog box. A field number has been assigned by HyperCard, corresponding to the field's order. It was the last field created, so it will be last in order.

4. Name the field *Manager* and select the checkboxes for Wide Margins, Auto Tab, and Fixed Line Height. Leave the style set to Transparent.

5. Click the Font button. The Text Style dialog box appears. Select a font, size, style, and alignment for the text you will enter in your new field.

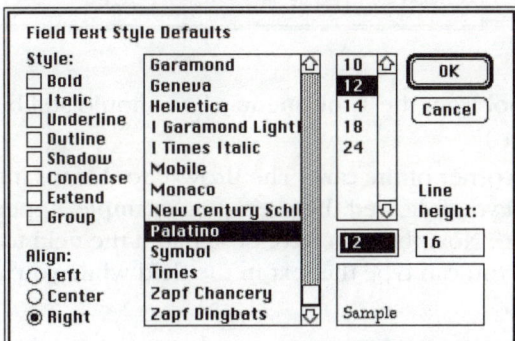

For example, select 12-point Palatino font. A sample of the text appears in the box in the lower right corner.

6

Entering Shared and Locked Text in a Field

The only thing left to do in this stack is enter your company name in the upper left corner field. Ordinarily, to make an object appear on every card in a stack, you would put the object in the background layer. In HyperCard, however, you cannot enter text in a field while you are in the background layer. Does that mean that you have to reenter your company name each time you create a new invoice? Fortunately not. That is what Shared Text is all about. You can set the shared text to be locked so that users cannot edit it in normal Browse mode.

Entering shared text can be a little tricky, so go slowly. First be sure that you are in the background layer, and then follow these steps:

1. Double-click the field in the upper left corner to access the Field Info dialog box. Click the Shared Text checkbox. (The Don't Search checkbox will automatically become selected as well.)

2. Click the Font menu and select the font type, style, and size you want. Then, click OK.

For example, select 14-point Palatino, Bold, Italic, and Center alignment. Click OK.

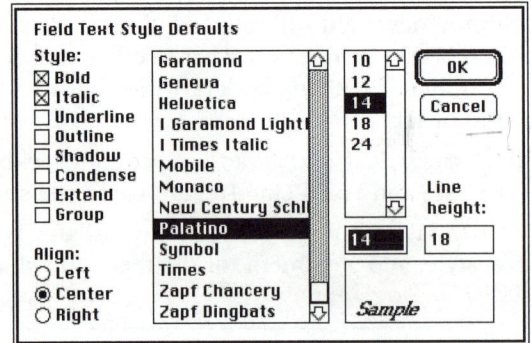

6

3. Select the Browse tool from the Tools menu. (You should still be in the background layer.)

4. Click the upper left corner of the card. The Browse tool turns into an I-beam cursor and, if you followed the preceding example, appears in the center of the field. Now that you have designated the field to contain shared text, you can type the text in the field while you are in the background layer.

Type your company name and address. You can change the font type and style on individual words or lines after you have typed the text.

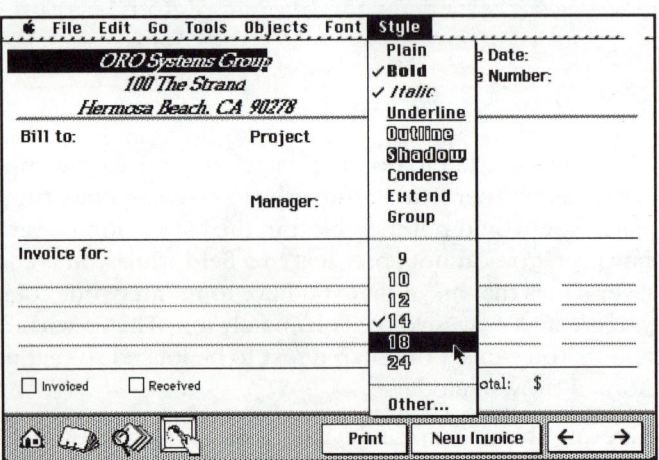

5. Pull down the Tools menu and select the Field tool.

6. Double-click the Company Name field again. Select Lock Text to disable editing of this field. Click OK.

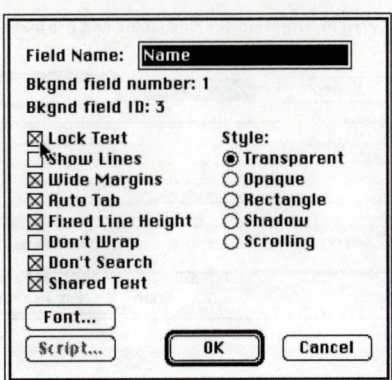

Here, Lock Text is selected.

Now the company name information cannot be edited, and it will appear on every card in the stack.

If at a later date you need to edit the information, click the field and deselect the Lock Text option. You will be able to edit the text.

7. Hold down ⇧Shift and select the Browse tool to leave the background layer and to see what your card now looks like. Position the Browse tool over the Company Name field to make sure that the Browse tool doesn't turn into an I-beam cursor. If it does, you did not "lock" the text and are able to edit.

8. Click the New Invoice button to go to the next card.

6

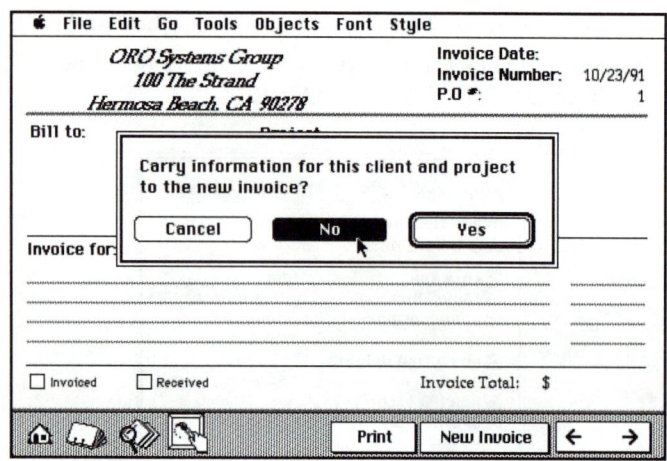

A dialog box appears, asking whether you want to carry over the client information.

9. Click No.

Your company name and address will automatically appear on every card, along with the current date and invoice number.

Modifying Field Order

Before you start using your new Invoice stack, you need to check the order in which the fields are set to receive information. Remember, when you add a new field to a card, the field is automatically given an ID number and a field number. The field number corresponds to the field's order in the card, or what is referred to as its *layer* in the card. Each time you add a new field to the card, you are adding another layer on top of the card. The first field on the card is on the first layer, or the bottom; the last field you add is on the last layer, or the very top. You can modify the order of the fields by sending a field farther down to the bottom layer, or bringing a field up closer to the top layer.

So, if you add a field to a card that already contains 10 fields, the new field will be numbered 11. When you press the Tab key to advance the text cursor from field to field, regardless of where you placed the new field in the card, the text cursor won't advance to the new field until you have cycled through the previous 10 fields. When you press the Tab key again, you start the cycle all over again with the first field on the very bottom layer.

To see this process, click the Invoice Date field in the Invoice stack you just created. Then, press $\boxed{\text{Tab}\updownarrow}$ to cycle through each field. The order in which you advance to each field is not necessarily what you might expect. Even though the P.O.# field is positioned right after the Invoice Number field, the text cursor doesn't advance to that field until after the Project field. The Manager field is positioned after the Project field. But, because it is the last field you added to the card, the Tab key won't advance the text cursor to that field until the end of the cycle.

Although you can get around this inconvenience by clicking the field you want to enter information into, you also can modify the field order so that you can tab from field to field in the order the fields are displayed.

To modify the field order in this Invoice stack, follow these steps:

1. Select the Field tool from the Tools menu and double-click each field to see the field numbers in the Field Info dialog box. If you followed the exact steps in this chapter to create the Invoice stack, the first six field numbers should be:

   Name : 1

   Date: 2

   Invoice Number: 3

   Client (Bill To): 4

   Project: 5

   P.O.#: 6

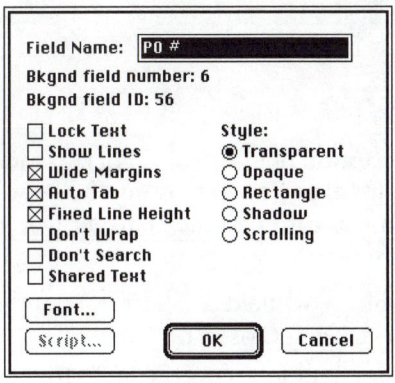

The P.O.# field is currently field number 6, which indicates that the field is on the 6th layer of the card. Assuming you want this field to be field number 4 (right after the Invoice Number field), you need to send the P.O.# field closer to the bottom layer.

2. Click the P.O.# field to select it. Then, pull down the Objects menu and select Send Farther, or press ⌘-⊟.

Here, Send Farther is selected from the Objects menu.

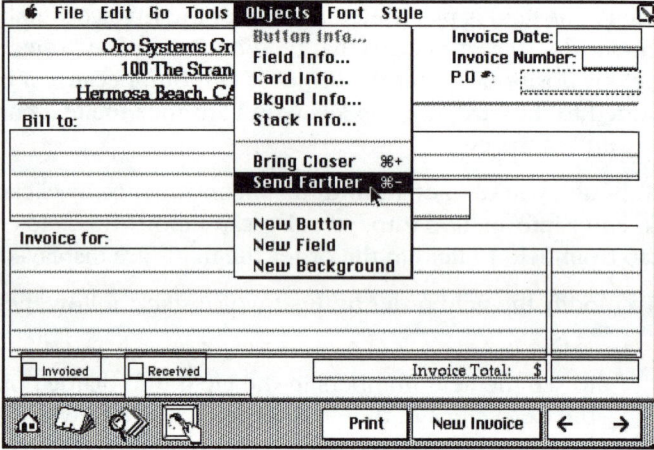

3. Double-click the P.O.# field to access the Field Info dialog box again. The field number should now be 5.

4. Repeat step 2 above to send the P.O.# field one more layer down to the bottom. The field number should now be 4.

    Now the first six fields should be:

    Name : 1

    Date: 2

    Invoice Number: 3

    P.O.#: 4

    Client (Bill To): 5

    Project: 6

Field number 7 is now the Description field (Invoice For). Assuming you want the Manager field to be the 7th field, you need to bring the Description field closer to the top layer, and then you can send the Manager field down to the bottom layer. Follow these steps:

1. Click the Description (Invoice For) field to select it. Then, pull down the Objects menu and select Bring Closer, or press ⌘-⊞.

2. Double-click the Description field to access the Field Info dialog box. The Field number should now be 8.

6

3. Now click the Manager field (which is currently field number 15). Pull down the Objects menu and select Send Farther 8 times so that the field is renumbered to be field number 7.

   Tab through the fields to be sure that you have renumbered them correctly.

Using Your Stack

Now take a few minutes and use your new Invoice stack to enter a sample invoice. Follow these steps:

1. Tab to (or click) each field and enter the appropriate information. If you don't remember your client's address, click the Address icon and look it up. After you have found the address, use the Recent command to go back to this card.

2. Click the Add Picture icon to go to the Art Bits stack. Choose a picture from the Small Treasures card and copy it. Then, select Back from the Go menu to return to this card.

3. Paste the picture into the card next to the company's name. Because you are pasting the picture into the card layer and not the background layer, the next invoice you create will not have the picture on it.

4. Tab over to the remaining fields and enter the invoice information. Click the Invoiced button, and the current date will be entered automatically.

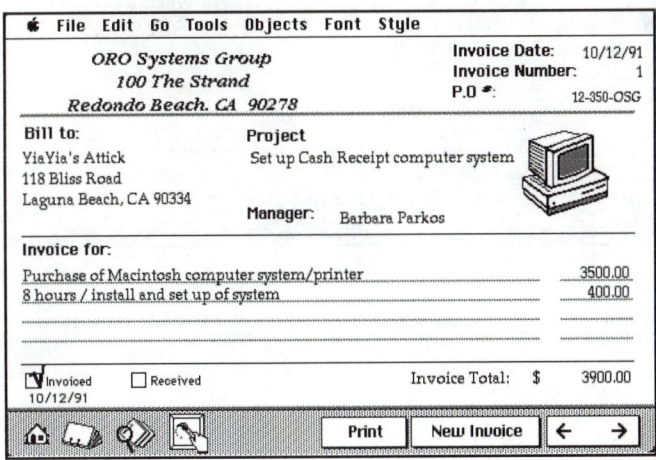

You can personalize each invoice quickly with a picture from the Art Bits stack.

5. Click the New Invoice button to enter a new invoice. A dialog box appears, asking whether you want to carry over the current client's name and information onto this new invoice. If you say yes, you will see a message about a missing Project Number field, because that was the field you removed. Click OK to proceed.

Linking Your Stack to Home

Now that you have created a useful stack, you may want to put it on one of your Home cards so that you can access it quickly and easily. Remember, you were provided with three empty Home cards just for this purpose. HyperCard has made it very easy for you to link your new stacks to Home. Follow these steps:

1. Click the Home button to go Home.

2. Click the Card 3 button to go to the third Home card, which is now empty.

3. Pull down the Home menu and select New Link to Stack.

The Home menu is new in Hyper-Card 2.0. Here, the New Link to Stack option is selected.

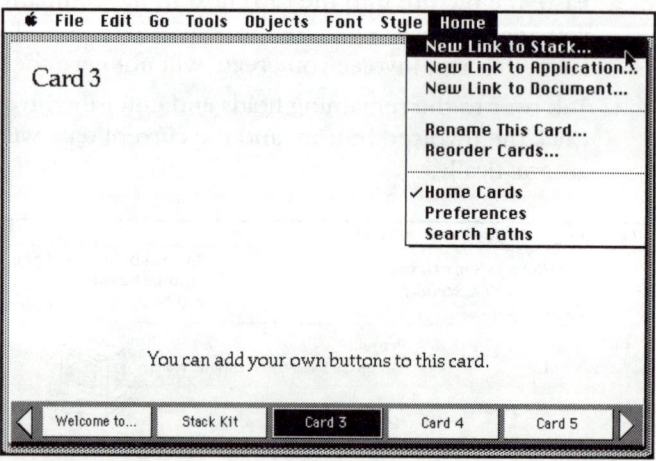

A dialog box appears, asking you to locate the stack you want to link to this Home card.

4. Select the Invoice stack. Click Open.

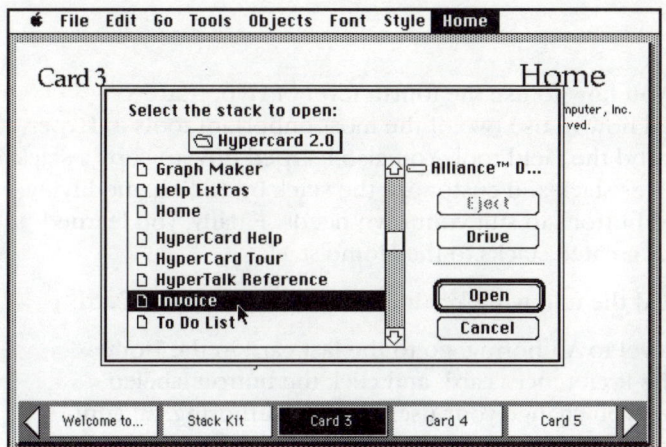

Here, the Invoice stack is selected.

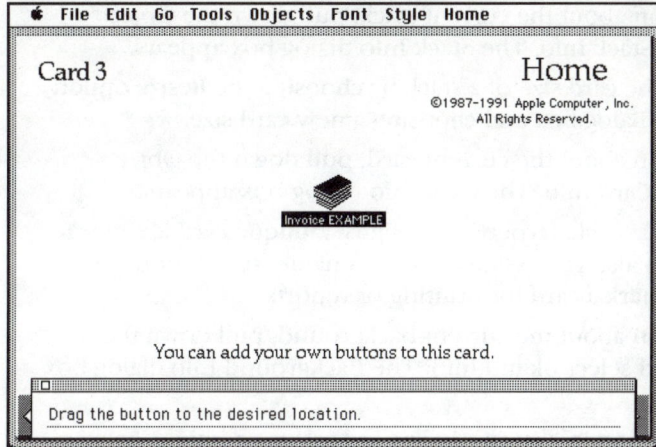

An icon for the Invoice stack is inserted into your Home card. A message box appears on the bottom of your card with instructions.

5. Click the icon and drag it to the desired location.

You have now established a link between your Invoice stack and the Home card. When you click this button, the Invoice stack will open. In the next chapter, you will create a new icon for this button.

Summary

This chapter showed you how to use the fourth level of HyperCard, Authoring. You learned how to use two of the most important tools in Hyper-Card: the Button tool and the Field tool. You also learned how to copy a stack from the Stack Templates stack and customize the stack by adding, modifying, and deleting fields and buttons to suit your own needs. Finally, you learned how to link your newly created stacks to the Home stack.

Specifically, you learned the following key information about HyperCard:

- To set the user level to Authoring, go to the last card in the Home stack, which is the Preferences card, and click the button labeled Authoring. When you change your user level to Authoring, an additional menu, named Objects, appears on the top menu line after the Tools menu.

- To get information about the current stack, pull down the Objects menu and select Stack Info. The Stack Info dialog box appears.

- You can change the card size of a stack by choosing the Resize option in the Stack Info dialog box and choosing a new card size.

- To get information about the current card, pull down the Objects menu and select Card Info. The Card Info dialog box appears.

- For every card in a stack, HyperCard assigns a unique card identification number. You also can assign the card a name, search or delete protection, and mark a card for printing or reports.

- To get information about the current background, pull down the Objects menu and select Bkgnd Info. The Background Info dialog box appears.

- For every background in a stack, HyperCard assigns a unique background identification number. You can also assign the background a name and search or delete protection.

- To see where the buttons are in any card, hold down ⌘ and Option at the same time. The thick gray rectangles indicate that the buttons reside in the background layer. The dotted rectangles mean that the buttons reside in the card layer.

- To add a new button to a card or a background, select the Button tool from the Tools menu and then select New Button from the Objects menu. Or, you can hold down ⌘ and drag the mouse to draw a button where you want it.

6

■ Whenever a button is created on a card or background, HyperCard automatically gives it a unique button number and a default style and attributes. You can change any of these attributes from within the Button Info dialog box. For example, you can change the style, the icon that represents the button, its visual effect, and the card or stack to which the button will link.

■ To access the Button Info dialog box, the Button tool must be selected in the Tools menu. Then, click the button to select it, and select Button Info from the Objects menu. Or, with the Button tool selected, double-click a button to access the Button Info dialog box.

■ You can move or resize a button in the same way that you move or resize a selected graphic image. To move a button, click the mouse near the center of the button to select it. Then, hold the mouse button down and drag the button to a new location. To resize a button, click any one of the button's corners, and drag the mouse in any direction to resize the button. You can hold down ⬆Shift to restrict your movement to a vertical or horizontal motion.

■ To clear or delete a button, first select the button, and then press Del or select Clear from the Edit menu. After you clear or delete a button, you cannot undo the operation. So, if you're not sure that you want to delete the button, use the Cut Button option in the Edit menu rather than Clear or Delete.

■ To copy a button from another card or stack, select the button you want to copy and select Copy Button from the Edit menu. Then, go to the card or stack you want to copy the button into and select Paste from the Edit menu.

■ To make a duplicate of a button in the same card, first select the button, then hold down Option and drag the mouse away from the button. A duplicate appears.

■ To assign a visual effect to a button, click the Effect button in the Button Info dialog box and select the effect you want to assign to the button.

■ To add or select a different icon that represents a button, click the Icon button in the Button Info dialog box. Then, select the icon you want from the dialog box and click OK. You then may need to resize the button so that the new icon fits the button.

6

205

■ To link a button to another card or stack, click the Link To button in the Button Info dialog box. Then, open the stack or card you want to link the button to and click This Card or This Stack in the Link To window that appears. You will return to your original card or stack, and the link will be established.

■ To see where the fields are in any card, hold down ⊙Shift, ⌘, and Option at the same time. The thick, gray rectangles indicate that the fields reside in the background layer. The dotted rectangles mean that the fields reside in the card layer.

■ To add a new field to a card or a background, select the Field tool from the Tools menu and then select New Field from the Objects menu. Or, you can hold down ⌘ and drag the mouse to draw a field where you want it.

■ Whenever a field is created on a card or background, HyperCard automatically gives the field a unique field ID number and a number that corresponds to its placement order in the card. HyperCard also gives the field a default style and attributes. You can change any of these attributes from within the Field Info dialog box.

■ To access the Field Info dialog box, the Field tool must be selected in the Tools menu. Then, click the field to select it and select Field Info from the Objects menu. Or, double-click a field to access the Field Info dialog box.

■ Normally, you cannot enter text in a field while you are in the background layer. To have a field's text appear on every card in the same background, you must first set the field's attributes to Shared Text, and then you can enter the text in the background layer. You also can lock the field's text so that it cannot be edited.

■ You can move or resize a field in the same way that you move or resize a button or a selected graphic image. To move a field, click near the center of the field to select it. Then, hold down the mouse button and drag the field to a new location. To resize a field, click any one of the field's corners and drag the mouse in any direction. You can hold down ⊙Shift to restrict your movement to a vertical or horizontal motion.

■ To clear or delete a field, first select the field, and then press Del or select Clear from the Edit menu. After you clear or delete a field, you cannot undo the operation. If you're not sure that you want to delete the field, use the Cut Field option in the Edit menu rather than Clear or Delete.

6

■ To copy a field from another card or stack, select the field you want to copy and select Copy Field from the Edit menu. Then, go to the card or stack you want to copy the field into, and select Paste from the Edit menu.

■ To make a duplicate of a field in the same card, first select the field, then hold down (Option) and drag away from the field. A duplicate appears.

■ To modify a field's order in the stack, first select the field and then select Bring Closer or Send Farther from the Objects menu. Bring Closer brings the field closer to the top layer of the card (which is the last field you entered). Send Farther brings the field farther down to the bottom layer (which is the first field in the card).

■ To put a new stack on one of your Home cards in the Home stack, select New Link to Stack in the Home menu. Select the stack to which you want to link. An icon for that stack is inserted into your Home card, and the link is established.

6

That's all it takes to be a HyperCard author. In the next chapter, you will learn how to use the new Icon Editor to customize any icon and create new icons to use in your cards and stacks.

7

Using the Icon Editor

The Icon Editor is a new feature in HyperCard 2.0. With the Icon Editor, you can create icons to add to your card or stack buttons, as well as modify icons. You can create pictures from scratch using the HyperCard graphics tools and then turn the pictures into icons, or you can "pick up" any bit-mapped art on a card and transform it into an icon. You also can copy an existing icon from another card or stack, modify its individual pixels, and save it as a new icon.

HyperCard has supplied you with several ready-made icons, and they may be quite sufficient for all the buttons you create. You may never need or want to create a new icon. However, if you recall from Chapter 6, buttons are the size of the rectangular square surrounding the icon, not the icon itself. When you size a button, therefore, you are not doing anything to the icon for that button, and in many cases your choices for an icon are limited to the size of the button. With the Icon Editor, you can modify the icon's individual pixels to increase its size to a maximum of 32 pixels by 32 pixels, or even transform a larger picture into an icon to fit your button.

In Chapter 6, you used the Button tool to create a new button in a stack. You selected the Icon option in the Button Info dialog box to display available icons, and you added an icon to the button by choosing one from the list. In this chapter, you will add your own icons to that list. First, you will learn how to use the Icon Editor to create a new icon from scratch. Then, you will "pick up" a bit-mapped graphic supplied in the Art Bits stack, modify the graphic, and transform it into a new icon. You then will add the new icon to the Invoice stack you created in Chapter 6.

Key Terms in This Chapter

Icon	A graphic symbol or picture that represents a file, folder, disk, application, or function. An icon for a stack should somehow reflect what the purpose of the stack is, just as an icon for a button should represent what the function of the button is.
Icon ID number	When an icon is created, HyperCard automatically assigns a unique ID number to it between the number 128 and 32767.
Drawing area	After you start the Icon Editor, the square area where the icon you are creating or modifying appears. The Icon Editor drawing area is similar to working with FatBits. The drawing is displayed in actual size next to an enlarged version of the icon in pixels.

7

What Is an Icon?

Icons are an integral part of the Macintosh. An icon is simply a picture. Every program that is created for the Macintosh has icons, and it is impossible to avoid them entirely. Icons are what make the Macintosh so easy to use. Clicking a picture to perform a function is far less intimidating than typing in a syntactically correct command.

As a HyperCard author, one of the things you should strive for, whether you are creating a stack for your own personal use or for distribution, is simplicity and an intuitive interface. If a button serves a particular function in the stack, then the icon for that button should somehow reflect the function. You should be able to guess what something does by the way it is represented on-screen. For example, in HyperCard the right and left arrows that lead to the next or previous card are actually icons for the buttons that perform those functions. When you are on a card, you know that to proceed, you click the right arrow, and to go back, you click the left arrow.

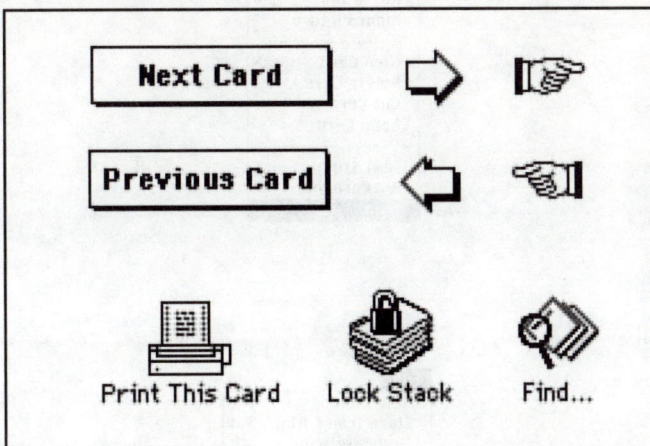

These buttons have icons that represent their function.

7

With the Icon Editor, you have the freedom and tools to create an icon for just about anything.

Viewing Icons

When you create an icon from scratch, it is saved with the current stack. For the icons that are supplied with HyperCard, the graphics are stored in a part of a particular stack file, the Home stack file, or in the HyperCard application itself. Even though the icon appears in the stack you are working in, the art for the icon may not reside there. If you want to edit the icon, you will be asked if you want to copy the icon art from where it resides. After you do that, you can edit the stack icon freely and save it as part of that stack.

To see the icon art for a particular stack, follow these steps:

1. Open the Addresses stack or any other stack that you prefer.
2. Pull down the Edit menu and select Icon, or press ⌘-⌶. The Icon Editor window appears, and four new menus replace the top menu line: File, Edit, Icon, and Special.

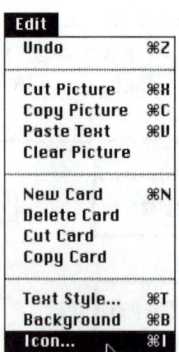

Here, the Icon
option is selected
from the Edit
menu.

7

This is the File
menu to use with
the Icon editor.

This is the Edit
menu to use with
the Icon editor.

This is the Icon menu to use with the Icon editor.

7

This is the Special menu to use with the Icon editor.

When an icon is created, HyperCard automatically assigns a unique ID number, between 128 and 32767, to the icon. You also can assign a name. The icon's name and ID number are displayed along with a picture of the icon art both in actual size and enlarged in the drawing area. The drawing area is separated into quadrants. You will find these quadrants useful when you use the commands in the Special menu.

213

The Icon Editor drawing area is similar to working with FatBits. The drawing is displayed in actual size next to an enlarged version of the icon in pixels.

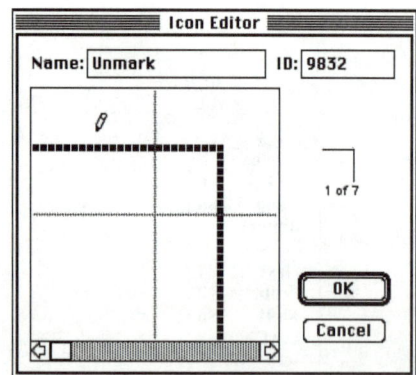

The icon for the Unmark card button appears first in the Icon Editor window for the Addresses stack. As you learned in Chapter 4, when you mark a card for printing or reports (in this stack), the left corner of the card is turned down. When you click again to unmark the card, the corner goes back up. The corner turning back up is what this particular icon represents.

3. Position the mouse pointer onto the Name field. The mouse pointer turns into an I-beam cursor, signifying that you can edit both the name and the ID Number field. Now move the mouse pointer over the drawing area of the icon. The mouse pointer turns into a pencil, as it does when working with FatBits.

4. Pull down the Icon menu and select Next (or press ⌘-3) to go to the next icon residing in the current stack. You also can choose First, Previous, and Last to cycle through all the icons residing in the Addresses stack. You will see the icon art for the small left and right arrow, the "glimmer" lightbulb, audio note, and small speaker. (These icons are not used in this particular stack, although that is where the icon art is stored.)

Note: You also can scroll through the icon art by using the scroll bar on the bottom of the drawing area.

Creating a New Icon

To create a new icon for the stack in which you are working, select New Icon from the File menu. The icon can be up to 32 pixels by 32 pixels, filling up the entire drawing area. It doesn't matter which stack you are in when you create

214

a new icon; you can copy the icon after you have created it to any other stack you want. You can either create a new icon using the Pencil tool, or you can copy a bit-mapped picture into the drawing area, modify the picture, and make it into an icon. You will try both methods in this chapter.

To create a new icon from scratch, follow these steps:

1. Pull down the File menu and select New Icon, or press ⌘-N. A blank drawing window appears, and the icon is given an ID number. The icon is positioned directly behind the one you were just viewing. Name the icon *Test*.

2. Position the mouse pointer over the drawing area so that it turns into the Pencil tool. Using the Pencil tool, fill in the top left quadrant with black pixels by clicking the mouse.

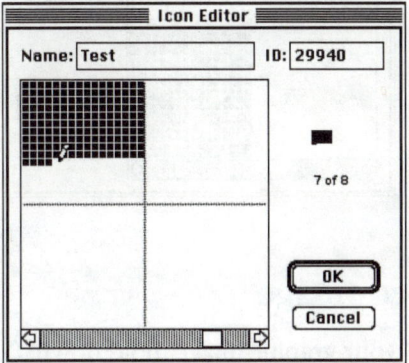

Remember, you can hold down ⇧Shift to restrict your movements horizontally or vertically.

Editing an Icon

To select a part of the graphic to work with, position the mouse pointer anywhere near the area you want to select and hold down ⌘. The mouse pointer turns into a cross cursor; you use it the same way you use the Selection tool when working with graphics. After you have selected part of a graphic, you can edit it in a number of different ways, as described in the sections that follow.

Moving the Selected Image

You can move all or part of the image in the drawing area in the same way you move any other graphic image. To move the image, follow these steps:

215

1. Hold down ⬚ and position the cross cursor on the left corner of the first quadrant. Hold down the mouse button and drag the cross cursor around the black box in the first quadrant. Release the mouse button.

2. Position the mouse pointer in the center of the selected image. Hold down the mouse button and drag the black box to the fourth quadrant of the drawing area. Click outside the selected area to deselect the image.

Here, the selected image is moved to the fourth quadrant of the drawing area.

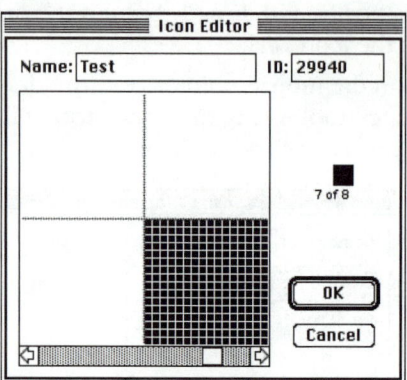

Duplicating the Selected Image

To duplicate a selected piece of your graphic image, hold down Option and drag the mouse away from the selected image. This procedure works exactly the same as with other graphics. To duplicate the image, follow these steps:

1. Hold down ⬚ and position the cross cursor on the left corner of the fourth quadrant. Hold down the mouse button and drag the cross cursor around the entire black box. Release the mouse button.

2. Position the mouse pointer in the center of the selected image. Press and hold down Option. Hold down the mouse button and drag the black box back to the first quadrant of the drawing area. Click outside the selected area to deselect the image.

216

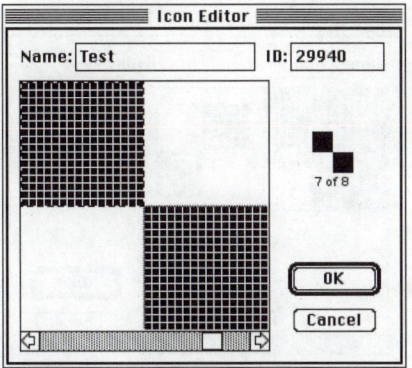

Here, the selected image has been duplicated onto the first quadrant of the drawing area.

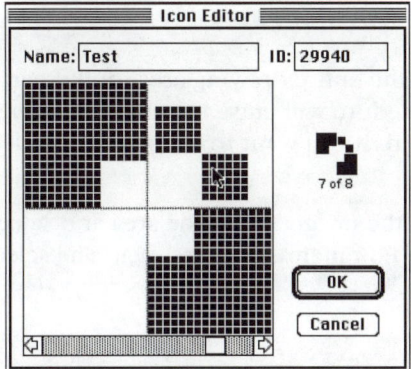

You also can move or duplicate a portion of the image.

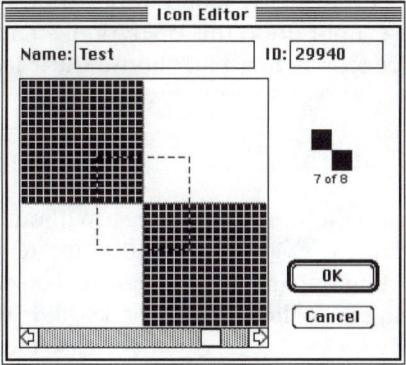

Here, a portion of the image has been selected.

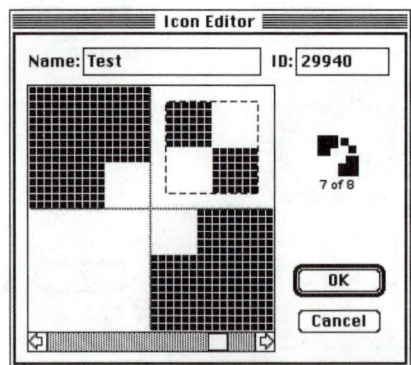

Here, the selected portion has been moved away from its original position.

Erasing the Drawing Area or Icon

If at any time, you want to erase the entire drawing area, pull down the Icon menu and select Erase. This procedure will erase the entire drawing area, even if you have a section selected. If you want to bring it back, select Undo from the Edit menu.

If you want to erase a portion of the image, select the area and select Cut Picture or Clear Picture from the Edit menu, or press Del. The selected area will erase.

Deleting an Icon

If you want to remove the entire icon from the Icon Editor window, select Clear Icon in the Edit menu. You cannot undo this operation, so make sure that you want to remove the entire icon before you choose Clear Icon.

Dragging an Image Out of View

Position the mouse pointer anywhere in the drawing area. Without any part of the icon selected, press and hold down Option. The mouse pointer turns into a small hand that you can use to drag the image into a particular section of the drawing area, or out of the drawing area altogether. When you drag a portion of the graphic out of the drawing area, however, do not release the mouse button until you are sure that you do not want to drag the graphic back into the drawing area. If you have released the mouse button, you cannot drag the graphic back into view. The only way to bring back the graphic is to

218

immediately select Undo from the Edit menu, or press ⌘-Z. Dragging a part of a graphic image out of the drawing area is actually a convenient way to erase part of a copied graphic that you do not want in your icon.

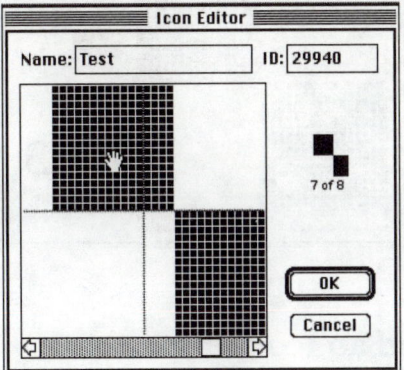

Hold down Option to turn the mouse pointer into a hand to drag a part of the image out of the drawing area.

Modifying an Icon

You can use the options in the Icon Editor Special menu on all or part of the image in the drawing area to modify an icon. The sections that follow describe a number of ways in which you can modify an icon.

Using Flip Horizontal and Flip Vertical

You can flip the entire image in the drawing area (or a selected portion) either horizontally or vertically around the dotted line of the quadrants. When you flip the image horizontally, it appears as if you are viewing the image from behind. When you flip the image vertically, it appears upside down.

1. Pull down the Special menu and select Flip Horizontal to flip the image. The image in the top left quadrant flips to the top right, and the image in the bottom right flips to the bottom left.

2. Pull down the Special menu and select Flip Vertical. The image in the bottom right flips to the top right and the image in the top left flips to the bottom left.

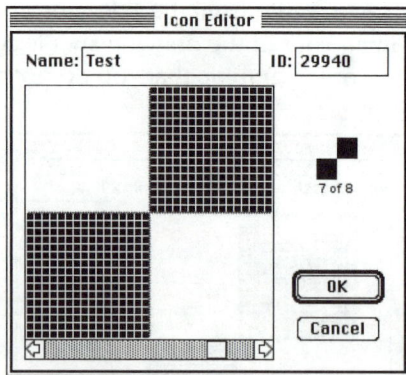

Here, the original image is flipped horizontally.

Creating a Frame around an Icon

Select Frame from the Special menu to insert a black frame around the entire icon picture. Or, select a portion of the image, and then select Frame to insert a black frame around the selected portion only.

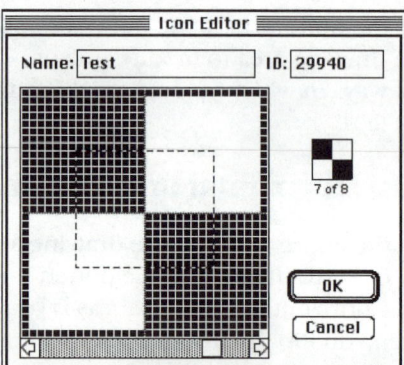

You can insert a frame around the entire drawing area.

220

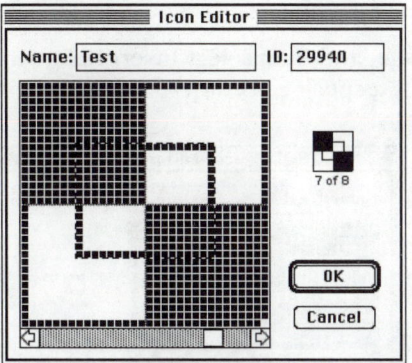

Or, you can insert a frame around a selected area.

Using the Grey Option

Select Grey from the Special menu to turn white every other black pixel in the drawing area (or selected portion of the area). The icon will appear greyed out.

7

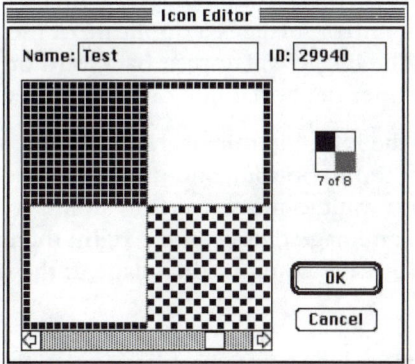

To grey out a portion of the graphic only, select the area first using ⊞ and then select Grey from the Special menu.

Inverting an Image

The Invert option on the Special menu turns black pixels to white and white pixels to black. When an image of an icon is inverted, it appears as it does when it is selected with the mouse.

1. Select Invert from the Special menu to invert the graphic image. Every black pixel will turn white, and every white pixel will turn black.

2. Select Invert again to reverse the effect.

3. Select a portion of the image, and then select Invert Image from the Special menu to invert only a specific portion of the graphic image.

Here, a particular section of the image has been selected and then inverted.

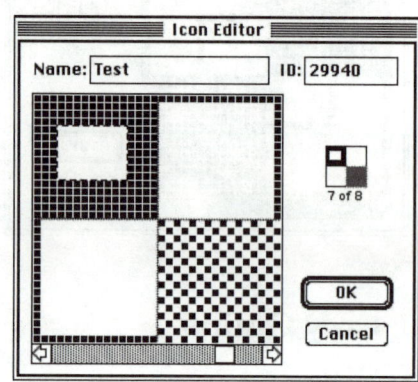

Mirroring an Image

Select Mirror Horizontal or Mirror Vertical from the Special menu to create a mirrored image of the graphic. A mirror image is a duplicate of the original image, as if viewed in a mirror. The image will appear backward or upside down and on the other side of either the horizontal or vertical axis.

You also can select a portion of the image to mirror. However, the mirror (vertical) image works only from top to bottom, and the mirror (horizontal) image from left to right. So, if you want to mirror vertical an image that is on the bottom or mirror horizontal an image that is on the right, then you first have to flip horizontally or flip vertically to move the image to the top or left quadrant.

Here is the original image in the top left quadrant of the drawing area.

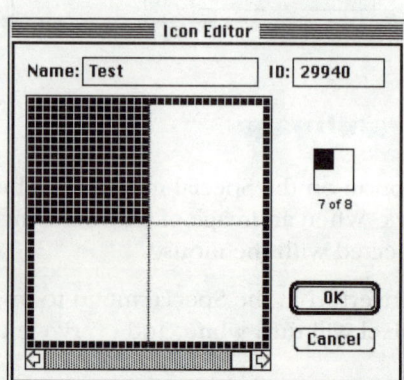

222

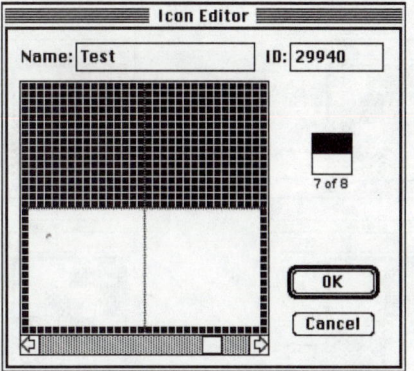

Here, the image in the top left quadrant has been "mirrored" horizontal to the top right quadrant.

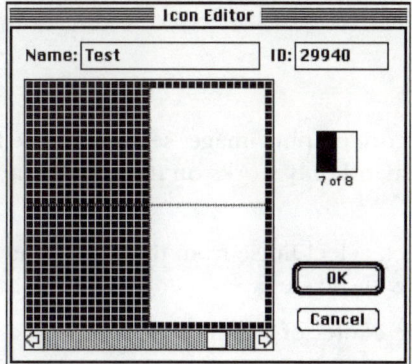

Here, the image in the top left quadrant has been "mirrored" vertical to the bottom left quadrant.

7

Rotating an Image

To rotate the graphic image 90 degrees at a time, select Rotate from the Special menu. The entire image will rotate 90 degrees each time you choose the option.

To rotate a section of the graphic image, select the portion first using ⊞, and then select Rotate from the Special menu.

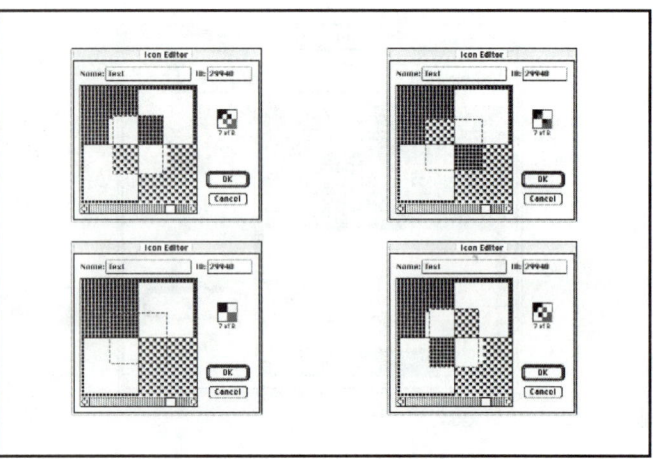

If you rotate an image (or a selected piece of the image) four times, the image will return to its original position.

Drawing a Shadow

7

To draw a shadow around the entire graphic image, select Shadow from the Special menu. The Shadow command only works on the entire graphic image, not on a selected portion.

To demonstrate the shadow effect, select Erase from the Edit menu to clear the drawing area, and then follow these steps:

1. Draw a simple square in the center of the drawing area.

2. Select Shadow from the Special menu. Select Shadow a second time to increase the shadow depth.

Each time you select Shadow, you increase the depth of the image.

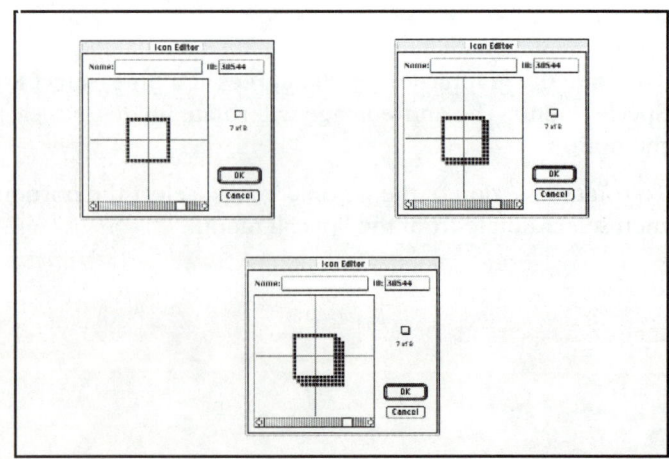

Saving Your Changes

To save changes to the icon as you work, pull down the Icon menu and select Keep, or press ⌘-K. Every time you keep your changes, you can continue experimenting. If you want to go back to the last saved version, pull down the Icon menu and select Revert. You will return to the last graphic image you saved.

HyperCard will automatically save your work when you click OK. When you click the scroll bar to move to another icon, HyperCard will ask whether you want to save your changes.

After you have created the artwork for your icon, you can save the icon as a new button or assign it to any other button. Be sure to save your work before you save it as a new button. When you select New Button, HyperCard will attach the last saved version of the picture, which may not necessarily be the one that is currently on your screen, to a new button and place the button in the center of the card currently on-screen.

To create a button from the sample icon you created, follow these steps:

1. Pull down the Icon menu and select Keep, or press ⌘-K.

2. Pull down the Edit menu and select New Button.

    You will immediately be taken out of the Icon Editor and returned to the stack you were in.

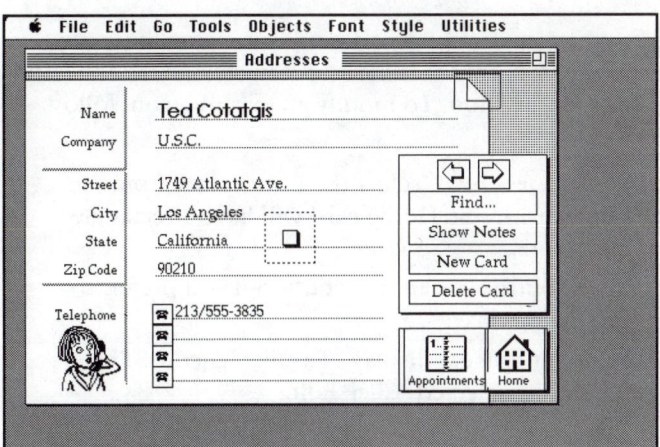

The icon you just created will be converted into a button and will appear in the middle of the card on your screen.

3. Double-click the new button to access the Button Info dialog box.

4. Select Icon from the Button Info dialog box. A display of icons appears. You will notice that the icon you just created now appears in the visual display of available icons and is selected. The icon's name, ID number, and stack address are displayed on the top line.

From here you can click the Edit button to go back into the Icon Editor. For this exercise, click Cancel and then delete the button from the Addresses stack. Then, press ⌘- H to go home.

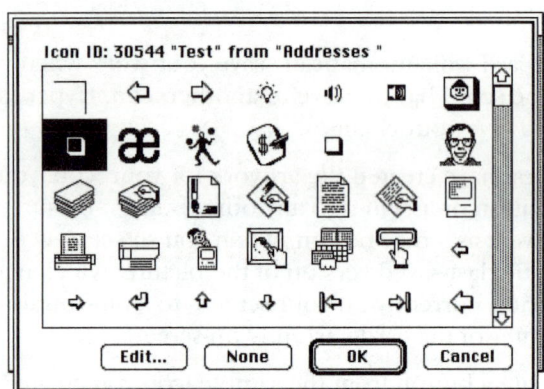

Making Several Modifications to an Existing Icon

You can choose an icon in the visual display and modify it, using the same methods described previously. A simple modification can change the look and feel of an icon to serve another function. To modify an existing icon, follow these steps:

1. With the Home card on your screen, select the Button tool from the Tools menu. All the buttons on the Home card will have a rectangle around their respective icons.

2. Double-click the Practice button, or another button if you prefer, to access the Button Info dialog box.

3. Click the icon button to get a visual display of available icons. The current Practice Stack icon is selected. Click Edit.

226

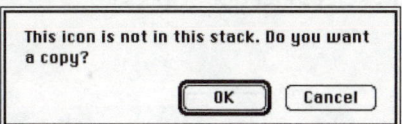

If the icon does not reside in the current stack, this dialog box appears. If you want to edit the icon, it must reside in the current stack. Click OK.

4. Modify the icon as you like. For example, hold down ⊞ and select the juggler's middle ball. Then, select Grey from the Special menu. Click OK to save your changes and leave the Icon Editor.

7

You can modify all or part of any available icon.

5. Select the Browse tool from the Tools menu to proceed.

Creating an Icon from a Picture

A fun way to create an icon is to take a snap shot of a picture and turn it into an icon. The two cards named Icon Ideas in the Art Bits stack supplied with HyperCard provide several samples. You can choose any of those samples, or you can select any other bit-mapped art from another stack and turn the picture into an icon. To create an icon from a picture, follow these steps:

1. Open the Art Bits stack and click Icon Ideas. Go to the second page of the Icon Ideas card.

227

2. Pull down the Icon Edit menu and select Icon to access the Icon Editor window. If you need to, move the window anywhere on your screen.

3. Pull down the Icon menu and select Pickup, or press ⌘-P.

The mouse pointer turns into a square with a cross inside of it, representing a miniaturized version of the drawing area.

4. Move the square over the picture you want. Then, click the mouse. The picture will be "picked up" onto the drawing area. From there, you can modify the picture as you want with any of the options in the Special menu.

Here, the Icon Editor is about to "pick up" a graphic image and place it into the drawing area.

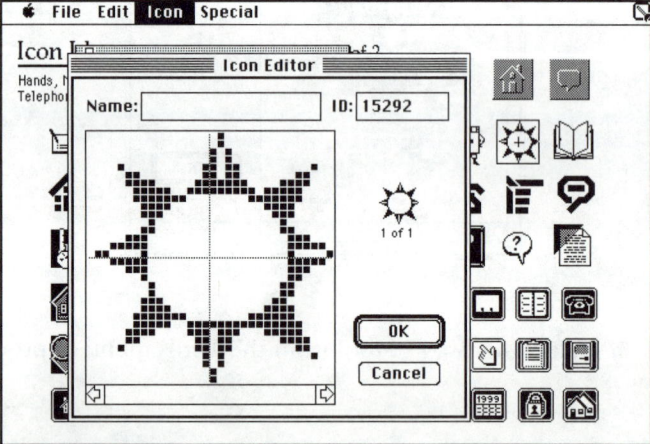

228

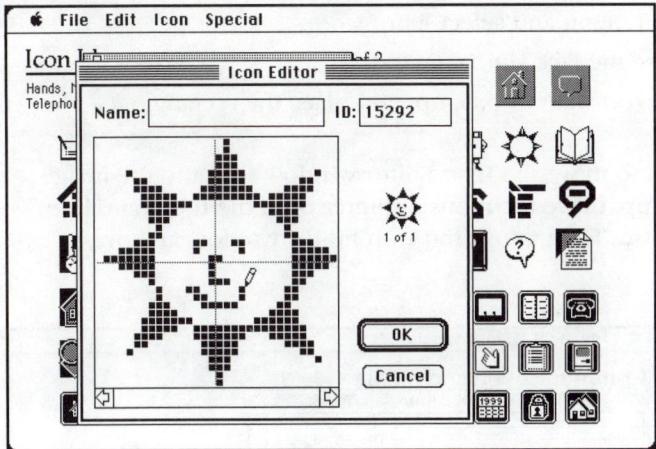

After an image has been picked up, you can modify it as you like.

You can perform these same steps and "pick up" any other picture and turn it into an icon. The Art Bits stack contains several graphic images and others that would make good icons.

7

Creating an Icon for the Invoice Stack

Now that you know how to create an icon for any button in any stack, you can create an icon for the Invoice stack you created in the last chapter. To create this icon, follow these steps:

1. Go to the second Communication and Media card in the Art Bits stack.

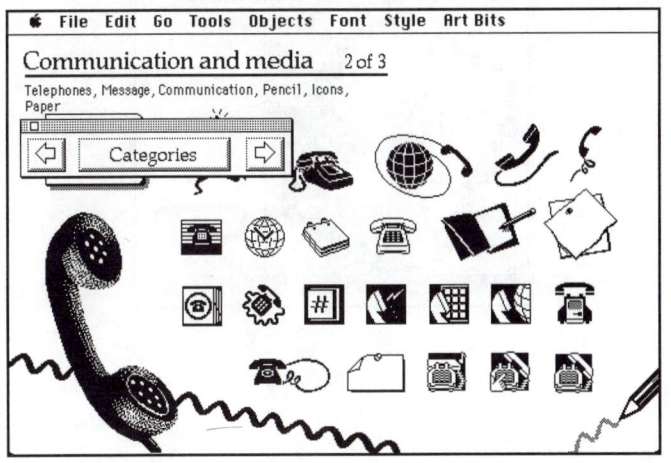

This is the second Communication and Media card in the Art Bits stack.

229

2. Pull down the Edit menu and select Icon.

3. Press ⊞-P to use the Pick Up command.

4. Choose an image you want to pick up, and place the rectangle around it.

   Note: If you need to move the Icon Editor window to get to the image you want to pick up, move the mouse pointer onto the top menu line and click the mouse. Then, move the Icon Editor window and press ⊞-P again.

Here, the pencil in a book image is picked up.

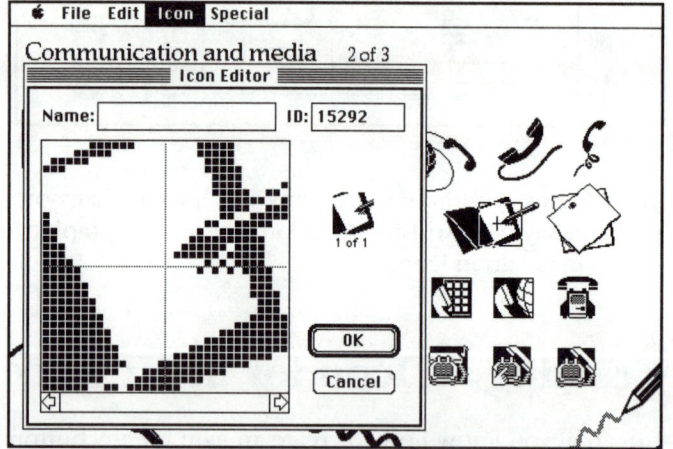

Modify the picture by drawing a dollar sign symbol, as shown.

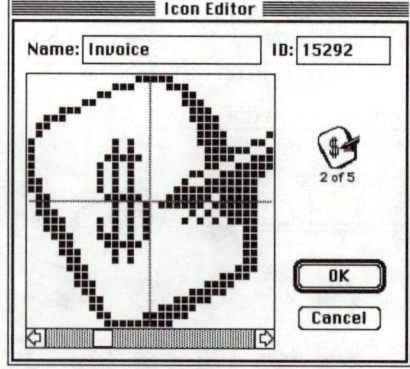

230

5. Name the icon *Invoice*, and then pull down the Icon menu and select Keep to save your changes.

Copying an Icon into Another Stack

After you have created an icon, you can copy it into any other stack. The most convenient stack to copy the icon into is the Home stack. If the icon is in the Home stack, you can access it easily. To copy the icon into the Home stack, follow these steps:

1. Pull down the Edit menu and select Copy Icon.
2. Pull down the File menu and select Close Icon Editor, or press ⌘-W.
3. Press ⌘-H to go back to the Home stack. Then, press ⌘-I to go back into the Icon Editor.
4. Pull down the Edit menu and select Paste Icon. The icon will be pasted into the Home stack for you to use as you like.

Attaching a New Icon to Your Stack

Now that the icon is available from the Home stack, you can attach the icon onto the button you created for your Invoice stack. To attach the icon, follow these steps:

1. Go to the third card of the Home Stack. Select the Button tool and *double* click the Invoice Stack button.
2. Click the Icon button to display a visual list of all the icons available. Select the icon you just created. Click OK.

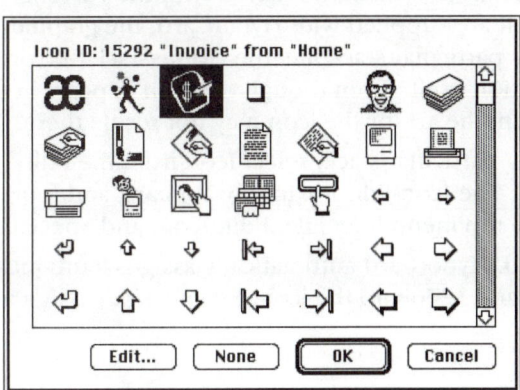

After you have copied an icon into the current stack, you can choose the icon to modify any button in the stack.

3. Resize the Invoice button to accommodate the new icon. Then, select the Browse tool from the Tools menu to see how the icon looks.

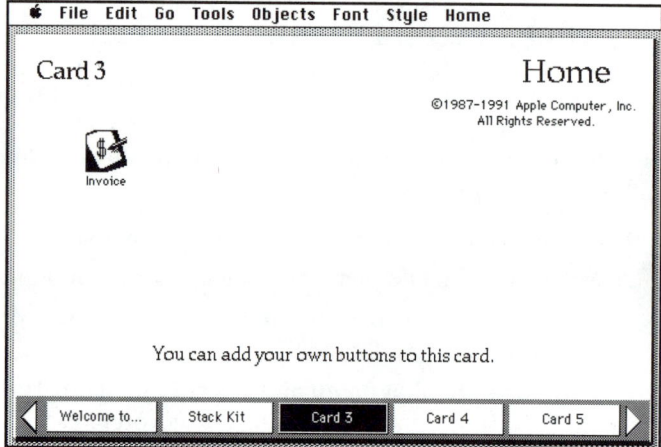

Here, your new Invoice icon is displayed in the Home stack.

Summary

This chapter showed you how to use the new Icon Editor that is provided with HyperCard 2.0. You learned how to create new icons from scratch to add to your card or stack buttons, as well as modify existing icons. You also learned how to convert any bit-mapped art on a card and transform it into an icon.

Specifically, you learned the following key information about HyperCard:

■ When you create an icon from scratch, it is saved with the current stack. For the icons that are supplied with HyperCard, the graphics are stored in a part of a particular stack file, the Home stack file, or in the HyperCard application itself. Even though the icon appears in the stack you are working in, the art for the icon may not reside there.

■ To see the icon art for a particular stack, select Icon from the Edit menu, or press ⌘-I. The Icon Editor window appears, and four new menus replace the top menu line: File, Edit, Icon, and Special.

■ When an icon is created, HyperCard automatically assigns a unique ID number, between 128 and 32767, to the icon. You also can assign a name to the icon.

■ The Icon Editor is similar to working with FatBits. The drawing is displayed in actual size next to an enlarged version of the icon in pixels.

■ To go to the next icon residing in the current stack, pull down the Icon menu and select Next, or press ⌘-3. You also can scroll through the icon art by using the scroll bar on the bottom of the drawing area.

■ To create a new icon for the stack in which you are working, select New Icon from the File menu. The icon can be up to 32 pixels square, filling up the entire drawing area.

■ Regardless of which stack you are in when you create a new icon, you can copy the icon after you have created it to any other stack.

■ To select a part of the graphic to modify, position the mouse pointer anywhere near the area you want to select and hold down ⌘. The mouse pointer turns into a cross cursor; you use it the same way you use the Selection tool when working with graphics.

■ You can move all or part of the image in the drawing area in the same way you move any other graphic image.

■ You can duplicate all or part of the image in the drawing area in the same way you duplicate any other graphic image. Select the image, and then press and hold down Option and drag the mouse away from the selected image.

■ To erase a portion of the image, select the area and select Cut Picture or Clear Picture from the Edit menu, or press Del.

■ To erase the entire drawing area, pull down the Icon menu and select Erase. If you want to bring it back, select Undo from the Edit menu.

■ To delete an icon from the Icon Editor window, select Clear Icon in the Edit menu. You cannot undo this operation.

■ If you hold down Option, the mouse pointer turns into a small hand that you can use to drag the image into a particular section of the drawing area, or out of the drawing area altogether. When you drag a portion of the graphic out of the drawing area, after you release the mouse button, you cannot drag the image back into the drawing area.

■ To flip all or part of the image either horizontally or vertically around the dotted line of the quadrants in the drawing area, select Flip Horizontal or Flip Vertical from the Special menu.

■ To insert a black frame around the entire icon picture (or a selected portion), select Frame from the Special menu.

7

■ To make the icon appear greyed out, select Grey from the Special menu. This option will turn white every other black pixel in the drawing area (or selected portion of the area).

■ To mirror all or a selected part of the image in the drawing area, select Mirror (Horizontal or Vertical) from the Special menu. A mirror image is a duplicate of the original image, as if viewed in a mirror. The mirror image only works from top to bottom or left to right.

■ To rotate all or part of the graphic image 90 degrees at a time, select Rotate from the Special menu.

■ To draw a shadow around the entire graphic image, select Shadow from the Special menu. The Shadow command only works on the entire graphic image, not on a selected portion. Each time you select Shadow, you increase the depth of the image.

■ To save your changes to the icon as you work, select Keep from the Icon menu, or press ⌘-K. If you want to go back to the last saved version, select Revert from the Icon menu.

7

■ You can save your new icon as a button by choosing New Button from the Icon menu. The icon you created converts into a button and appears in the middle of the card on your screen.

■ To create an icon from a bit-mapped image, select Pickup from the Icon menu, or press ⌘-P. Move the square over the picture you want, then click the mouse. The picture will be "picked up" onto the drawing area.

Now that you know how to create and modify icons to add to any card or stack buttons, the possibilities are endless. Take a few minutes and go through any art images you might have to see if you would like to make any into icons. Then, move on to the next chapter to create another useful HyperCard stack.

Creating a New Stack

Now that you have experimented with all the tools available to you, in this chapter you will create a new stack from scratch and build into it circular links to the Invoice stack you created in Chapter 6 and also to your word processing application. You then can cut and paste information to and from one application or stack to the other. Also, you will learn how to work with multiple windows in HyperCard so that you can have more than one stack open on your desktop at one time and can exchange easily information from one window to the next.

When you have finished building the stack, you either can design an icon for your stack using the Icon Editor, or you can turn a graphic image into a button to open your stack. Then, you will link your new stack to Home.

The stack you will create in this chapter will serve as a client "tickler" file, a home base for all your client information and work history. You will start out by copying the background from the Names and Addresses template supplied in the Stack Templates stack. Then, you will copy several elements from other stacks, as well as create a few new ones. You will apply the tools and practices you have learned so far. Your new stack will look quite different from the template you started out with.

Copying a stack template

Designing a stack

Working with buttons, windows, and fields

Testing your new stack

Key Terms in This Chapter

Client tickler file   A stack to keep track of names, addresses, and contact history of clients.

Background graphics   Graphics that appear in the background layer of the card and therefore are shared by more than one card.

Scroll window   A window that lets you change the size of the window in which a particular card is displayed. By using the scroll window on a standard size Macintosh display, you can view more than one window at a time (thereby viewing more than one card or stack at a time).

Application link button   A button that can link you to an application. By clicking the button, you will go out of the HyperCard program and into the specified application.

Copying a Stack Template

8

The Names and Addresses template that is supplied in the Stack Templates stack is different from the Address Book stack supplied with HyperCard that you used in Chapter 3. You can use either one, but for the purpose of this exercise, the Names and Addresses template is preferred.

Note: You are not limited to the stacks in the Stack Templates stack to create a new stack. You can choose any stack you want and then create a new stack based on it by selecting New Stack from the File menu. You will find, however, many good examples in the Stack Templates stack that you easily can use and modify to handle several different applications.

To copy the Names and Addresses stack template, follow these steps:

1. Go to the Stack Kit Home card and click the Stack Templates icon. (Or, select Open Stack from the File menu and choose Stack Templates.) The Stack Templates stack opens. The first card appears.

2. Click the Names and Addresses button.

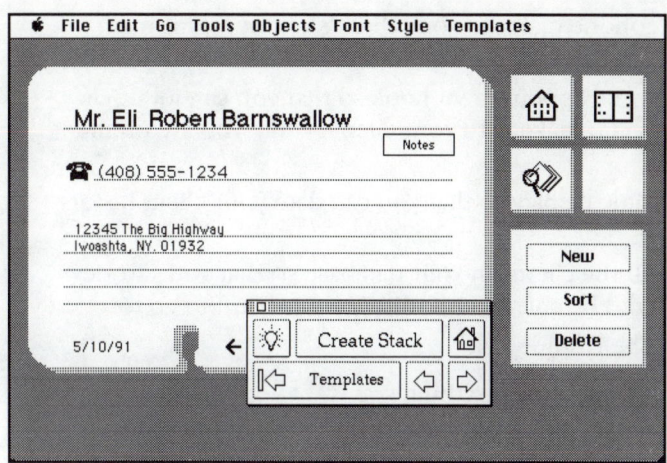

The Names and Addresses card is displayed.

3. Click the Create Stack button on the navigational palette. Name the new stack *Clients*, or whatever name you want, and press ⌐Return⌐ . In a few moments, your stack will be created.

8

Designing a Stack

Before you sit down to build a stack or to modify an existing one, you should know what you want your stack to accomplish and where you want the buttons and fields. You might sketch on a piece of paper some of the things that are important in accomplishing your task. If you are currently using a "paper system" to keep track of this information, you may want to review your records to make sure that you have included all the necessary information in your stack.

Because this stack will be a basis for all your client work, you may want to include the following items:

- Client name/address/contact information
- Client history (notes on what's been happening with this client in terms of contacts, proposals, and work performed)
- A link to the Invoice stack where you can automatically insert the client's name, address, or job description
- A link to a word processing program where you can automatically insert the client's name and address in a letter or proposal

- An automatic telephone dialer to your client's phone, voice mail, or fax

- A circular link to your Appointment book so that you can jot down any appointments you make with your clients while you are on the phone with them

- A continual date/time display so that you can date your client history notes

- A running list of all the clients in your database so that you can view them at all times and be able to click the one you want to go to

- A circular link to the Home stack

Now that you have written down everything you want your client stack to accomplish, decide on a layout for all these things. To determine the layout, get the buttons and fields in your stack, and then move them around until you're happy with the way your stack looks.

When you sit down to design a stack (whether you have initially designed the stack on paper or as you go along), the majority of the decisions you make come simply by trial and error. Try one layout and if you don't like it, try another icon for the button, or resize the field, or add another link that leads to another stack. In other words, building a stack is not a clean and simple process. You build as you go along, and you take things apart and put them back together until you're happy with the end result. If you find that after using the stack for awhile, you would like to add some new features, you can always go back in and change the stack to suit your needs.

The stack you are about to create in this chapter has gone through an evolution much like the one described in the preceding paragraph. Now that the final decisions have been made, you can follow the steps it took to get to the final outcome, not the steps of trial and error! Feel free as you build this stack to change as much or as little as you desire, so that the stack you end up with will fit your own needs.

Working with Buttons

You will begin your work in this stack by modifying the buttons in the template and adding a few more. First, press and hold ⌘-Option to see where the buttons reside, and then press ⇧Shift-⌘-Option to peek at both the buttons and the fields. Now that you have an idea of what you have to work with, follow these steps:

1. Press ⊞-Ⓑ to get into the background layer. (Or, select Background from the Edit menu.)

2. Select the Button tool from the Tools menu.

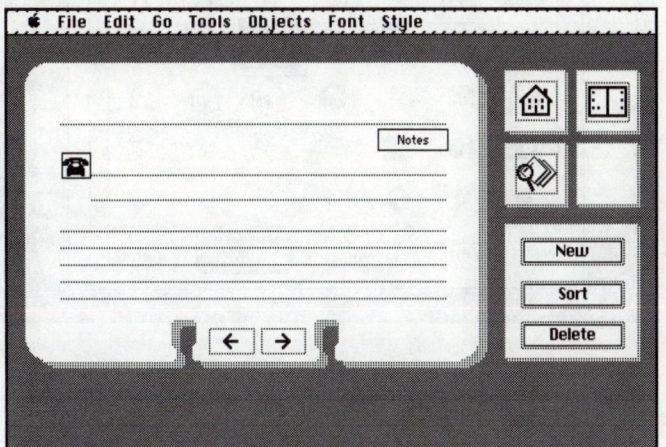

All the buttons in the card are enclosed in rectangles.

8

If you want to make any changes to any of the button icons or styles, double-click the button to access the Button Info dialog box and make any changes you desire. For example, to change the icon representing the Appointment Book stack, follow these steps:

1. Double-click the Appointment Book icon. The Button Info dialog box appears.

2. Click the Icon button. Scroll down the window and select another icon for the button (or, click Edit to modify the current one). Click OK. The new icon replaces the old one.

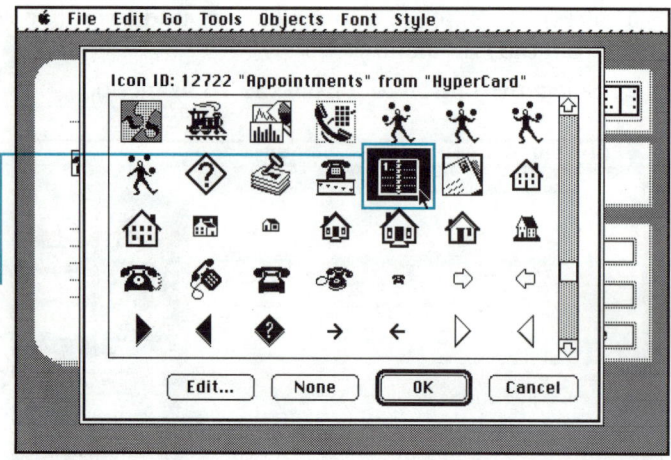

Here, a new icon for the Appointment Book button is chosen.

3. Because you want the two button areas below the Home and Appointment Book icon reserved for links to the Invoice stack and your word processing application, move the Find button down below the card graphic.

4. Double-click the Find button. The Button Info dialog box appears. Select the options you want for the Find button, and deselect the options you don't want.

For example, select Show Name and select Round Rect for the button style. Then, click the Icon button and click None.

Now make the button a little larger to accommodate the changes you have made. To enlarge the button, click the button to select it. Click one of its corners and, while you hold down the mouse button, drag the mouse to resize the button.

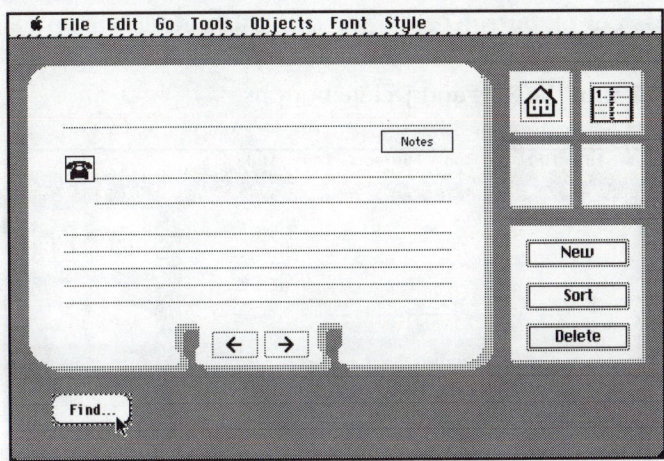

Here, the Find button's style and icon have been changed, and the button is moved to the bottom of the screen.

5. Move the New, Sort, and Delete buttons next to the Find button to make room on the card to add another field. Also, change their style to round rectangle and size them so that all four buttons look alike.

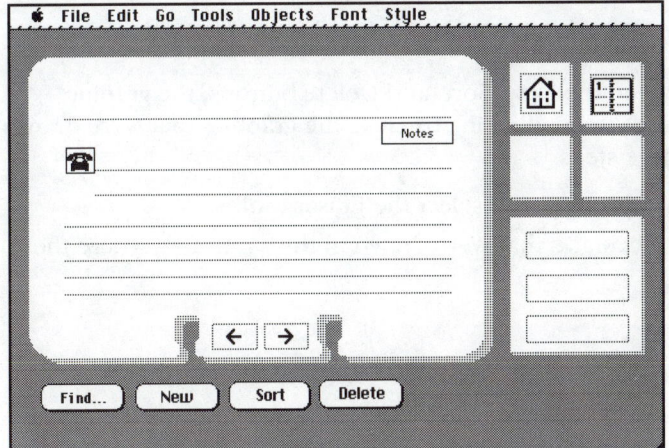

Here, all four buttons have a similar style and have been moved together.

To make sure that the New, Sort, and Delete buttons are exactly the same size as the Find button, follow these steps:

1. Pull down the Go menu and select Message. The message box appears.

2. Type **Set the height of bg button "NEW" to the height of bg button "FIND..."**. Press Return .

241

3. Type **Set the width of bg button "NEW" to the width of bg button "FIND..."**. Press [Return].

4. Repeat steps 2 and 3 for the Sort and Delete buttons.

Here is the completed message box.

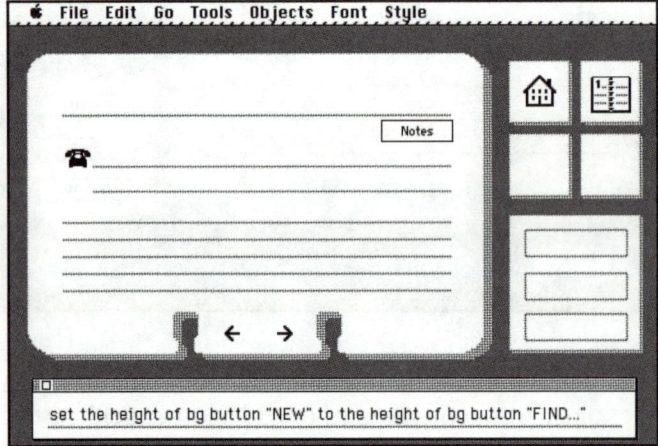

8 Working with Background Graphics

Now that you have moved the New, Sort, and Delete buttons, the graphic laying below them needs to be filled in. To erase the graphics that were drawn in that area, follow these steps:

1. Pull down the Tools menu and select the Eraser tool.

2. Erase the three rectangles that were drawn in the white area where the buttons were.

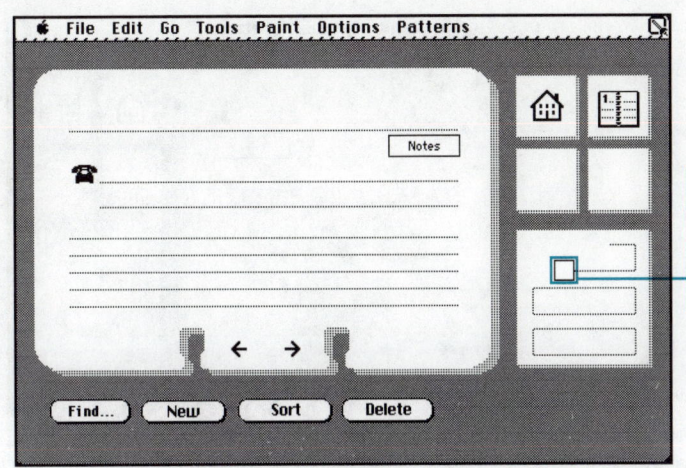

Here, the Eraser tool is used to clean up the area where the buttons were located.

3. Pull down the Tools menu and select the Fill (or Paint Bucket) tool.

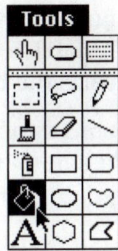

The Fill tool is selected from the Tools menu.

4. Pull down the Patterns menu and select the pattern that matches the background.

The background pattern is chosen.

5. Position the Fill tool inside the white area and click the mouse once.

243

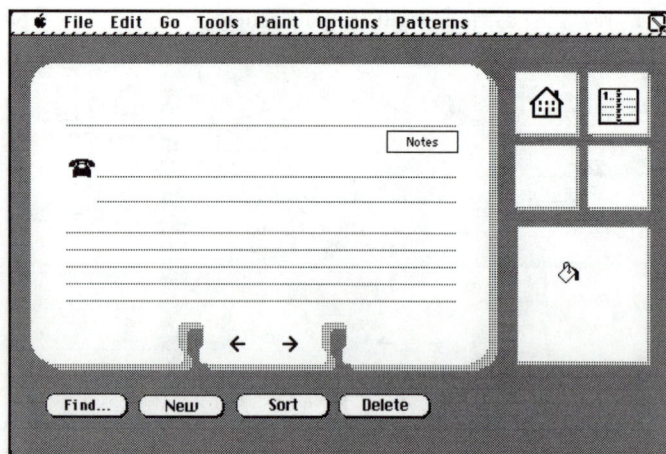

The white area
will be filled in
with the back-
ground pattern.

Pasting a Button from Home

Now, you can add a link to the Invoice stack and to a word processing application. You can either create a new button and establish the desired link, or
copy a button from another stack that already has the link established.

First, you will add a button that will link to your Invoice stack. Because you
already have the button and the link established in your Home stack, you can
copy it from there. Follow these steps:

1. Hold down ⇧Shift and select the Browse tool. (Remember, holding
   down ⇧Shift moves you out of the background layer.)

2. Click the Home button to go Home. Then, click the Card 3 button
   where your Invoice Stack icon resides.

3. Select the Button tool from the Tools menu, and then select the
   Invoice button.

4. Press ⌘-C to copy the button. (Or, select Copy Button from the Edit
   menu.)

5. Pull down the Go menu and select Back to return to the Clients stack
   you were creating. (You may have to select Back a few times, depending on which Home card you were initially taken to.)

6. Press ⌘-B to get back into the background layer. (Or, select Background from the Edit menu.)

7. Press ⌘-V to paste the Invoice button into your stack. (Or, select
   Paste Button from the Edit menu). Move the button to the third white
   square in the right corner of the card.

244

8. Double-click the button to access the Button Info dialog box so that you can change the style to Opaque and deselect Show Name. Then, size the button so that it fits into the white square.

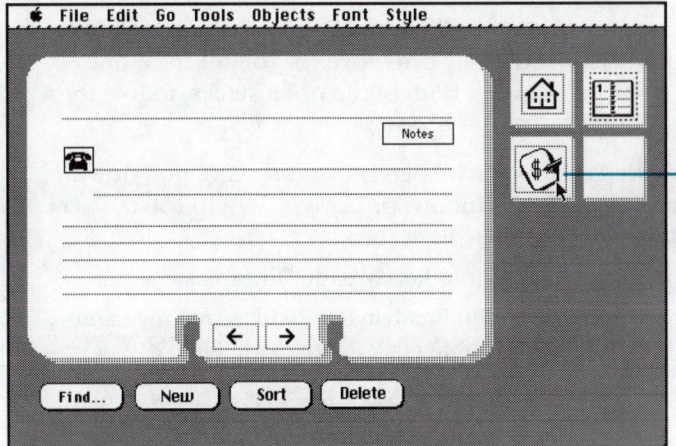

Here, the Invoice Stack button has been changed to opaque, no name showing, and sized to match the others.

Note: To make this a circular link when you have finished creating this Client stack, go into the Invoice stack and create a new button to link the stack to this Client stack. From both places you can get to the other stack.

Working with Windows

Now that you have established a link to take you Home and you can get back to this stack easily, copying a button from the Home stack is easy. Now you will copy a few more buttons (and fields) from a few other stacks. Instead of opening and closing stacks to copy and paste buttons, have all the stacks you need to work with open at the same time in different windows on your desktop. Then, to move from one window to the next, just point and click.

First, open the Readymade Buttons stack. This stack contains the button you will copy into the current stack. To open this stack, follow these steps:

1. Press ⌘-B to leave the background layer. (Or, select Background from the Edit menu.)

2. Press ⌘-O. (Or, pull down the File menu and select Open.)

3. Select the checkbox labeled Open stack in new window, and double-click the Readymade Buttons stack to open it. The stack opens in a new window.

245

Note: To automatically open a stack in a new window, you can use the key combination ⇧Shift-⌘-O. Remember, ⌘-O is the key combination to open a new stack. By pressing ⇧Shift-⌘-O, you select the option to open a stack in a new window.

Now you have two windows open: the Client stack you were working on and the Readymade Buttons stack. You easily can move (or rotate) from one window to the next. To move between both of the open stacks, follow these steps:

1. With the Readymade Buttons stack open on your screen, pull down the Go menu and select Next Window, or press ⌘-L to rotate to the next open window, which is the Client stack.

2. Press ⌘-L again to go back to the Readymade Buttons stack.

3. Now open another window to the Readymade Fields stack the same way. Press ⇧Shift-⌘-O and double-click Readymade Fields.

Here, Readymade Fields is selected. The key combination ⇧Shift-⌘-Option has automatically selected the checkbox labeled Open stack in new window.

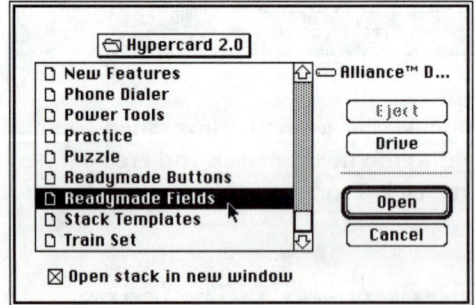

Scrolling a Window

Although you have three windows open at the same time, if you are using a standard nine-inch Macintosh display (Plus, SE series, or Classic series), you are probably viewing one window at a time on your screen. HyperCard 2.0 has a new feature called *Scroll* that enables you to resize stack windows so that you can view more than one on your screen at one time. In fact, you are limited only by the amount of memory your Macintosh has. The Scroll window is also helpful when you want to display large cards on a small screen. Remember that you are not actually changing the size of the card when you use the Scroll window, you are changing only the window in which it is displayed. This feature is handy when you want to copy buttons, fields, or graphics from one card or stack to another.

Now that you are in the Readymade Fields stack and you also have opened the Readymade Buttons stack (and your Client stack), you can use the Scroll feature to view all three open stacks on-screen at one time. To use the Scroll window, follow these steps:

1. Pull down the Go menu and select Scroll, or press ⌘-E.

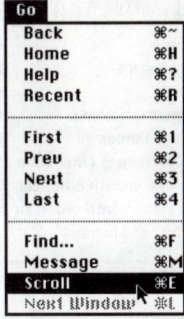

The Scroll window is selected from the Go menu.

A small window appears in the lower left corner of the screen. The Scroll window works like the Hand tool when you are working on a graphic in FatBits.

2. Position the mouse pointer near an edge in the Scroll window. The cursor becomes a double-headed arrow.

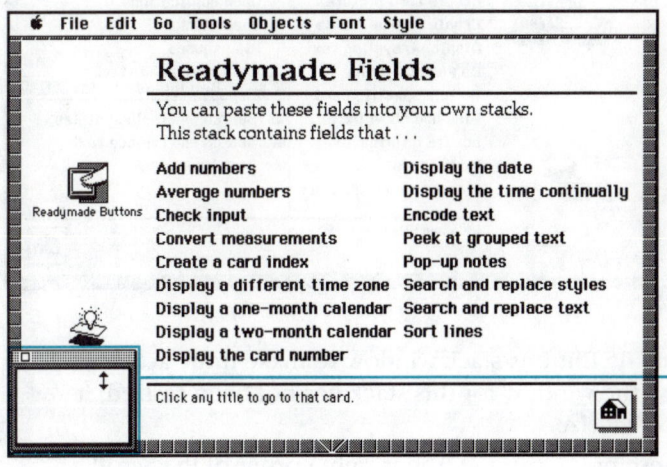

Here, the Scroll window is displayed with the mouse pointer near the edge of the window.

8

3. Drag the double-headed arrow from the top left corner to the bottom right corner of the scroll window to resize the Card window.

Here, the window is being resized with the Scroll window.

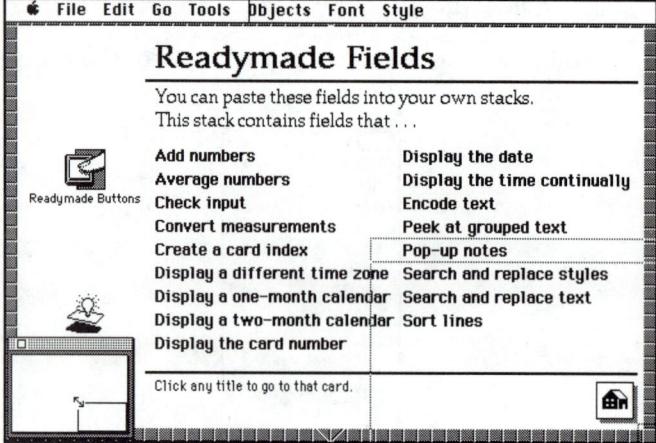

8

When you release the mouse button, the top window (Readymade Fields) is resized, and the window below it (Readymade Buttons) is visible.

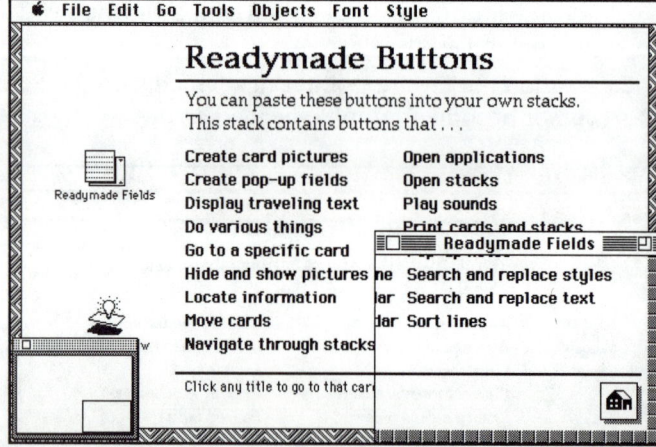

4. Click the Readymade Buttons stack window to make it the active window. Because the window for this stack has not been resized, it appears at its normal size.

5. Position the mouse pointer in the upper right corner of the Scroll window and drag the window down to the lower left corner. Now the Client stack window below is visible.

248

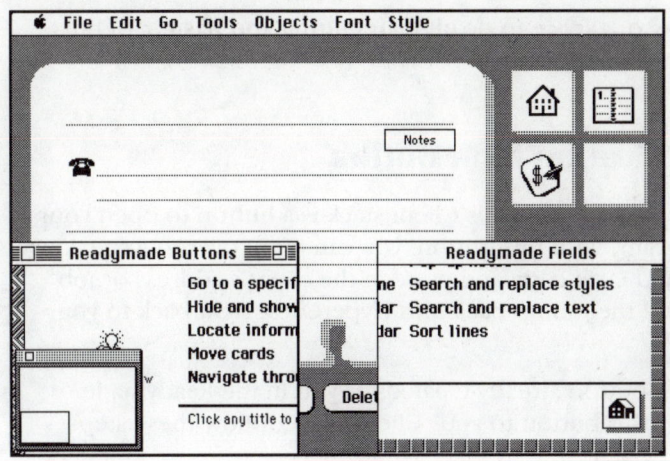

Here, all three
windows are
visible at one
time.

To resize any of the windows on the screen, click in the window to
make it active, and then resize it in the Scroll window. Or, to resize
any of the windows back to their original size, double-click in the
Scroll window, and the active window will return to its full size.
Double-clicking in the Scroll window a second time will reduce the
window again.

6. Click the close box of the Scroll window to close the window. (Or, you
   can drag the window to the upper left corner of the screen in case you
   need to use it during your work session.)

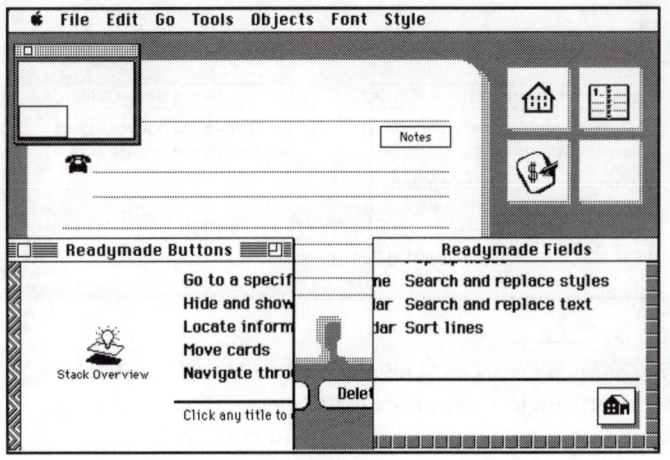

Move the Scroll
window wherever
you want on your
screen.

Now you have a great work space to do all your cutting and pasting of buttons, fields, and graphics.

Creating an Application Link Button

The next button you will copy into this Client stack is a button to open your word processing program. With this button, you can jump over to write your client a quick letter (and even copy and paste in the client's address or job order information), and then jump back into HyperCard, right back to your Client stack.

There is an application button already created for you in the Readymade Buttons stack. To copy this button to your Client stack, follow these steps:

1. Click the Readymade Buttons window to make it active.

2. Click the Open applications line in the Readymade Buttons stack window. (If you can't see it, position the mouse cursor near the center of the Scroll window and drag the little hand over so that you can bring that line into view.) Or, double-click the Scroll window to expand the window.

8

Drag the Hand tool in the Scroll window to view different areas of the active window.

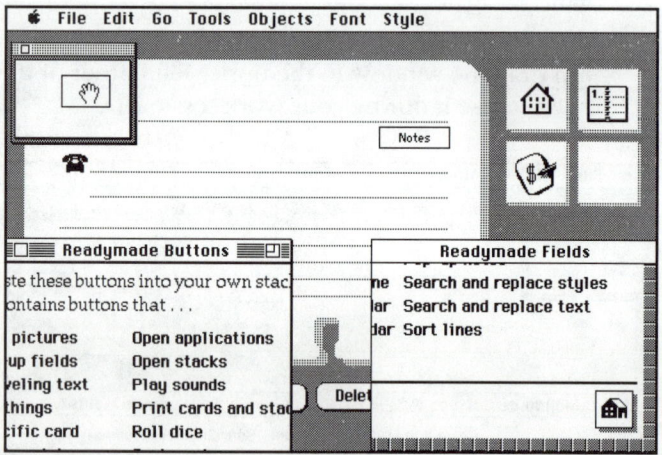

Notice the button that takes you to MacPaint and to MacWrite II. There is also a generic button labeled <application name> that you can customize to take you to whatever application you choose.

3. Select the Button tool from the Tools menu, and then select the <application name> button you want. Press ⌘-C to copy it.

250

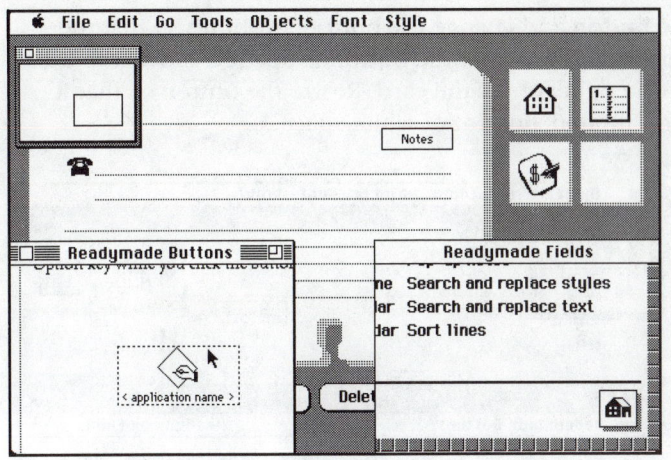

Here, the
<application
name> button is
selected in the
Readymade
Buttons stack.

4. Click in the client database window to make it the active window. Size the window in the Scroll window so that you can still see the other two windows.

8

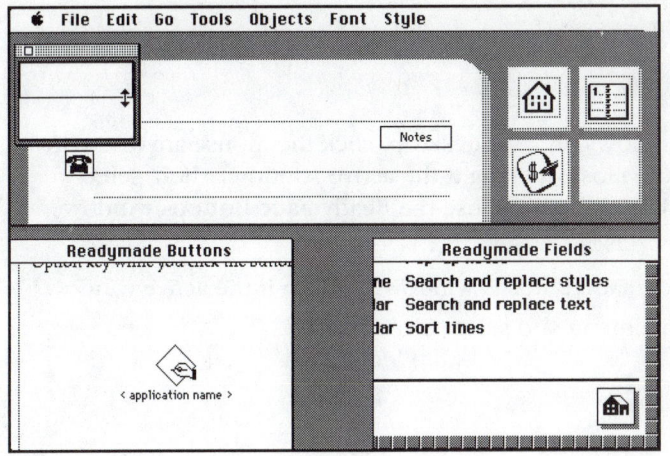

Here, the Client
stack has been
sized so that you
can view all three
windows again.

5. Press ⌘-B to go into the background layer, and then press ⌘-V to paste in the button (or, select Paste Button from the Edit menu).

You will be asked to select the application you want the button to open. The application name will appear as the name of the button.

251

6. Double-click the button and change the button attributes so that the name is not displayed, and so that the button is opaque. Move it to the white square on the right side of the card. Resize the button so that it fits neatly into the allotted amount of white space.

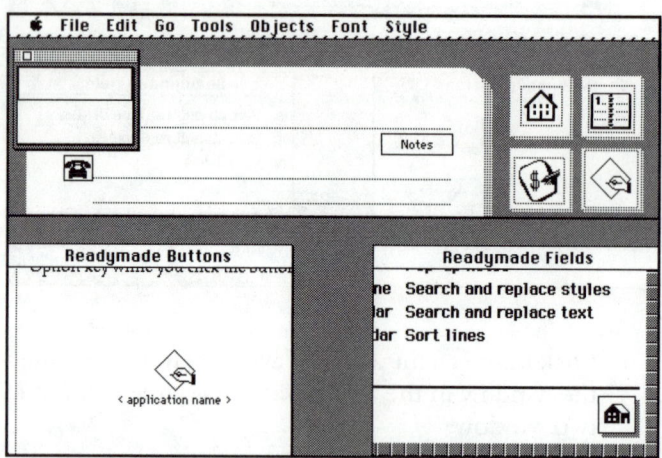

Now, you have four buttons linking you to stacks and applications.

Closing Windows

To close any of the windows on your desktop, click the mouse anywhere in the window you want to close, making it the active window. Then, select Close Stack from the File menu. To close the Readymade Buttons window, follow these steps:

1. Click in the Readymade Buttons window to make it the active window.
2. Pull down the File menu and select Close Stack.

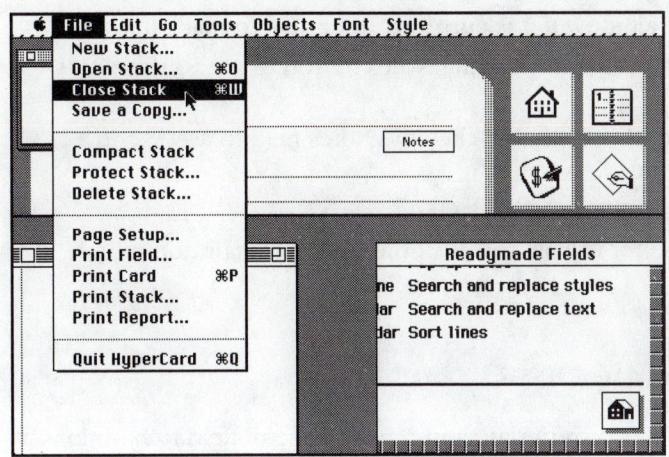

Close Stack is
selected.

Note: You also can close a stack by clicking the close box in the upper left corner of the window.

3. Resize the Readymade Fields window so that you can view more of it.

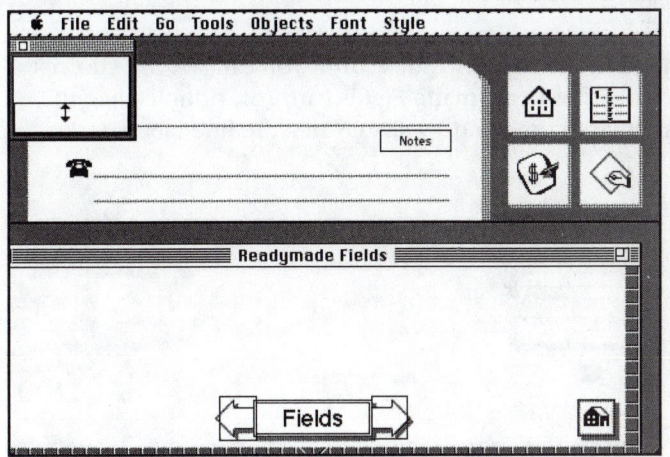

Here, the
Readymade Fields
window has been
resized from the
Scroll window.

Working with Fields

Now you will add some fields to your stack from the Readymade Fields stack. But first, modify the Notes field that is already in your stack and make it a scrolling field so that you can enter as much information as you want in that field. To make the Notes field a scrolling field, follow these steps:

253

1. Click the Clients window if it is currently not active to make it active.

2. Select the Browse tool and click the Notes button to access the Notes field.

3. Select the Field tool and double-click the Notes field to access the Field Info dialog box.

4. Set the style to Scrolling and click OK.

5. Select the Browse tool again and click the Hide Notes button to hide the Notes field.

Adding a Date/Time Display Field

A continual display of the current date and time is a useful field to have in a client database stack. The Readymade Fields stack contains two fields already set up to display the date and time. To copy the fields into your stack, follow these steps:

1. Click the Readymade Fields window to make it active.

   Note: If you are still in background mode, you won't see anything on the card. Everything in the stack is on the card layer. Press ⌘-B to go into the card layer.

2. Move the little hand in the Scroll window until you can see the choices in the right column of the Readymade Fields card (or, double-click the Scroll window to enlarge the window size). Click the line labeled Display the date.

Here, Display the date is selected.

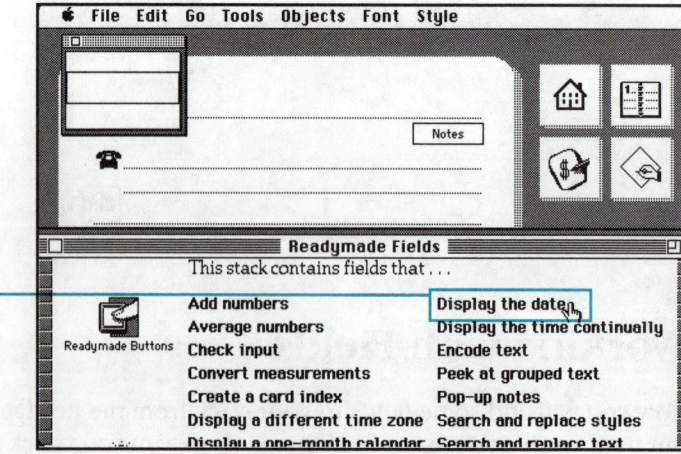

254

3. Select the Field tool, and then select the Date field displayed. Press ⌘-C to copy the Date field.

4. Click the mouse pointer back in the Client window to make it active and press ⌘-B to go to the background layer. Then, press ⌘-V to paste the Date field.

5. Double-click in the Scroll window so that the Client stack assumes its full size. Move the Date field into the lower right corner of the screen.

6. Double-click the field to access the Field Info dialog box. Press the Font button to modify the font selected for the contents of this field. Change the font to Avant Garde (or any other font you have available), bold, 10 point, extend, so that the field doesn't have to be quite so large. Then, size the field so that it fits in the bottom right corner of the screen.

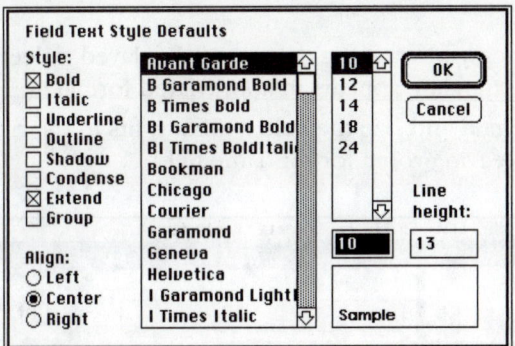

Here, the font style and type is changed so that the field can be smaller.

8

7. Select the Browse tool and click the Date field. A dialog box appears, asking what kind of format you want the date to be displayed in. Select Abbrev.

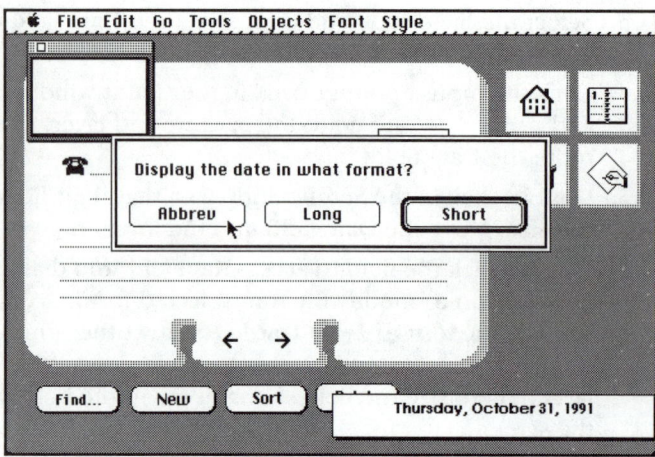

The default is
Short, although
currently the Date
field is set to
Long.

Then, when asked when you want the date to be displayed, select
card. After a moment, the date appears in abbreviated format.

8. Select the Field tool again and size the field so that it fits in the right
corner of the screen, leaving room for the Time field.

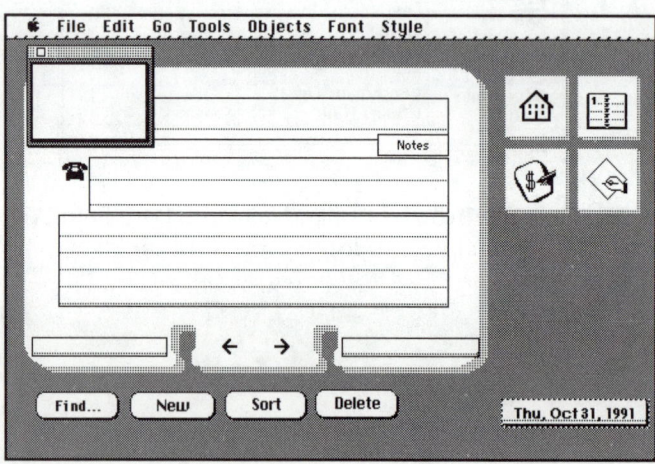

Here, the Date
field has been
sized and posi-
tioned in the
lower right corner
of the card.

Copying the Current Time Display Field

Now that the Client stack is taking up the whole window, press ⌘-L to view
the other open window, which is the Readymade Fields stack.

1. With the Readymade Fields window active, press ⌘-B to leave the
   background layer so that you can view the fields in the card layer. The
   current date card will be displayed.

2. Press → to go to the next card. There, you see the Readymade Field
   for the current time display.

3. Go through the same steps as you did with the Date field to copy the
   Time field into your Client stack (and change the font and size of the
   field). Place the Time field under the Date field. Don't forget to copy it
   into the background layer of the Client stack and not the card layer.

   Note: The time will not be displayed in the Time field until you leave
   the background layer.

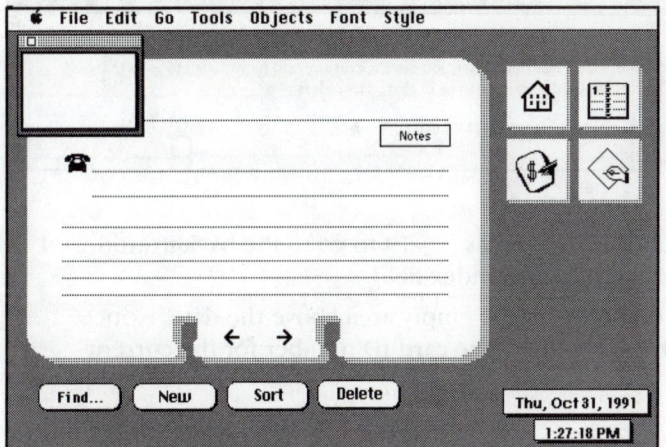

Here, the Date
and Time fields
have been added
to the Client
stack.

Creating a Card Index Field

Next, you will put into this stack a Card Index field. If you name the cards in
this stack the name of each client, you can scroll through the list of clients (or
cards), click whichever card you want, and you will go there. The Card Index
field is a great way to create a field that acts like a button.

To copy the Card Index field from the Readymade Fields stack, follow these steps:

1. Press ⊞-Ⓛ to view the Readymade Fields stack window. Press → to cycle through the cards until you get to the card labeled Create a card index field in the Readymade Fields stack.

2. Select the Field tool and select the Card Index field. Press ⊞-Ⓒ to copy the field.

Here, the Card Index field is selected.

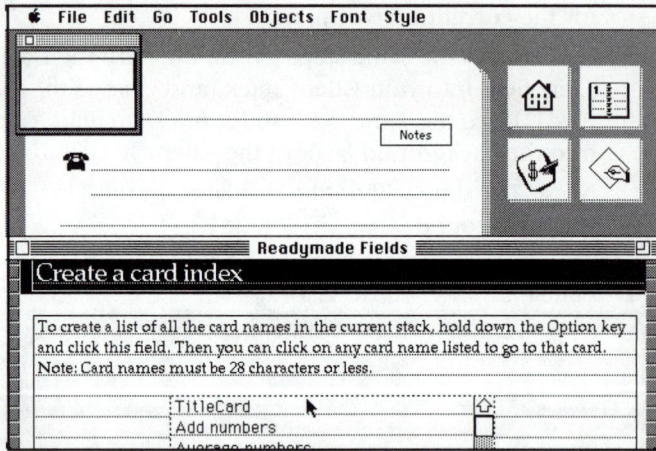

3. Go back to the Client stack, press ⊞-Ⓑ to go to the background, and press ⊞-Ⓥ to paste the Card Index field.

4. Size the field so that it fits in the empty area above the date. Notice how the first entry in the field, the card ID number for the current card, is already there.

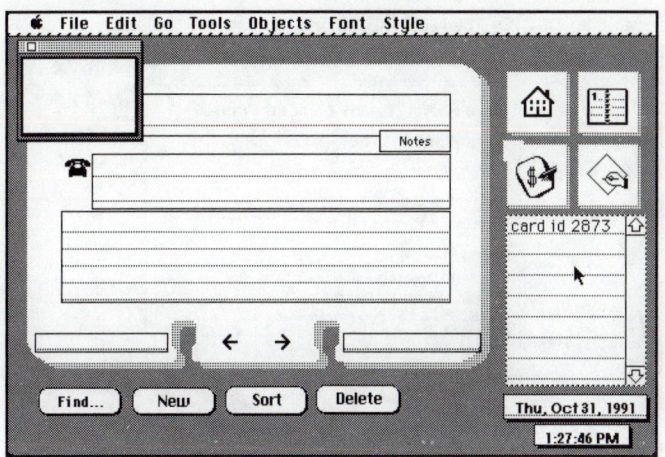

The Card Index field is put into place.

Testing Your New Stack

Now it's time to test your new stack and see how it works. Hold down ⌖Shift and select the Browse tool to leave the background layer.

1. Click the close box of the Scroll window to close it.

Here, the Scroll window is being closed.

2. Enter the name of your first client on the top line. Then, select the client's name and press ⌘-C to copy it.

3. Pull down the Objects menu and select Card Info. Press ⌘-V to paste in the client's name as the card name. Click OK.

Here, the client's name is pasted in as the card name.

(Dialog box shows:)

Card Name: EMJAY Computer Careers

Card number: 1 out of 1
Card ID: 2873

Contains 0 card fields.
Contains 0 card buttons.

☐ Card Marked
☐ Don't Search Card
☐ Can't Delete Card

[Script...]   [OK]   [Cancel]

4. Enter additional information about the client, and then click the New button and enter another client to your stack. Enter as many as you like.

5. To use the Card Name field to view the clients in your database, position the Browse tool in the Card Name field, hold down Option, and click the mouse once. Your card list will be generated.

8

The card index displays all your card names (or client names). Click any one to go to that card.

(Second screen shows:)

Nova Development Corp.

☎ 818-992-3222

23801 Calabasas Road, Suite 2050
Calabasas, CA 91302
Attn: Roger Bloxberg

10/30/91

Emjay Comput
Langa Products
Nova Develop
Que Corporatio
SanSoft, Inc.

If you forgot to name any one of your cards, the card ID number will be displayed. Click the ID number to go to that card and give it a name.

260

Copying and Pasting Information between Stacks and Programs

It is easy to copy your client's address (or history) information and paste it into a document with your word processing program or an invoice created with your Invoice stack. To copy and paste the information, follow these steps:

1. Select the Address line for any of your client cards, and press ⌘-C to copy the information.

2. Click the Application button to jump out of HyperCard and into your word processing program.

3. Open your letter template (or create a new one), and press ⌘-V to paste the address information.

   Note: When you quit your word processing program and go back into HyperCard, you will return to this client card.

You also can copy and paste text (either the Address or Notes field) into your Invoice stack to create a new invoice for the client. Or, you can copy and paste information in and out of your Appointment Book stack just as easily.

8

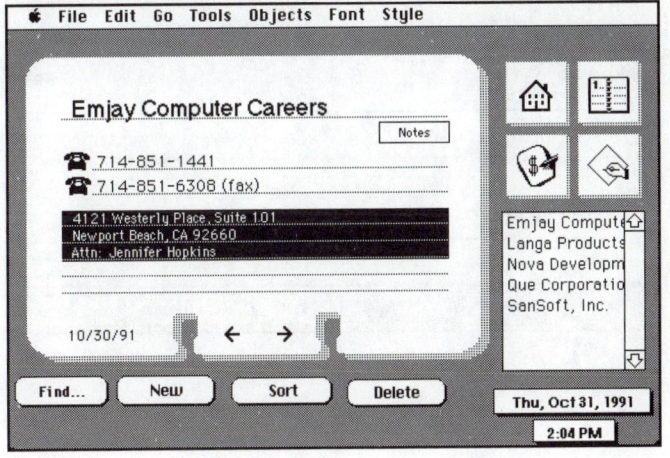

Copy information from your Client stack.

Paste the information into your word processing program.

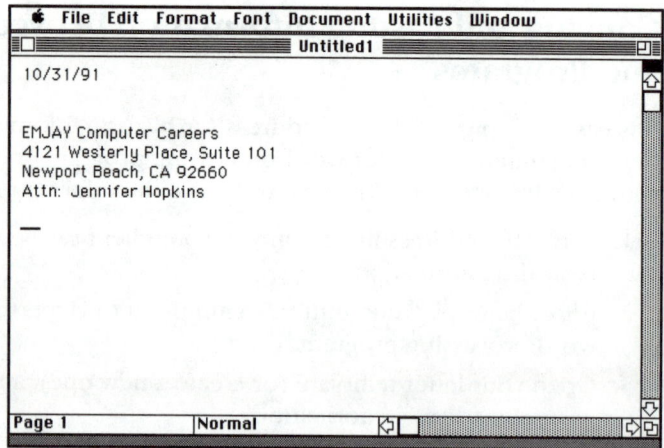

```
 ⌘  File  Edit  Format  Font  Document  Utilities  Window
▣□▭▭▭▭▭▭▭▭▭▭ Untitled1 ▭▭▭▭▭▭▭▭▭▭▭▭▭⊞▤
  10/31/91                                                    ⇧


  EMJAY Computer Careers
  4121 Westerly Place, Suite 101
  Newport Beach, CA 92660
  Attn: Jennifer Hopkins

  ─



                                                              ⇩
  Page 1            │Normal        │◁□▬▬▬▬▬▬▬▬▬▷⊡
```

Copy and paste information between your Client stack and your Invoice stack.

```
 ⌘  File  Edit  Go  Tools  Objects  Font  Style
        ORO Systems Group           Invoice Date:   10/12/91
          100 The Strand            Invoice Number:        1
        Redondo Beach, CA  90278    P.O #:
  Bill to:                      Project
  EMJAY Computer Careers
  4121 Westerly Place, Suite 101
  Newport Beach, CA 92660
  Attn: Jennifer Hopkins        Manager:
  Invoice for:
  ........................................................
  ........................................................
  ........................................................
  ........................................................
  □ Invoiced    □ Received              Invoice Total:  $

  ⌂ ▱ ◇ ▨              Print      New Invoice    ←    →
```

8

262

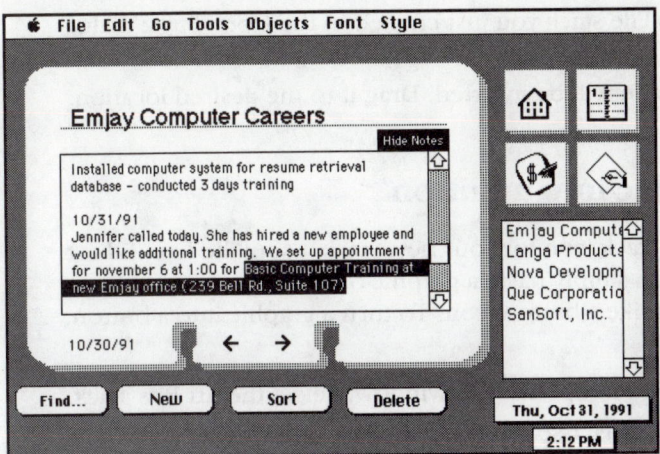

Copy information from your Client stack.

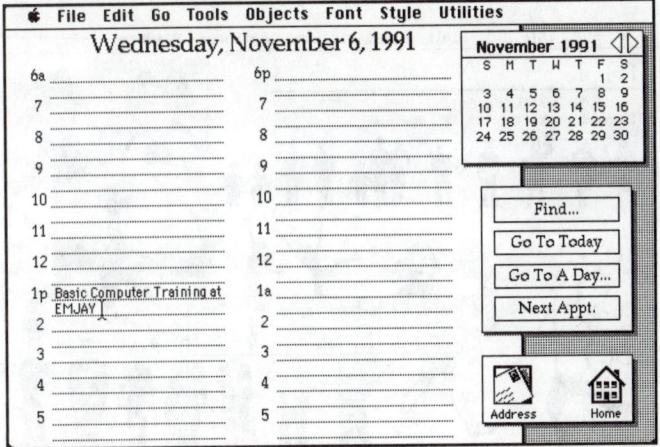

Paste the information into your Appointment Book stack.

8

Linking Your Client Stack to Home

Now that you have designed a useful stack, you should link it to Home. To link your stack to Home, follow these steps:

1. Click the Home icon to go home. Go to the Card 3 Home card where your Invoice stack resides.

2. Pull down the Home menu and select New Link to Stack.

3. Select the Client File stack you just created in the Open Stack dialog box.

   A generic stack icon will be inserted. Drag it to the desired location.

Turning a Graphic into a Button

Now you can create a stack icon for your new stack, using the Icon Editor. Or, if you want, you can simply paste a graphic over a transparent icon to make the graphic look like a button icon. To turn a graphic into a button, follow these steps:

1. Press ⇧Shift-⌘-O to open a new window. Select the Art Bits stack.
2. Flip through the cards. Use the Rectangular or Lasso selection tool to select a graphic that will represent your Client stack. Press ⌘-C to copy the graphic.

Choose any graphic you want to represent your new stack.

3. Press ⌘-L to go to the next open window, which in this example is your Home card.
4. Press ⌘-V to paste the graphic you copied.
5. Move the graphic over the Client stack.

264

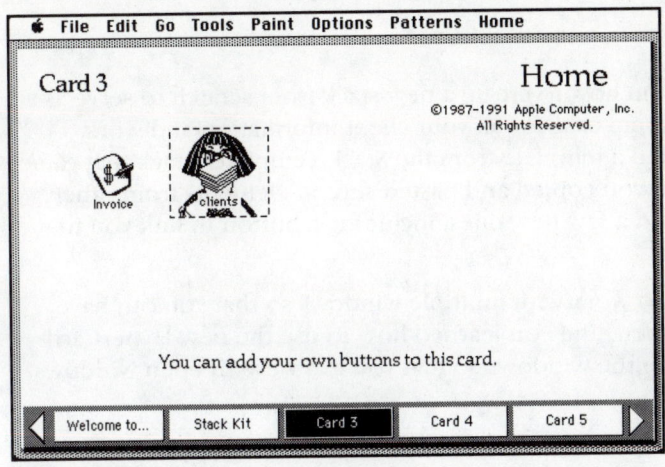

The graphic you paste appears to be underneath the stack icon.

6. Select the Button tool from the Tools menu and change the style of the Client stack so that the stack name is not displayed and the icon is set to None.

Now you have made a graphic image look like a button. When you click the graphic, you will activate the button underneath. In this case, you will open your Client stack.

8

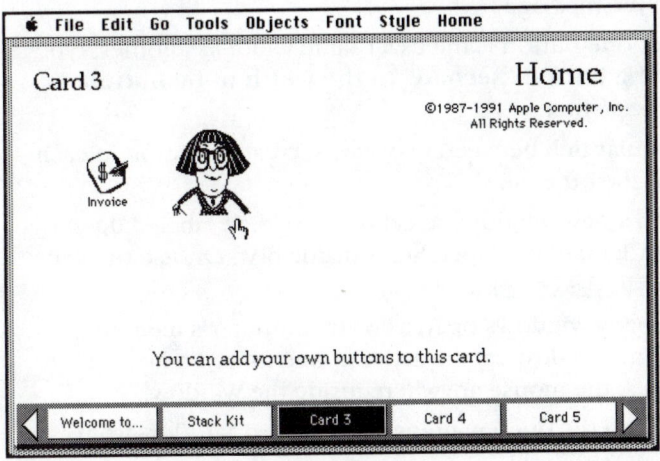

A transparent button over a graphic image looks like a button icon.

265

Summary

This chapter showed you how to create a new stack from scratch to serve as a client "tickler" file, a home base for all your client information and work history. First, you copied a template from the Stack Templates stack that came with HyperCard. Then, you copied and pasted several elements from other stacks, as well as created a few new ones, including a button to link you to another application.

You also learned how to work with multiple windows so that you can have more than one stack open, and you learned how to use the new HyperCard 2.0 Scroll feature to size the windows so that you can view all open windows at one time.

Specifically, you learned the following key information about HyperCard:

- Before you sit down to create a new stack from scratch, decide what you want your stack to accomplish. Then, lay out a general design of the buttons and fields you want to include.

- To see where the buttons in a stack reside, press ⌘-Option.

- To see where the fields in a stack reside, press ⇧Shift-⌘-Option.

- To make sure that one button is the exact same height as another, type **set the height of bg button "second" to the height of bg button "first"** in the message box.

- To make sure that one button is the exact same width as another, type **set the width of bg button "second" to the width of bg button "first"** in the message box.

- To establish a circular link between two stacks, create a button in each stack that links to the other stack.

- To open a stack in a new window, select the checkbox labeled Open stack in new window in the Open Stack dialog box. Or, use the key combination ⇧Shift-⌘-Option.

- You can have as many windows open as your computer's memory allows, but only one window can be active at one time. To make a window active, click the mouse anywhere inside the window.

- To rotate between all the open windows, select Next Window from the Go menu, or press ⌘-L.

- HyperCard 2.0's Scroll feature enables you to resize windows so that you can view more than one on your screen at one time. To open the Scroll window, select Scroll from the Go menu, or press ⌘-E.

■ To resize any of the windows on the screen, click inside the window to make it active, and then move the mouse pointer in the Scroll window in any direction to resize the active window.

■ To resize any of the windows back to their original size, double-click inside the Scroll window. The active window returns to its full size. Double-clicking inside the Scroll window a second time reduces the window again.

■ Drag the Hand tool in the Scroll window to view different areas of the active window.

■ You can move the Scroll window anywhere on your screen in the same way that you move any other window. To close the Scroll window, click its close box.

■ To close any of the windows on your desktop, click the mouse any-where inside the window you want to close, making it the active window. Then, select Close Stack from the File menu.

■ To create a button to link you to an application, copy the <applica-tion name> button from the Readymade Buttons stack that came with HyperCard.

■ To add fields that will provide a continual display of the current date and time, copy the date and time fields from the Readymade Fields stack that came with HyperCard.

■ To create a Card Index field, copy the Card Index field from the Readymade Fields stack. The Card Index field is a great way to create a field that acts like a button. You can scroll through the list of cards, click whichever card you want, and you will go to the card.

■ It is easy to copy information between stacks and programs. Simply select the text you want to copy, press ⌘-C to copy the information, then click the button to go to another application or stack and press ⌘-V to paste the text in.

■ You can paste a graphic over a transparent button icon to make the graphic look like a button icon.

Now that you know how to design and create your own stacks for a variety of applications, you are ready to take a look at what's behind these stacks. The next chapter will introduce you to the world of scripting in HyperCard so that you can go beyond the supplied buttons and fields and actually create your own scripts to perform menu selections and functions.

8

Introducing Scripting

Up until now, you have modified and created new stacks simply by copying elements from other stacks supplied with HyperCard. Using those elements, along with selecting menu items and typing commands in the message box, you may never need to go beyond the Authoring level. However, after you find out how easy it is to write a script for a button or card to accomplish those same tasks, you may want to explore the next level of HyperCard, called *Scripting*.

Also, when you are creating a new stack based on an existing one, you may want to make slight modifications to the original stack's script. For example, if the names of buttons are embedded in the script for that stack and you change one of the button's names, you will get an error message when you click that button. Therefore, you need to go into the script and change the names of the referenced buttons.

Every HyperCard object (buttons, fields, cards, backgrounds, and stacks) has a script. Scripts are instructions that tell HyperCard what you want it to do. Scripts in HyperCard are written in a language unique to Hyper-Card, called *HyperTalk*. HyperTalk commands tell the object what to do, such as go to the next card, add a column of numbers, sort a stack, or dial a phone.

Setting the preference level to Scripting

Looking at scripts

Creating a button script

Creating a Library stack

In this chapter, you will look at scripts that have been written for the Home stack and cards. Then, you will experiment with creating your own button scripts to perform various functions you are already comfortable using. You will create a new stack based loosely on the Music Library stack template and modify the stack's script as well as create a few new button scripts for the stack.

Key Terms in This Chapter

Scripting

The fifth and most advanced user level of Hyper-Card. When you change your user level to Script-ing, an additional item in all of the Objects dialog boxes appears (named *script*) that gives you access to view, modify, or create new scripts for that particular object.

HyperTalk

HyperCard's built-in script language.

Script

A series of commands written in HyperTalk to make a particular object do something.

Objects

In HyperCard, there are five different objects (buttons, fields, cards, backgrounds, and stacks). Each of these objects may have an associated script that belongs to it.

Script window

The window that appears when you click the Script button in any object's dialog box that displays the object's script.

Script handler

A block of statements in a script that begins with the word *on* and ends with the word *end*. HyperTalk has message handlers and function handlers. Both *on* and *end* must be followed by the name of the message or function it is to execute. Any message you enter in the message box could be inserted between a message handler in a script.

Setting the Preference Level to Scripting

To use the Scripting level of HyperCard, you need to change the user prefer-ence. Follow these steps:

1. With the Home card on your screen, click the left-arrow button (or press ⌘-4) to go to the Preferences card.

2. Click the Scripting button.

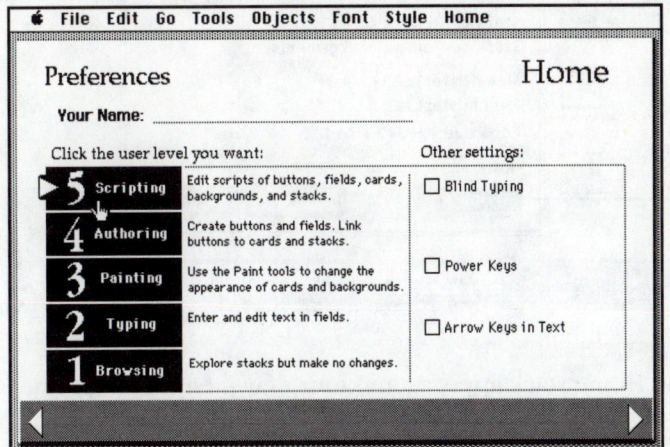

Here, the user level is set to Scripting.

3. Click the right-arrow button to go back to the Home card.

When you change your user level to Scripting, an additional button, named *Script*, will appear in all the Objects dialog boxes. Clicking the Script button opens the script that controls the object.

9

Looking at Scripts

In HyperCard, there are five objects (button, field, card, background, and stack) that can have a script associated with them. Each of these objects has an Info dialog box that you can access from the Objects menu. You can look at the scripts for each of these objects by clicking the Script button in their respective dialog boxes.

Looking at Stack Scripts

To look at the script for the Home stack, follow these steps:

1. With the Home card on your screen, pull down the Objects menu and select Stack Info.

2. Click the Script button.

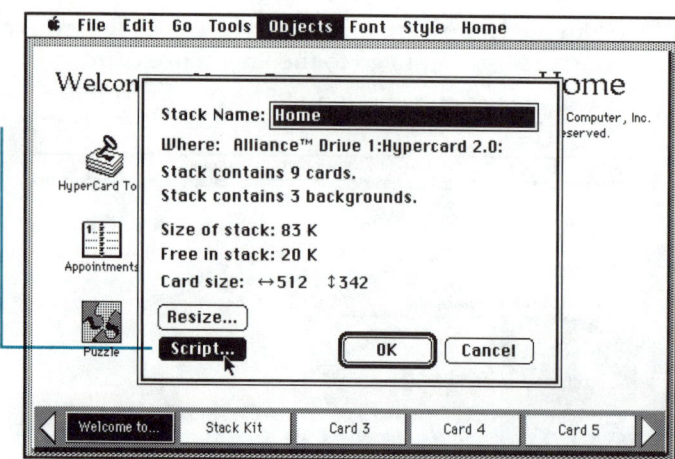

When you changed your user level to Scripting, this new button, labeled Script, became enabled.

The script for the Home stack appears, and four new menus appear on the top menu line.

The script for the Home stack is displayed.

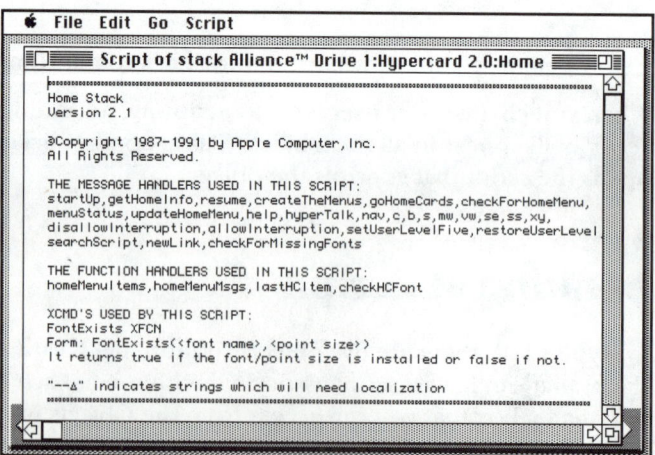

Here is the File menu.

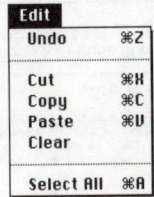

Here is the Edit menu.

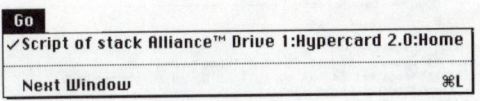

Here is the Go menu.

Here is the Script menu.

9

3. Scroll down the window to look at the script for the Home stack to see what a stack script can look like.

4. To close the Script window, pull down the File menu and select Close Script. Or, click the upper left corner close box.

   Note: As a shortcut, you can press ⌘-Option-S to open the script of the current stack.

Looking at the Background Script

You also can view the script for the background object of the stack in the same way. To view the background script, follow these steps:

1. With the Home card on your screen, pull down the Objects menu and select Bkgnd Info.

2. Click the Script button of the Background Info dialog box.

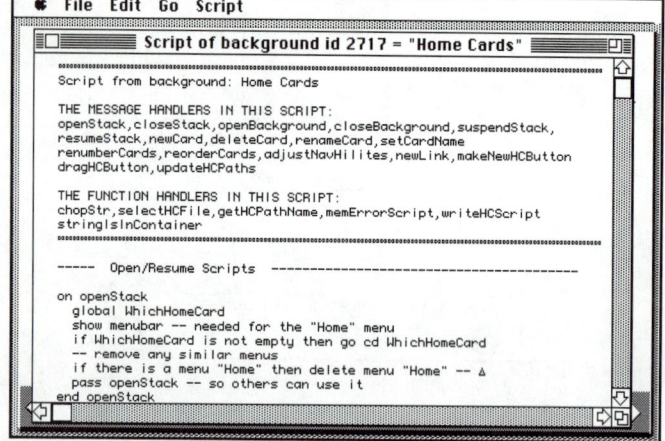

The script for the
Home stack
background
appears.

3. Click the close box to close the Script window.

Note: As a shortcut, you can press ⌘-Option-B to open the script of the current background. You also can press ⌘-Option-C to open the script of the current card. Use ⌘-Option-S to open the script of the current stack.

Looking at Button Scripts

You also can view the script for a particular button in a stack in the same way. To view the script for the button that takes you to the Client stack you created in the last chapter, follow these steps:

1. Go to the Card 3 Home card, or wherever your Client stack button resides.

2. Select the Button tool from the Tools menu and select the Client button.

3. Double-click the Client button to access the Button Info dialog box.

4. Click the Script button.

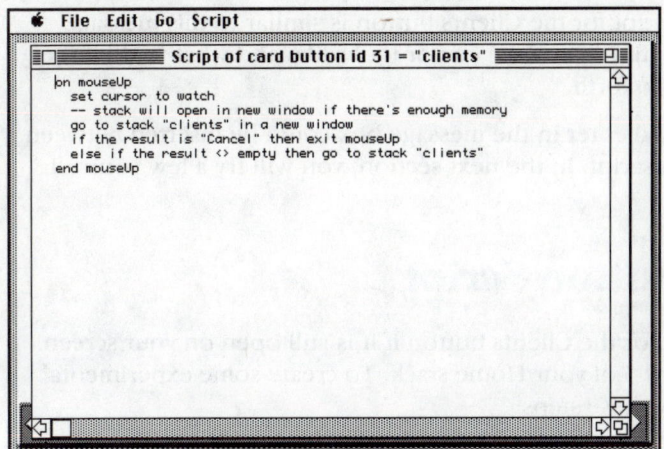

Here, the script
for the Client
stack button is
displayed.

Note: As a shortcut, press ⌘ and Option, and then click the button for which you want to view the script.

Looking at Script Handlers

You will notice that the script for the Client stack button begins with the words on mouseUp and ends with end mouseUp. These two statements together are called a *message handler*. HyperTalk has message handlers and function handlers. The first line of a handler always begins with the word on, and the last statement of a handler begins with the word end. Both on and end must be followed by the name of the HyperTalk message or function.

On mouseUp means that when the mouse is clicked and released, this object will do something. The statements between the on mouseUp and end mouseUp tell what the object will do, which in this case is open the Clients stack.

This is an example of a simple message handler:

```
on mouseUp
  go to stack "stackname"
end mouseUp
```

9

As you can see, the script for the Clients button is similar to this message handler, but it also defines what the cursor looks like and what to do if the result is Cancel, and so forth.

Any message you could enter in the message box could be inserted between a message handler in a script. In the next section, you will try a few yourself.

Creating a Button Script

First, close the script for the Clients button if it is still open on your screen. You should be at Card 3 of your Home stack. To create some experimental button scripts, follow these steps:

1. Select the Button tool from the Tools menu.

2. Pull down the Objects menu and select New Button.

3. Double-click the new button to access the Button Info dialog box. Name your button *Test Scripts*, and then click the Script button.

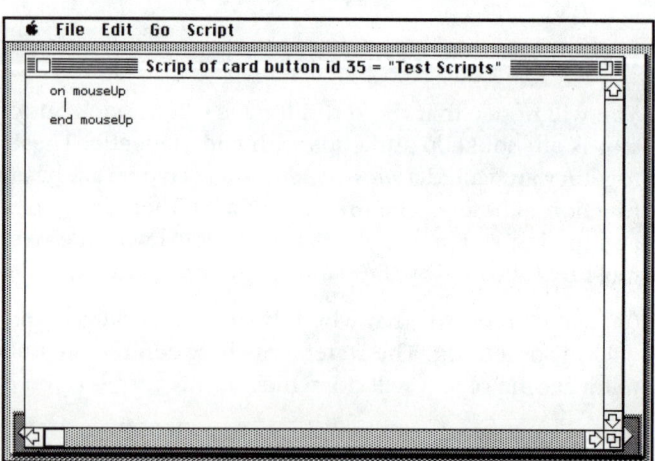

The message handler on mouseUp and end mouseUp are already inserted for you.

4. Type go to next card .

276

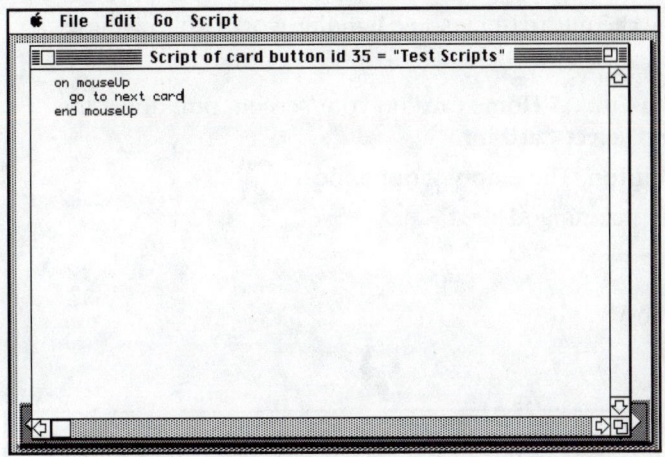

The script is completed.

5. Pull down the File menu and select Close Script, or press ⌘-Ⓦ (or click the close box). Click Yes to save your changes, or press Return .

6. Select the Browse tool and try your new button. It should take you to Card 4.

You have scripted a button. Now try a few more messages on your Test Scripts button:

- go to first card
- go to last card
- go to previous card
- go to card "cardname" (for example, go to card "Welcome to...")
- go to stack "stackname" (for example, go to stack "Art Bits")

Using the On Idle Message Handler

The other message handler that is easy to use is the on idle and end idle message handler. You can use this message handler when you do not want to click the mouse to execute a script. For example, in a script for a self-running demo, where you do not want to click your way through the cards in the stack, use the on idle and end idle message handler.

For an example of how the `on idle` message handler works, follow these steps:

1. With the "Welcome to. . ." Home card on your screen, pull down the Objects menu and select Card Info.

2. Click the Script button. The empty script appears.

3. Type the following commands:

   on idle
   wait 5 seconds
   go next card
   end idle

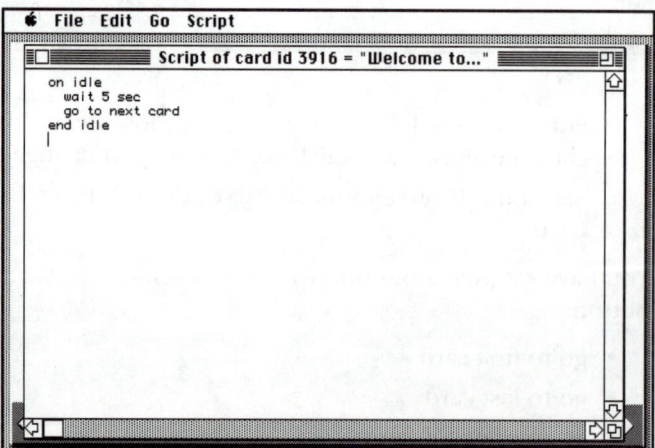

The `on idle` and `end idle` message handlers are automatically indented for you.

9

4. Click the close box and save your changes.

5. Now wait five seconds, and the next card, Stack Kit, should appear.

To delete the script for the "Welcome to..." card, select any other tool in the Tools menu. Then, press ← on your keyboard to go back to the Welcome card. Then, open the card's script (by pressing ⌘-Option-C), and delete the commands you entered.

Creating Button Scripts for Menu Selections

You also can create button scripts to execute any menu command. Use the HyperTalk doMenu statement followed by the name of the menu item to execute.

Try these examples:

- doMenu "New Card"
- doMenu "Background"
- doMenu "Card Info"
- doMenu "Delete card"
- doMenu "Print card"

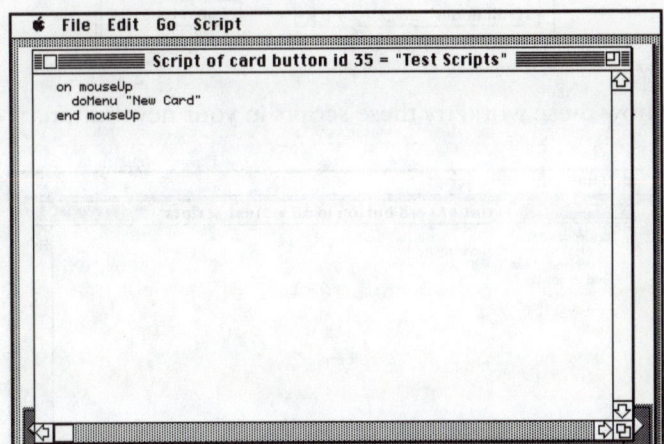

Here, the script to execute the Edit menu command New Card is displayed.

9

Adding Visual Effects in Scripts

New to HyperCard 2.0 is the capability to add visual effect commands to your button scripts. As you recall from the Button Info dialog box, there is an option for effects, with several different effects to choose from, along with four speeds. You can add any of these to your button scripts.

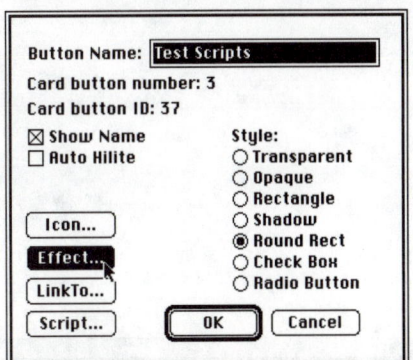

Choose the Effect option.

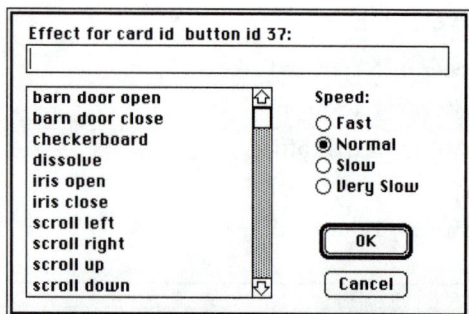

All the effects you
can include in
your button
scripts are listed.

For some examples of how these work, try these scripts in your new button.

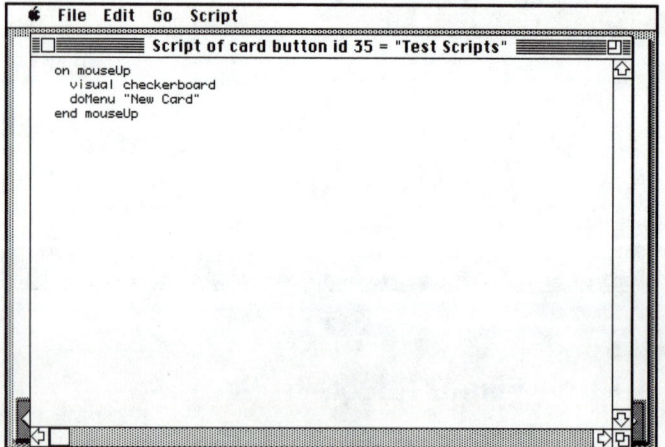

Here is a script
that uses a visual
effect with a
menu command.

9

Here is a script
that uses a visual
command with a
speed specified to
go to the last
card.

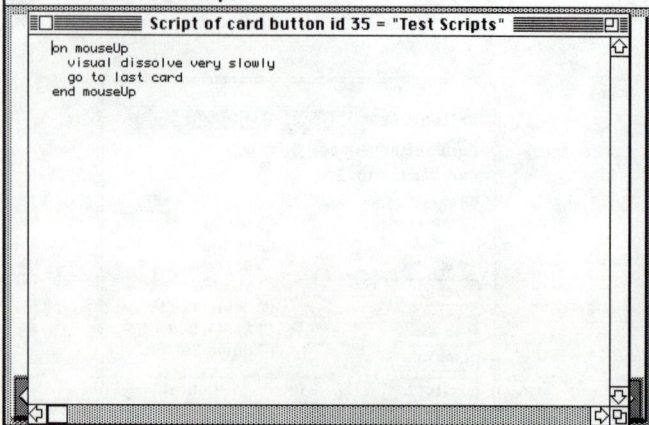

280

Creating a Library Stack

Now that you have an idea of what scripting is all about and how much you can do with some very simple scripts, you will create a new stack for a library based on the Music Library stack template. You will modify some of the scripts for the buttons and create a few new ones as well. To begin, follow these steps:

1. Click the Stack Templates button on the Stack Kit Home card. (Or, open the Stack Templates stack by selecting Open Stack from the File menu.)

2. Click the Music Library button to access the card for a Music Library template.

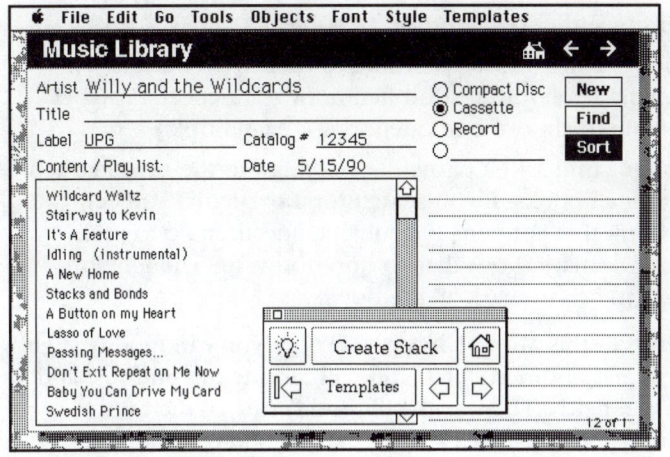

The Music Library template card is displayed.

9

3. Click the Create Stack button on the navigator palette. Name your new stack *My Library*, and click the Save button (or press Return).

Note: When a button is outlined, as it is in this dialog box, you can press Return to activate the button. In this case, pressing Return has the same effect as clicking the Save button.

After a few moments, your stack is created and you are at the first card. Click OK, or press Return .

Now that you have a basis from which to begin, you can change all the fields, buttons, or graphics you want to convert this Music Library stack into a book Library stack.

Designing Your New Stack

First, think about the things you will need to add or change in this Music Library stack to make it into a useful book library stack.

Some useful items might be:

- Book Title and Author fields.
- Label field (the physical label on the book).
- ISBN Number and Date Published field.
- Subject or Category field.
- Additional Notes field to write anything else about the book that would be useful to the browser.
- Buttons to add a new book, to find a particular book or subject, and to sort the books by either title, author, or subject.
- Buttons to categorize the books according to their type, such as primary, intermediate, or young adult fiction or nonfiction. (You should only be able to choose one category for each book.)
- Buttons to mark (or unmark) a particular book, go to the next marked book, and unmark all books. If you search for a particular subject, you can mark each book that contains the subject, and then go to each marked book and unmark those that you do not want. Then, before another search, you can unmark all the books.

There are several things in this Music Library stack that you can modify slightly to accomplish the task just outlined. First, you will modify the buttons, and then you will modify the fields. Then, you will modify one of the button scripts so that you can use the features already established but with the different button names. You also will create a few new buttons with scripts to accomplish some other tasks.

Working with Buttons

First you will work with the buttons in this stack. You will modify those that can be used and create new ones as needed. According to the design outlined previously, the buttons needed for this stack include:

282

- Buttons to add a new book, to find a particular book or subject, and to sort the books by either title, author, or subject.
- Buttons to categorize the books according to their type, such as primary, intermediate, or young adult fiction or nonfiction.
- Buttons to mark (or unmark) a particular book, go to the next marked book, and unmark all books.

To create these buttons, follow these steps:

1. Press ⌘-B to go to the background layer and select the Button tool from the Tools menu.

2. Change the following button names and sizes if needed:

Current Name	New Name
Artist	Title
Title	Author
Catalog #	ISBN #
Content/Play list	Subject List

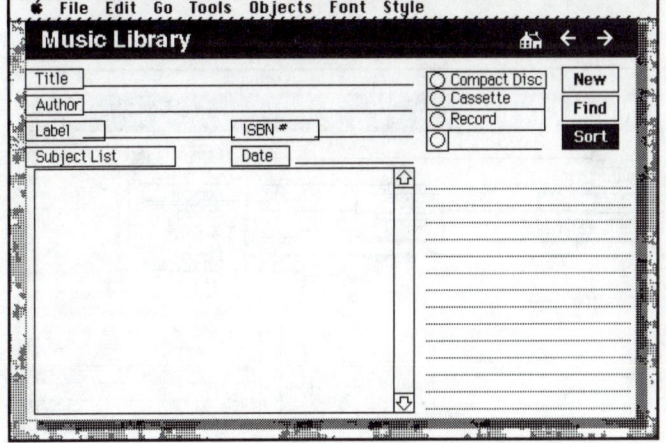

Here, the button names have been changed.

3. Move the New, Find, and Sort buttons to the bottom of the card to make room for additional buttons. Also, change their style to Shadow if you want.

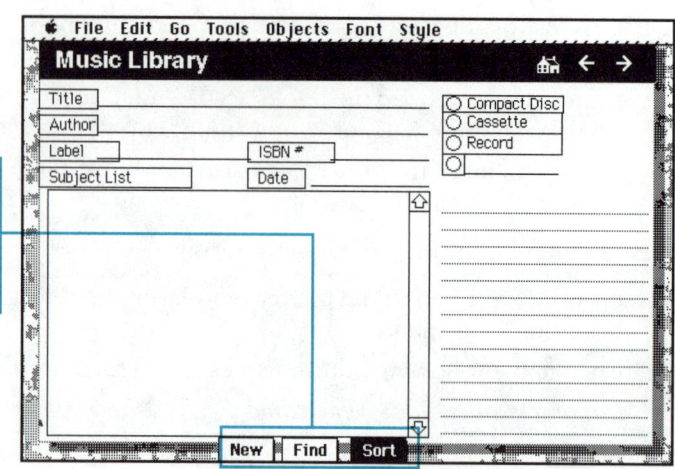

Here, all three buttons have a shadow style and have been moved together.

4. Delete the unnamed button below the record button and erase the line next to it with the Eraser tool. Then, select the Button tool again.

5. Select the Record button, hold down ⟨Option⟩ and pull away a duplicate of the button. Do this two more times so that you have six buttons all together.

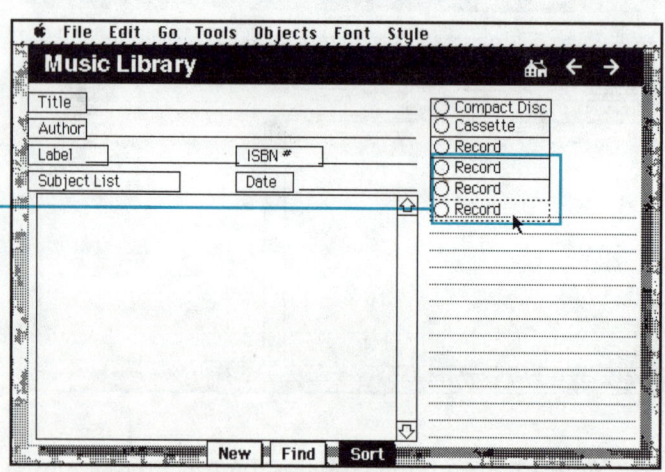

The Record button has been duplicated three times.

6. Change the button names so that they represent book types.

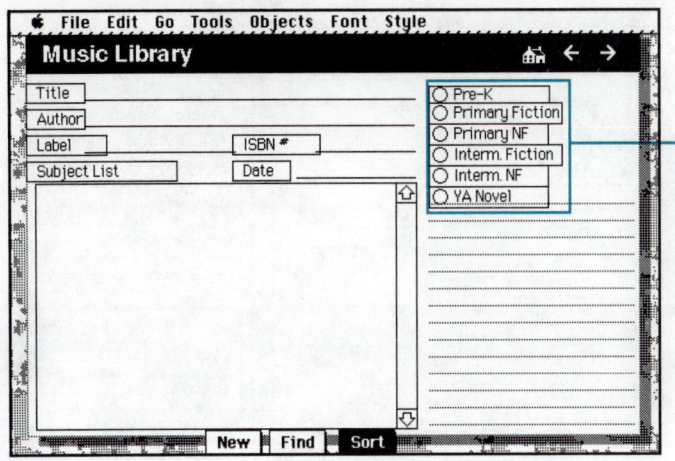

Here, the button names have been changed.

Working with Fields

Next, you will modify the fields in this stack to make room for the additional buttons you will need.

According to the preceding list, you need the following fields:

- Book Title and Author fields
- Label field (the physical label on the book)
- ISBN Number and Date Published field
- Subject or Category field
- Additional Notes field

To create these fields, follow these steps:

1. Select the Field tool from the Tools menu.

2. Double-click the field next to the Title button and change the field's name to *Title*. Then, change the name of the second field (next to the Author button) to *Author*.

3. Change the name of the field next to the ISBN # to *ISBN#*.

4. Because typically a book's ISBN number is longer than the physical label, make the Label field smaller so that you can enlarge the ISBN # field. Then, use the Eraser tool to erase the line that was drawn under the field.

5. Select the Button tool and move the ISBN # button, and then select the Field tool again to enlarge the ISBN Number field.

9

285

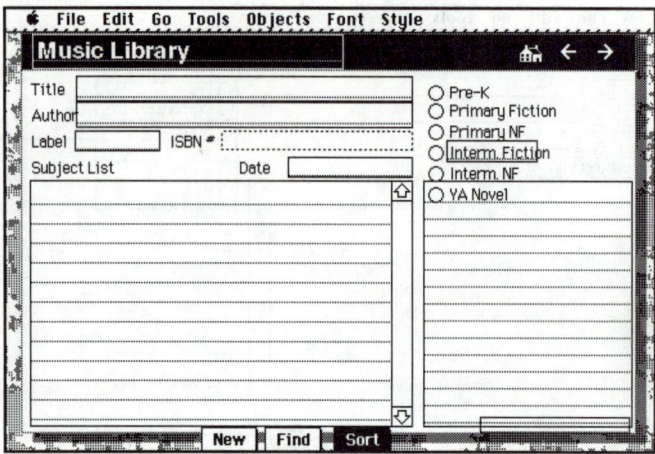

Here, the ISBN # field has been lengthened and the Label field shortened.

6. Select the Lasso tool to select the line drawn under the ISBN # field. Then, press 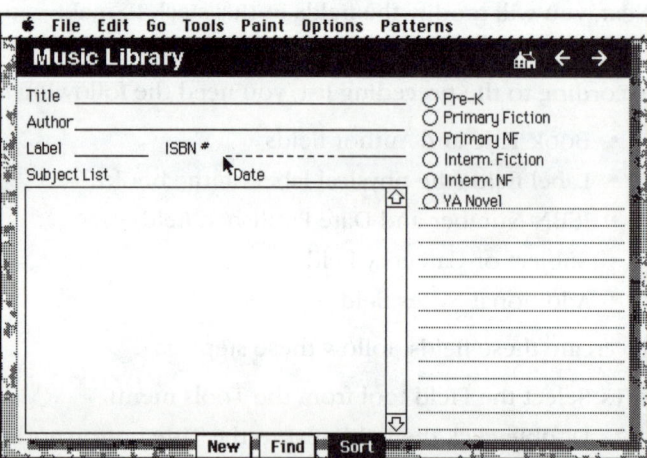 to stretch the line drawn under the ISBN # field.

Here, the line is stretched to accommodate the new field's size.

9

7. Select the Field tool again and double-click the Subject List field. Change its name to *Subject List* and its style to Shadow. Then, resize the field so that it is lined up below the Label field.

8. Move the field below the Primary NF button to see the area between the Subject List field and the Notes field. Then, Move the Book Category Buttons (Pre-K, Primary, Fiction, and so on) next to the Subject List field. (You also can move the New, Find, and Sort buttons up.)

286

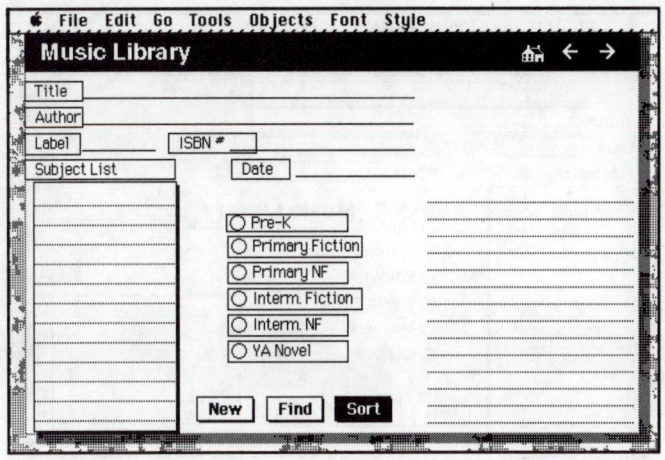

Here, the Subject field is resized, and the Book Category buttons (and also the New/Find/Sort buttons) have been moved.

9. Select the Field tool again and double-click the Notes field on the right side of the card and change its style to Scrolling. Then, resize the field so that it is about half its original height.

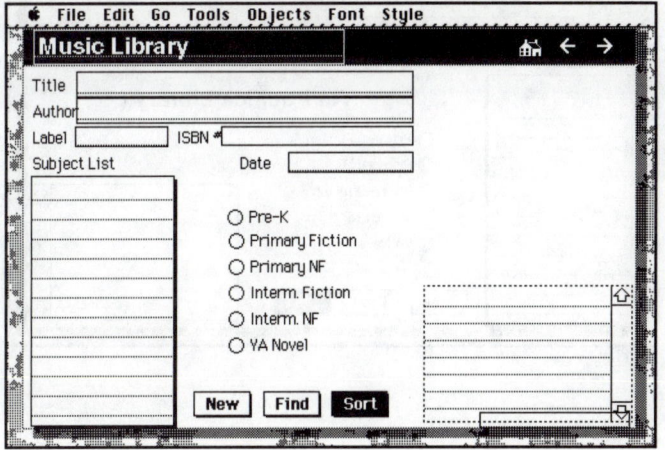

Here, the Notes field has been sized to take up about half its original area.

10. The last field that needs to be changed is the Title field that now reads Music Library. Because that field resides under a shared hilite button, the easiest way to edit its contents is to move the field down to another area in the card, select the Browse tool, and edit its contents; then, select the Field tool and move the field back up to the black area.

287

First, move the field to an area easy to work in.

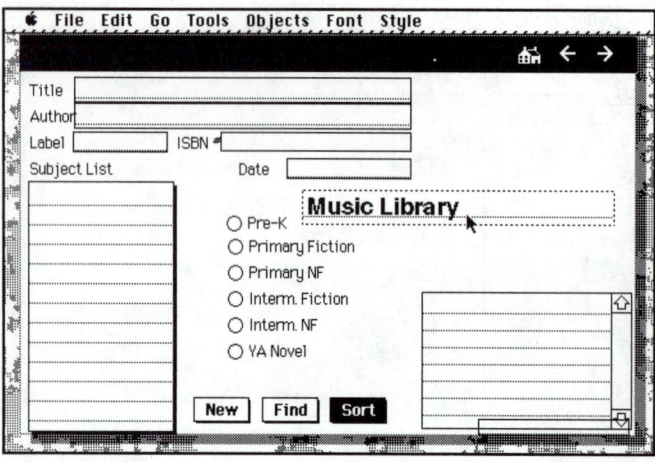

9

Then, select the Browse tool and edit the contents.

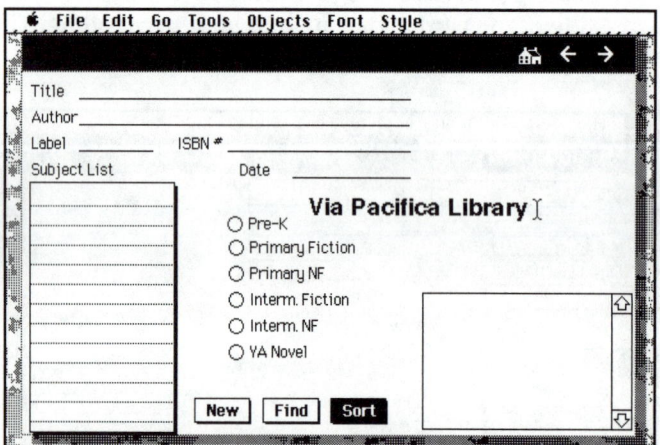

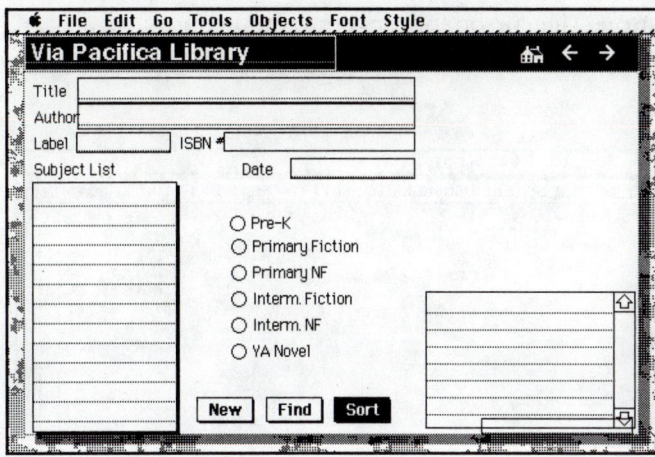

Last, select the Field tool again and move the field back up to its original location.

To check out your work so far, select the Browse tool and leave the background layer.

Writing New Button Scripts

Now you will create buttons to mark, unmark, and go to the next marked card. You can copy the Mark and Unmark buttons from the Readymade Button stack, but you have to create your own for the Go to Next Marked Card button. For the purpose of this exercise, you will create your own for all four new buttons. To create your buttons, follow these steps:

1. Press B to go to the Background layer.

2. Pull down the Objects menu and select New Button. Place the button in the upper right corner of the card.

3. Double-click the new button to access the Button Info dialog box. Give the button the following properties:

    Name: Mark This Card

    Style: Transparent, Auto Hilite, and deselect Shared Hilite

9

4. Click the Script button. The cursor appears between the message handlers. Type the following message between the handlers:

   Mark this card

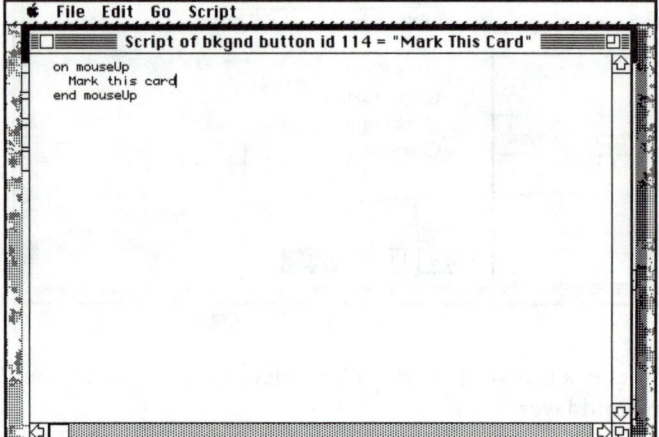

The script is
completed.

5. Click the close box and save your changes.
6. Duplicate this button three times (using the Option-drag method) and modify the other three buttons names and scripts so that they will be Unmark This Card, Go Next Marked Card, and Unmark All Cards.

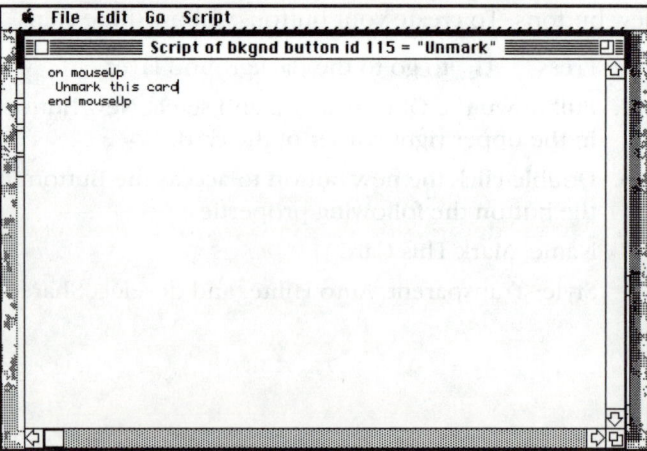

Here is the first
button script.

9

290

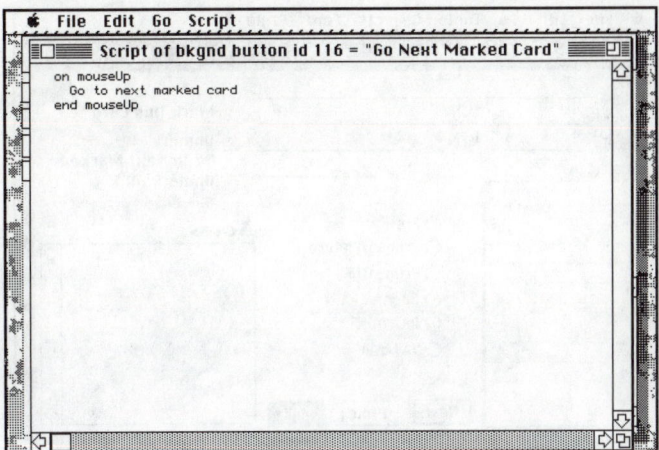

Here is the second button script.

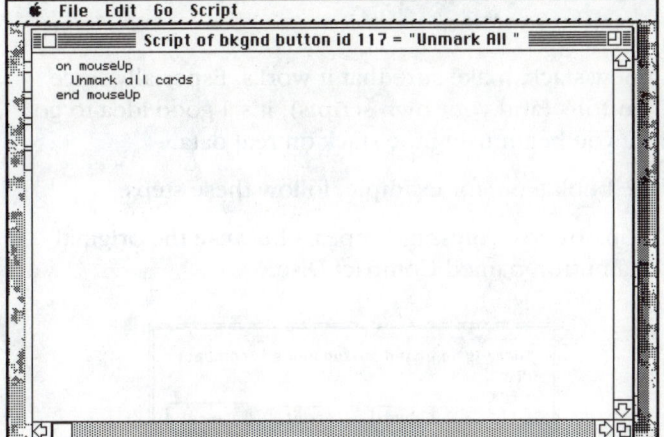

Here is the third button script.

9

7. Size the buttons and select the Browse tool to check your work.

Adding Background Graphics

Now, you can add a few background graphics to the stack to make the stack look more appealing. In this example, the Text tool was used to create the graphic above the Notes field, and the Push Pin graphic was copied and pasted in from the Pages card in the Background Art stack. Refer to Chapter 5, "Using HyperCard Graphics," for assistance.

291

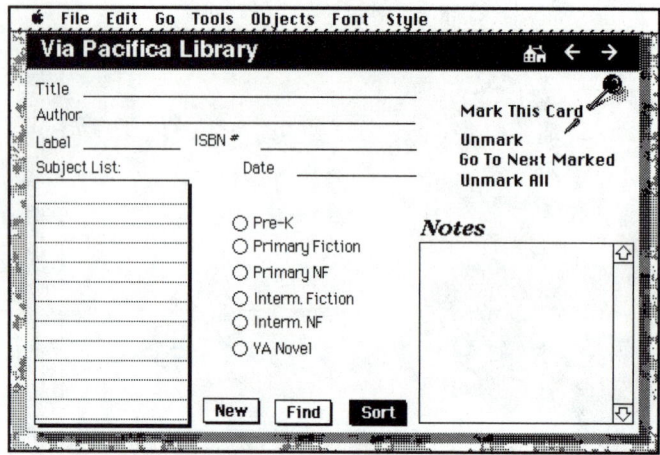

Background graphics have been added to this stack for effect.

Testing and Debugging Your Stack

After you have created a new stack, make sure that it works. Especially since you have added several buttons (and your own scripts), it's a good idea to go through a few tests before you begin using the stack on real data.

To test the buttons for the book type, for example, follow these steps:

1. Click the Pre-K button. An error message appears because the original script is looking for a button named Compact Disc.

Here, the error message is displayed.

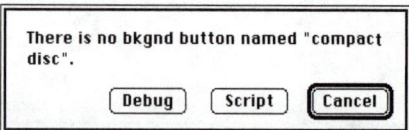

2. Click the Script button.

292

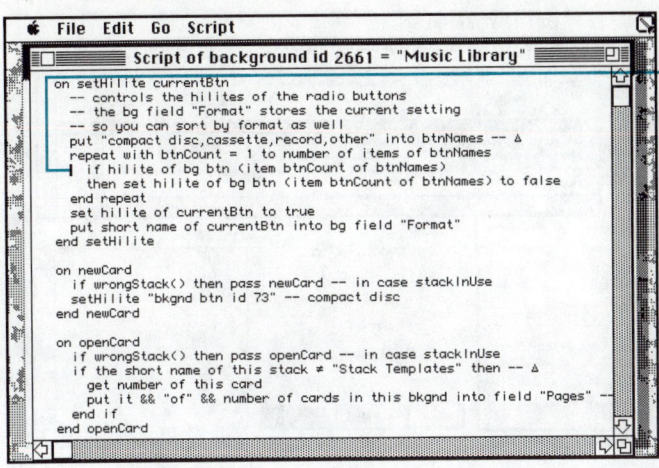

Your cursor is placed near the area the script could not understand.

3. Note how the names of the original buttons are written into the script. You need to edit the script by adding the new button names. Select the line in the script that calls out the buttons names and type your new button names (Pre-K, Primary Fiction, Primary NF, Interm.Fiction, Interm.NF, YA Novel).

Note: You can move and size the Script window so that you can see the button names in your library stack.

9

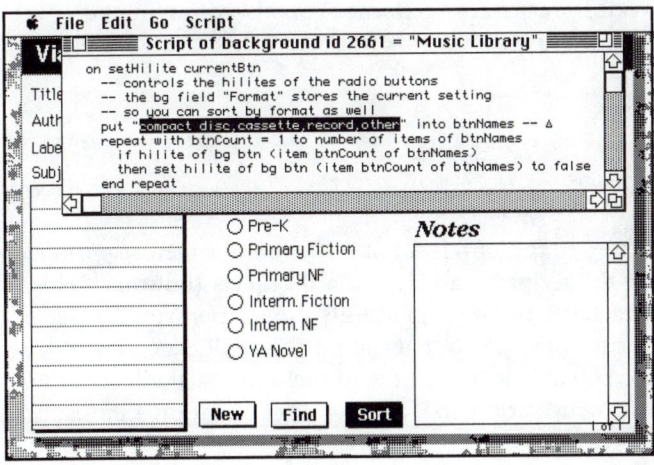

Here, the Script window has been moved and made smaller so that you can see the card below.

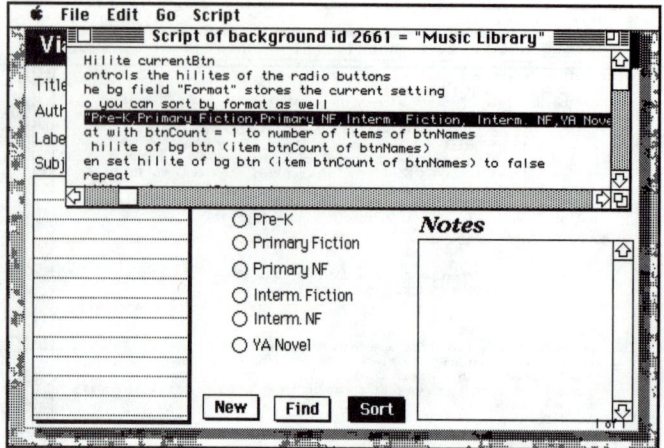

Here, the line in the script has been changed to reflect the new button names.

Note: There are no spaces after the commas separating the button names.

4. Close the Script window and save the changes you have made to the script. Then, test the buttons again to be sure that you didn't make any typographical errors.

    Now type in some information into a few cards and test the Mark and Unmark buttons you created.

The last step is to link your library stack to Home. You also can type the command **hide menubar** in the message box to make your stack look professional.

Summary

This chapter introduced you to the fifth level of HyperCard, called *Scripting*. You learned how to view the script for all HyperCard objects (buttons, fields, cards, backgrounds, and stacks) and how to modify the scripts. You learned how to create new scripts for buttons so that the buttons will execute a command or menu item. You also learned how to include visual effects in button scripts and how to write scripts that are not dependent on a mouse click to execute.

9

Specifically, you learned the following key information about HyperCard:

- Every HyperCard object (buttons, fields, cards, backgrounds, and stacks) has a script. Scripts are instructions that tell HyperCard what you would like it to do for you. Scripts in HyperCard are written in a language unique to HyperCard, called *HyperTalk*.

- To set the user level to Scripting, go to the last card in the Home stack, the Preferences card, and click the button labeled Scripting.

- When you change your user level to Scripting, an additional button, named Scripts, appears in all the objects dialog boxes. Clicking the Script button opens the script that controls the object.

- As a shortcut, you can press ⌘-Option-B to open the script of the current background. You also can press ⌘-Option-C to open the script of the current card, or ⌘-Option-S to open the script of the current stack.

- Press and hold down ⌘-Option and click an outlined button to open its script.

- Press and hold down Shift-⌘-Option and click an outlined field to open its script.

- HyperTalk has message handlers and function handlers. The first line of a handler always begins with the word *on*, and the last statement of a handler begins with the word *end*. Both *on* and *end* must be followed by the name of the HyperTalk message or function.

- On mouseUp means when the mouse is clicked, the object will do something. The statement between on mouseUp and end mouseUp tells what the object will do.

- Any message you enter in the message box could be inserted between a message handler in a script.

- When you create a new button, on mouseUp and end mouseUp are already inserted for you.

- Use the on idle message handler when you do not want to click the mouse to execute a script. For example, use the on idle message handler in a script for a stack that acts as a self-running demo.

- You also can create a script to execute any menu command, using the HyperTalk doMenu statement followed by the name of the menu item to execute.

9

295

■ You can add any of the visual effects that are listed in the Button Info dialog box to a button script.

■ When you copy a stack template and change button names, you can easily modify the stack's scripts to account for the new names.

In the next chapter, you will create another stack using more button and card scripts. The stack will be an automated résumé that acts like a self-running demo.

9

Creating an Automated Résumé Stack

In this chapter, you will create a different kind of HyperCard stack. The stack is called *HyperRe*s, and it serves as an automated Résumé stack that you can personalize. The script is similar to a self-running demo: it requires no action from you except to read what's on the screen and click the mouse to make choices.

The entire HyperRes "application" is comprised of two stacks. One stack is for the basic résumé, and the other is for a portfolio of additional graphics, or whatever you might want to include. When you click the Portfolio button, the Portfolio stack opens. When you are through viewing the stack, you are returned to the original résumé stack.

The stack is simple to create. It consists of six introductory cards, each consisting of simple graphics or text. The cards are scripted so that, without any intervention from the browser, each one will dissolve into the next one; the first six cards look like a slide show or demo.

After the introductory cards, the next four cards show the beginning of the résumé, one card at a time, with each card adding additional information to the previous one. So by the fourth Résumé card, you are looking at a full page of text. Then, you are offered a button to "click to continue."

The Continue button takes you to the next card, which is a Main menu. The menu contains three buttons: one to view a Work History card, one to take you to the Graphics portfolio, and a third to take you to a card that contains references.

If you choose the Work History button, you go to a card with a work history summary, and buttons to take you to other cards that contain detailed information about each job. Each Job Description card contains a button to take you back to the Main menu.

The entire Résumé stack is comprised of 19 cards. All the cards share the same background, and several of the cards share the same information as well, so it's easy to create the stack by copying one card to the next and then changing or adding information. Several of the cards have a script associated with them, and several include buttons with their own script.

The 19 cards in this stack can be categorized as follows:

- 6 Intro Graphic cards
- 5 Résumé Overview cards
- 1 Main Menu card
- 1 Intro Portfolio card (that will take you to the other stack)
- 1 Work History card (that lists 4 jobs)
- 4 detailed Job Description cards (one for each job)
- 1 References card

10

First, you will learn about each card display, and then you will see the script for each card.

Creating a New Stack

This stack doesn't start out with any template, so follow these steps to begin a new stack from scratch.

1. Pull down the File menu and select New Stack. The New Stack dialog box appears.

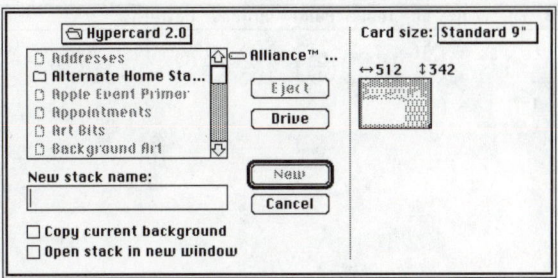

Here, the New
Stack dialog box
is displayed.

2. Name the stack *My Résumé*. Do not select the Copy Current Background option.

   A white screen appears, which is the first card of your new Résumé stack.

Creating Introductory Cards

The first three cards of this Résumé stack are all similar. You will create the first one, and then copy it to the next two. First, you will create the card graphics, and then the script.

Creating Card 1

The first card in this stack is an introductory card that displays the name of the HyperCard application. You may want to include this first card as part of your Résumé stack. For the purpose of this exercise, follow these steps to create the card; you always can delete it later, if you want.

Creating the Card Graphics

First, you will create some simple card graphics, and then define the background.

To create the card graphics, follow these steps:

1. Select the Text tool from the Tools menu.

2. Press ⌘-T to open the Text Style dialog box. Select Times font, 48 point size, and Outline for the style. Press Return to select OK.

3. Click anywhere on the card and type **HyperRes**.

10

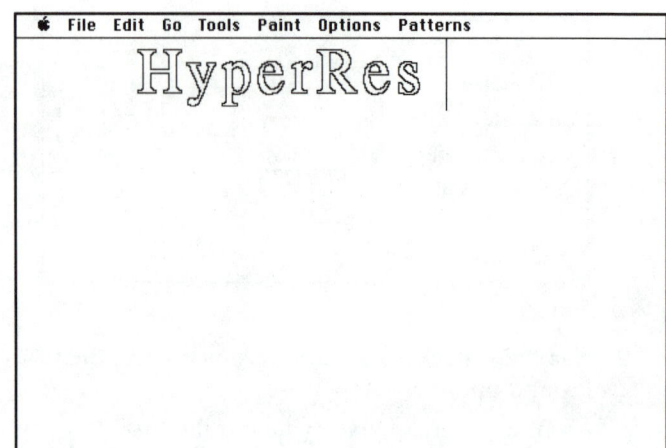

Here, the outlined text is painted on the card.

4. Select the text with the Selection tool, and move the text to the upper left corner of the card.

5. Press ⌘-B to go to the background. Then, select the Fill tool from the Tools menu and the black square from the Patterns menu.

6. Click the Fill tool anywhere on the card to fill the entire screen black. Then, press ⌘-B to leave the background layer. The outlined text you painted remains visible.

7. Click the Fill tool in the rectangle around the text and in the middle of the letters that need to be filled in. If you can't get to the small areas, select the Pencil tool and use FatBits to fill in the areas.

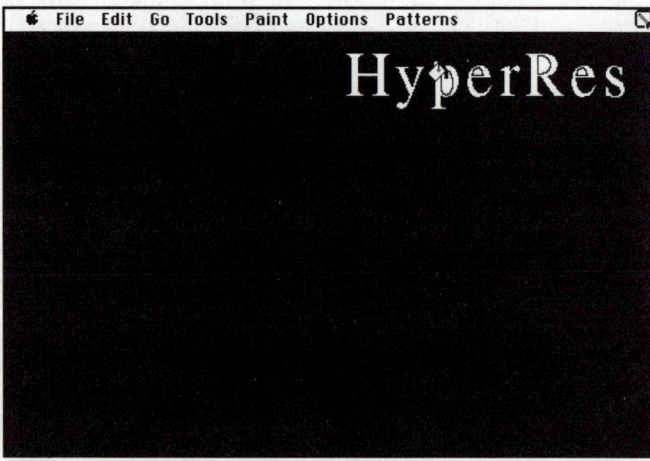

Fill in behind each outlined letter.

10

Creating the Card Script

Now that the first card looks the way you want it to look, you will write a script for the card so that it acts the way you want it to act. Follow these steps to create the card script:

1. With the first card on your screen, press ⌘-Option-C to get to the card's script. It is currently blank.

2. Type the following in the Script window:

   on idle

       wait 1 second

       visual dissolve

       go to next card

   end idle

3. Close the Script window and save your changes.

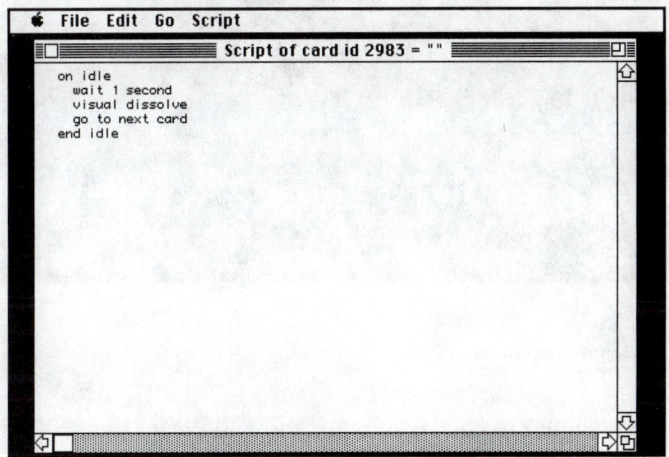

The first card's script is completed.

10

Note: The script will not work until the Browse tool is selected. For now, don't select the Browse tool until you finish creating the next five cards.

Creating Card 2

To create the next introductory card, you will copy the contents of the first card (including the script), and then add another line in the bottom right corner. Follow these steps to create Card 2:

1. With the first card still on your screen, pull down the Edit menu and select Copy Card.

2. Pull down the Edit menu and select Paste Card, or press ⌘-Ⓥ.

   If you press ⌘-Ⓞⓟⓣⓘⓞⓝ-Ⓒ to open the script for this card, you will see that it has also been copied.

3. Select the Text tool again, and press ⌘-Ⓣ to open the Text Info dialog box. Change the font size to 36. Click OK.

4. Click anywhere on the screen and type **by: <your name>**. Fill in the areas that need to be filled in with the Fill tool, and then move the text to the lower right corner of the screen.

The second card is completed.

Creating Card 3

The next four cards are all similar to each other. So, you will create the first, and then copy the next three in succession. Follow these steps to create Card 3:

1. Pull down the Edit menu and select New Card, or press ⌘-Ⓝ. The black background appears.

2. Select the Text tool and press ⌘-Ⓣ to open the Text Info dialog box. Change the font size to 24. Click OK.

3. Click in the middle of the screen and type your full name. Then, fill in the white areas with the Fill tool.

This is what the third card looks like.

4. Press ⌘-Option-C to open the card's script. Type the following script:

on idle

   wait 1 second

   visual dissolve very slowly

   go to next card

end idle

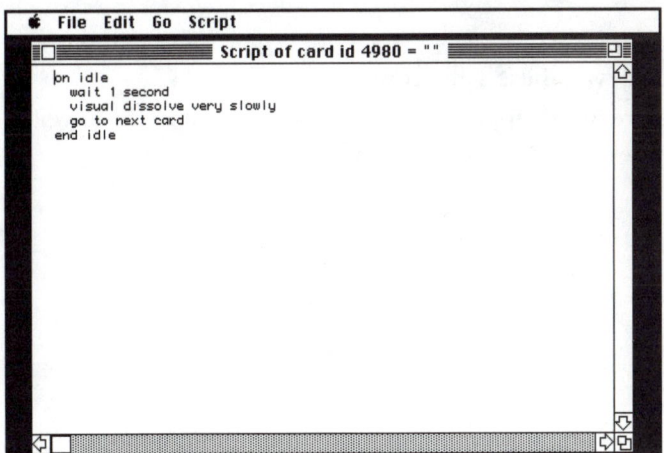

10

Here, the script for the third card is displayed

Creating Cards 4, 5, and 6

To create Cards 4, 5, and 6, follow these steps:

1. Pull down the Edit menu and select Copy Card.

2. Press ⌘-V to paste the previous card template.

3. Add a picture to the upper right corner (paste one in from Art Bits or draw your own), and add text in the lower left corner that highlights one of the main skills outlined in your résumé.

Here is an example of what the fourth card might look like.

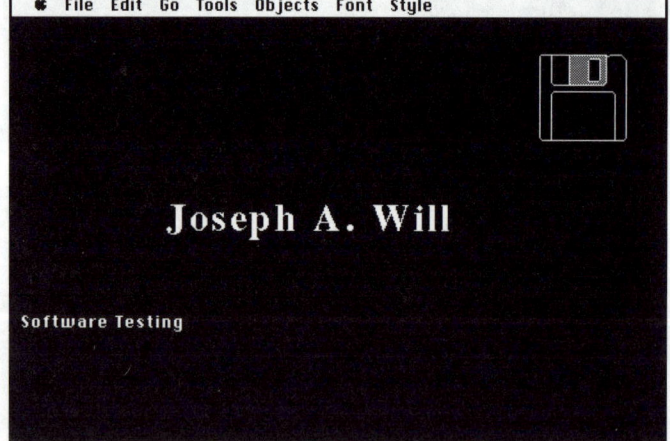

10

4. Pull down the Edit menu and select Copy Card. Then, press ⌘-V to paste in a new card with these same contents.

5. Add another picture in the upper left corner and add text in the lower right corner to add another résumé highlight.

304

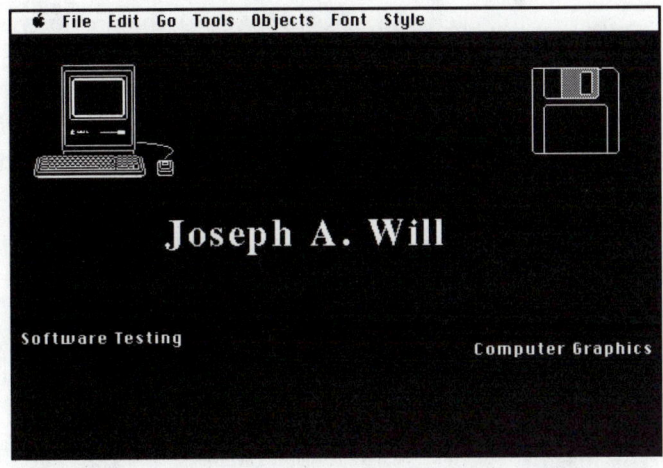

Here is an example of what the fifth card might look like.

6. Copy this card to another, and then add one more picture and text in the lower middle area.

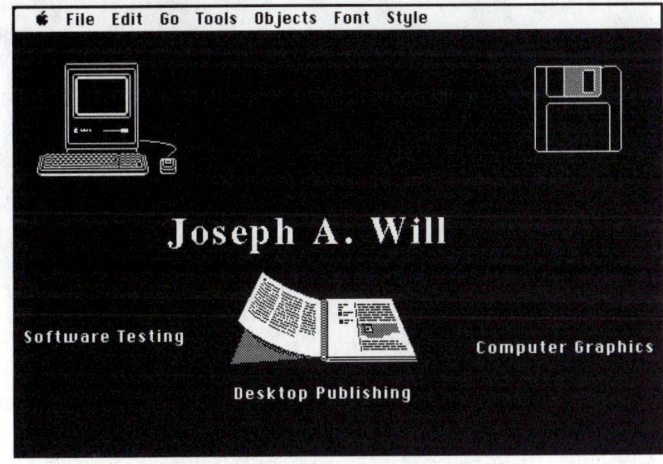

Here is an example of what the sixth card might look like.

Creating Five Résumé Overview Cards

The next five cards you will create are Résumé Overview cards. The information in these cards is similar to what would be in the top section of your résumé, such as an Overview section or Summary of Qualifications. This particular résumé has three paragraphs of overview information, so it is broken down into five cards. Again, each one starts as a copy of the previous card.

Creating Card 7

Before creating Card 7, you will copy the text graphic of your name that is in the center of Card 6 so that you can paste it into Card 7. Then, you will create the additional résumé overview information on each succeeding card. Follow these steps:

1. Select the Selection tool from the Tools menu.

2. Select your name and press ⌘-C to copy it.

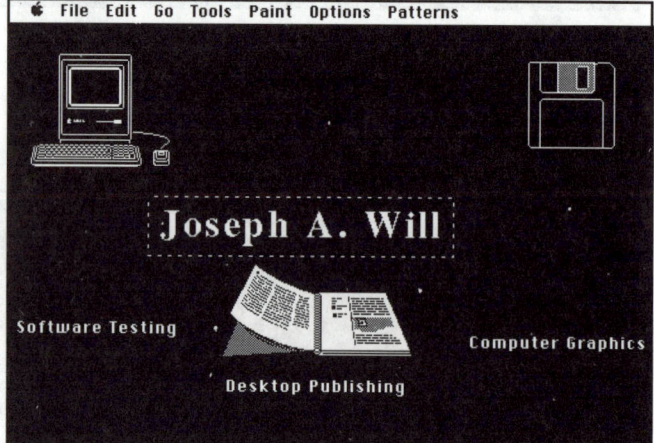

Here, the painted text is selected to copy.

3. Press ⌘-N to create a new card. Then, press ⌘-V to copy the painted text into the card. The text is pasted in the center of the new card.

4. Move the selected text to the upper right corner of the screen.

5. Press ⌘-T to open the Text Info dialog box, and select Chicago, 12 point size, Outline. Then, select the Text tool and type **Summary of Qualifications** in the upper left corner. Fill in any white areas, if needed.

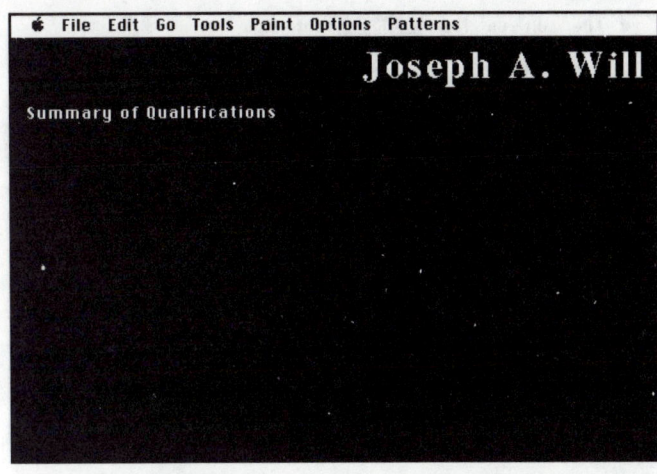

Here is an example of what the seventh card might look like.

6. Press ⌘-Option-C to open the card's script. Type in the following commands:

on idle

    wait 2 seconds

    visual dissolve

    go next card

end idle

Creating Card 8

10

The eighth card of the stack will include all the graphics currently on the seventh card. So, again you will start out by copying and pasting the card. Follow these steps to create Card 8:

1. Pull down the Edit menu and select Copy Card.

2. Press ⌘-V to paste in a new card.

   Note: If at any time you get confused about which card you are working on, select Card Info from the Objects menu to see the card number.

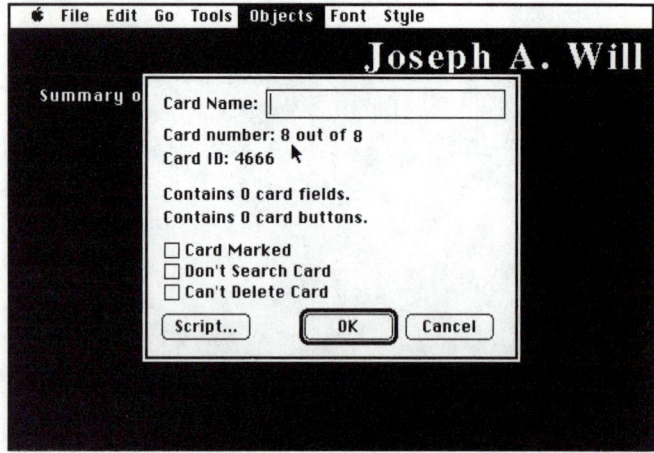

You can view the card number in the Card Info dialog box.

3. Select the Text tool and type in a Summary of Qualifications paragraph.

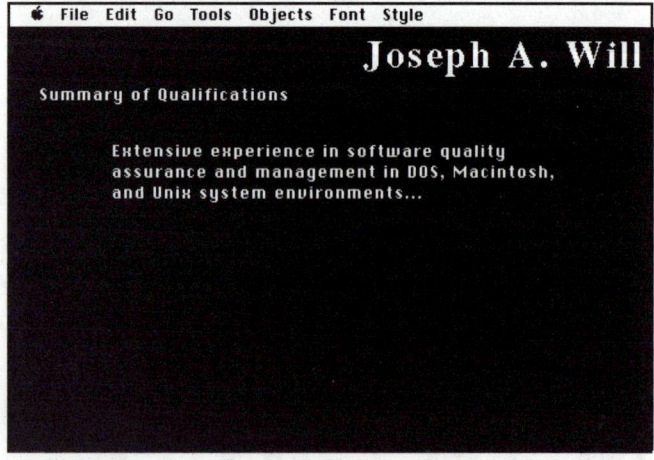

Here is an example of what the eighth card might look like.

Creating Cards 9 and 10

To create two additional cards with summary paragraphs, follow the steps in the preceding procedure. First, copy the card. Then, write an additional paragraph of summary information.

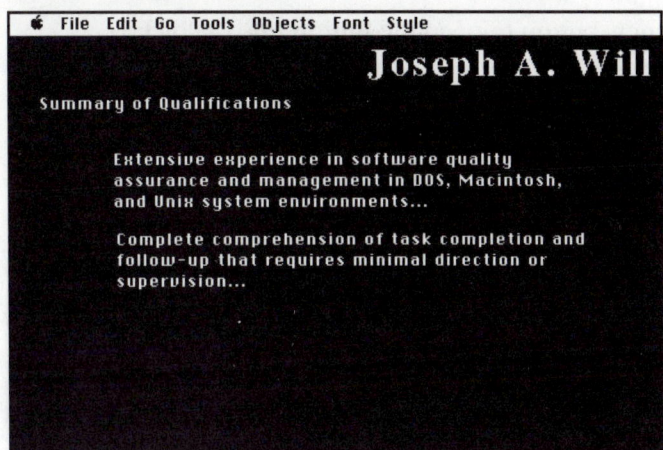

Here is an example of what the ninth card might look like.

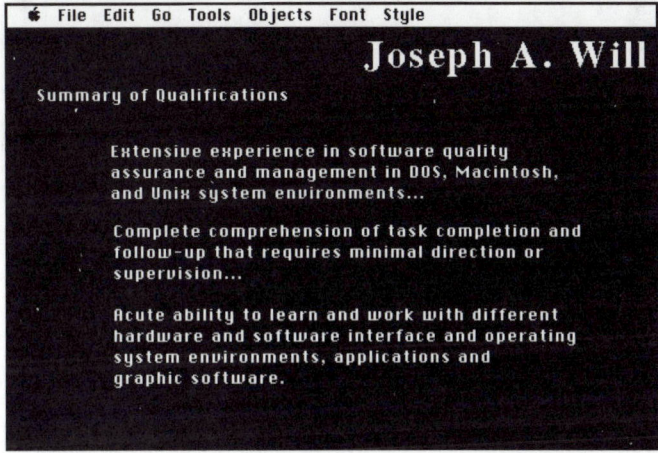

Here is an example of what the tenth card might look like.

10

Creating Card 11

The last card in the Résumé Overview set is exactly like Card 10 but also includes a Continue button on the bottom of the card. The card's script will also change. To create Card 11, follow these steps:

1. Copy Card 10, and then press ⌘-V to paste it for Card 11.

2. Select the Button tool from the Tools menu, and select New Button from the Objects menu.

3. Position the new button below the last paragraph.

4. Double-click the new button to open the Button Info dialog box. Name the button *Click to Continue*.

5. Click the Script button. Insert the following commands between the on mouseUp and end mouseUp handlers:

   visual dissolve

   go next card

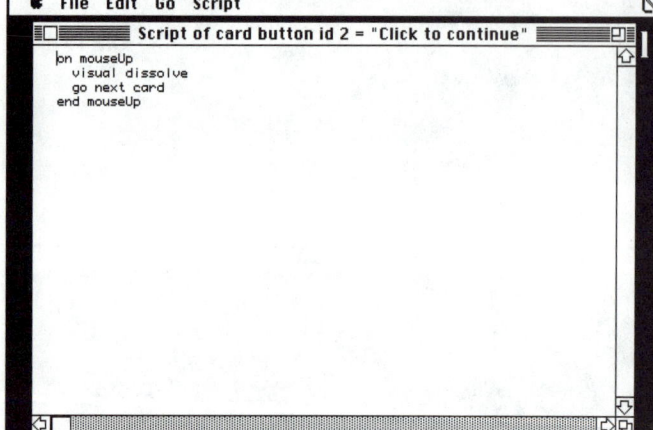

Here, the script for the new button is displayed.

6. Size the button so that you can read the entire Click to Continue name.

7. Press ⌘-Option-C to open the card's script. Delete the entire card script so that the button's script is the only one on this card.

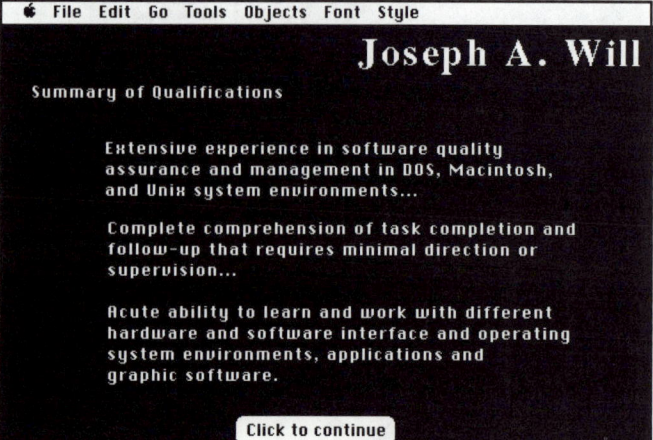

Here is an example of what the eleventh card might look like.

10

Now press ⊞-1 to go to the first card. Then, select the Browse tool and review your stack. When you get to the last card (Card 10), select the Button tool again so that you continue creating the remainder of the cards.

Creating the Main Menu Card

Before you create the Main Menu card, you will copy your name in the upper left corner so that you can paste it in the Main Menu card. Follow these steps to copy your name:

1. Use the Selection tool to select your name in the upper left corner. Press ⊞-C to copy.

2. Select New Card from the Edit menu, or press ⊞-N.

3. Press ⊞-V to paste your name in the upper left corner. Move the mouse to the upper right corner.

Now you're ready to design the Main Menu card. First, paint the text you want, and then create the buttons. For example, type **Menu** in the upper left corner, and then type three choices: to go to a Work History card, a Graphics portfolio stack, or a References card.

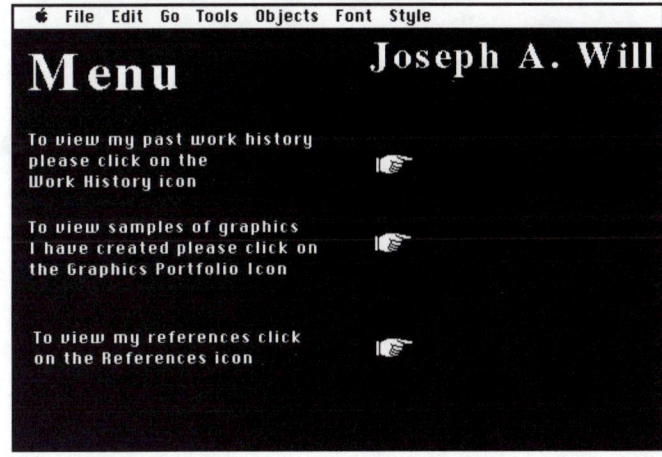

10

Here is an example of what the Main Menu text might look like.

4. Select the Button tool from the Tools menu. Then, select New Button from the Objects menu.

5. Double-click the new button to access the Button Info dialog box. Name the button *Work History*, set its style to Transparent, and

choose an icon for the button. Then, you can paint text under the button if you want.

This is an example of what the Work History button might look like.

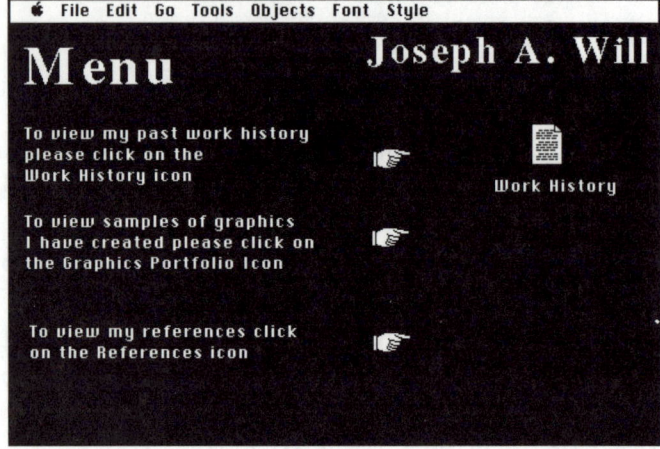

6. Double-click the button again to access the Button Info dialog box, and click the Script button. Write a script for the button to go to the Work History card; this card will describe your job experience.

Here is what the script for the Work History button might look like.

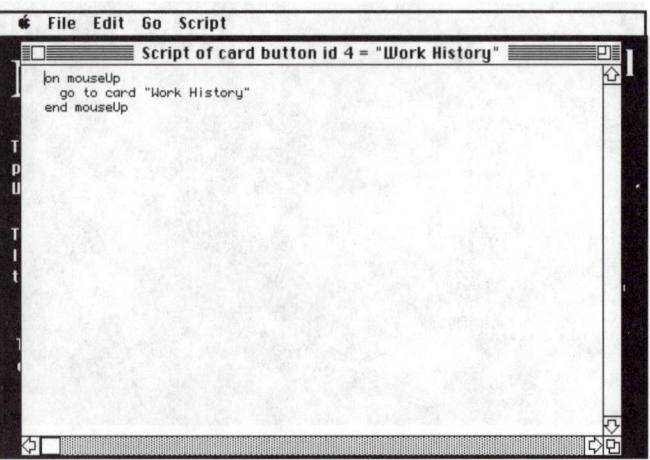

7. Follow steps 4–6 to create a References card button and a Portfolio card button. The scripts will be the same as the Work History button's, except that they will take the browser to a References card or a Portfolio card.

10

312

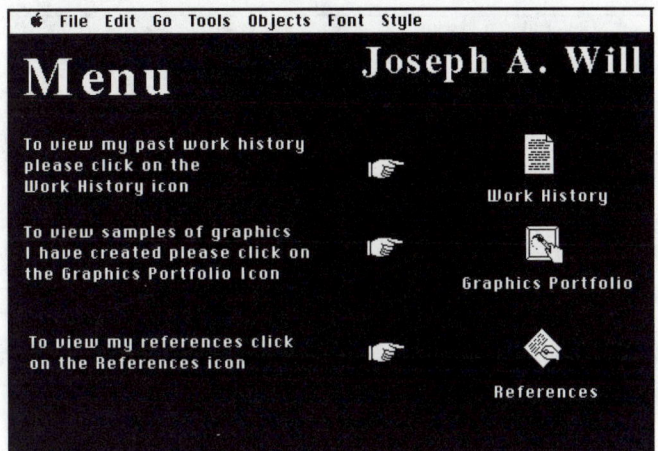

Here is what the Portfolio and References buttons might look like.

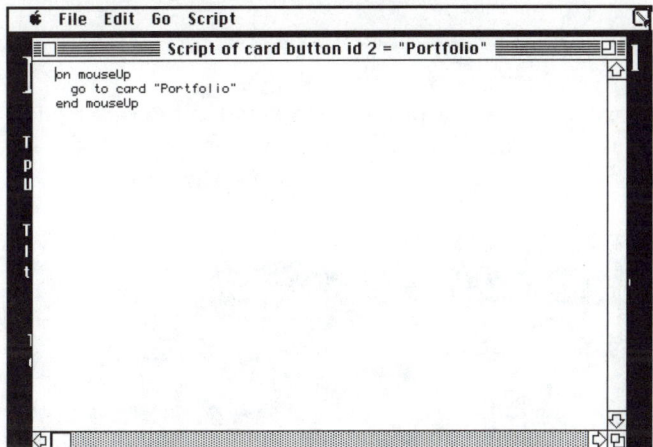

Here is what the script for the Portfolio button might look like.

10

313

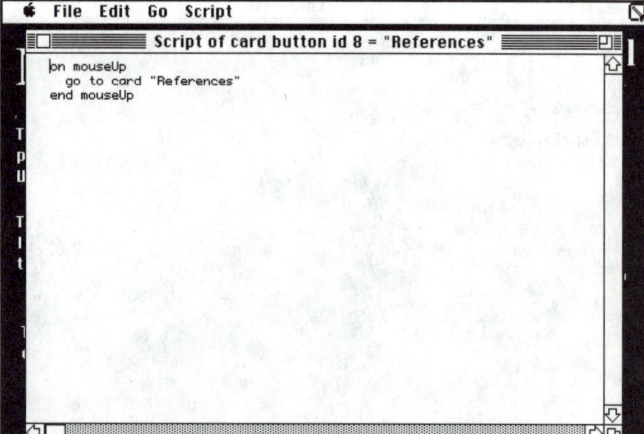

Here is what the script for the References button might look like.

Creating the Work History Card

Next create a Work History card with buttons to go to detailed Job Description cards. Each card should also include a button to take you back to the Main Menu card.

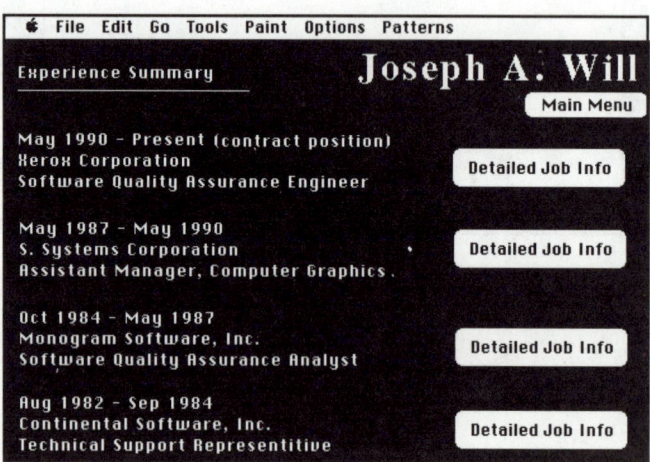

Here is an example of what the Work History card might look like.

Creating Detailed Job Info Cards

The next step is to create detailed Job Description cards for each of the jobs that are summarized in the Work History card. To create a sample Job Description card, follow these steps:

1. Type the name of the job title and company in the upper left corner.

2. Create a button in the upper right corner to take you to the Main Menu card.

3. Create a large scrolling field to enter detailed job information. After you enter the information, select the field and select Lock Text in the Field Info dialog box.

Creating the Portfolio Card

Next you will create a card to take you to another stack, where your graphics portfolio might be located. This card could include two buttons, one to take you to a "slide show" portfolio, and another to take you to a Portfolio stack where you can view the graphics separately. The only difference between the two stacks is the "slide show" portfolio's script has the message handler on `idle` and `end idle`, and the View Separately stack has the message handler on `mouseUp` and `end mouseUp`.

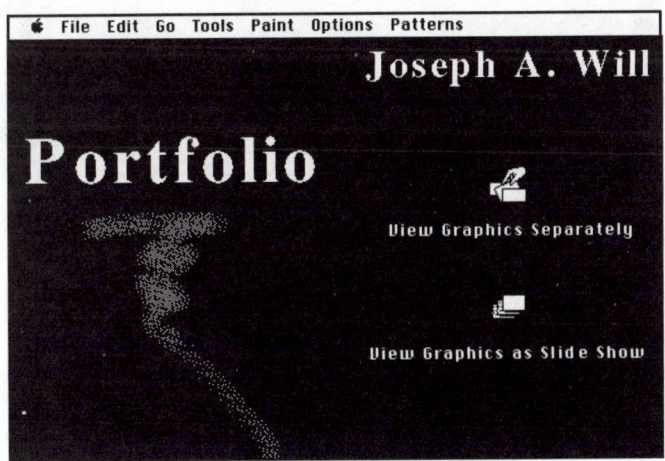

Here is what the main Portfolio card might look like.

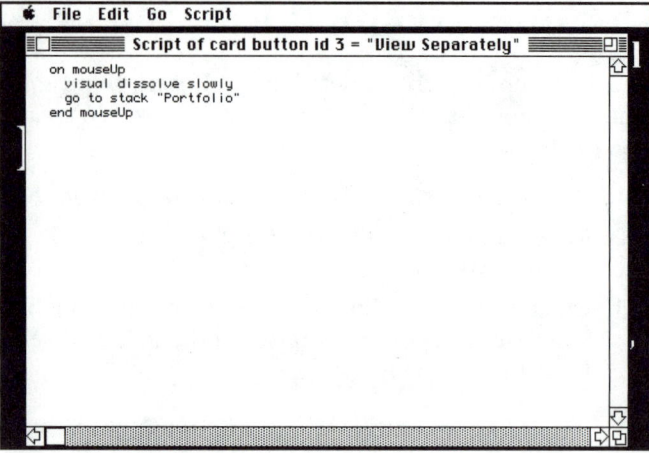

Here is what the first button's script might look like.

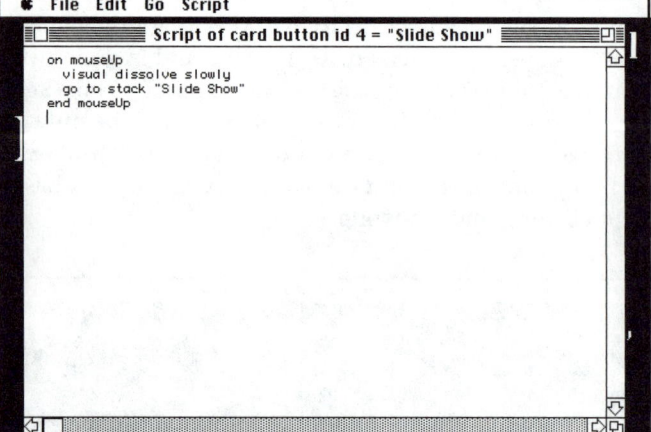

Here is what the second button's script might look like.

Completing Your Stack

Now, all that's left to do is create the Portfolio stack. This stack might contain your portfolio of graphics.

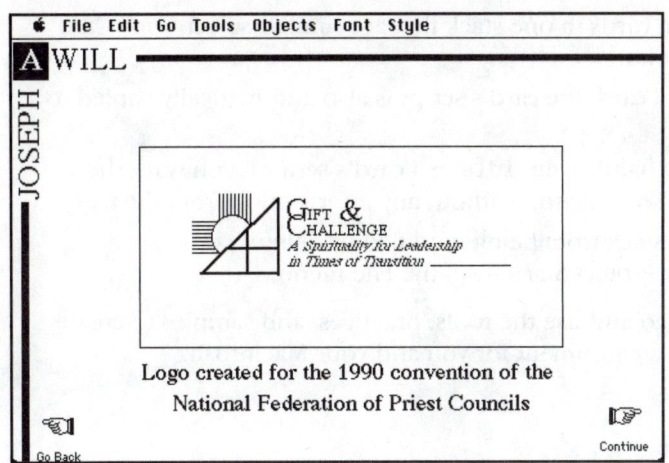

Here is an example of what the Portfolio stack might look like.

Protecting Your Stack

After you have created a stack that you intend to distribute, you might want to protect it so that a casual browser won't be allowed to modify your stack's contents. Protecting a stack is very simple to do. Just use the Protect Stack option in the File menu. You can protect your stack from being modified, deleted, etc. You can also assign a password to your stack or set the user level to not go beyond Browsing.

10

Summary

This chapter showed you how to create a new HyperCard stack that serves as an automated résumé and functions as a self-running demo. You learned how to create a new stack from scratch without copying a template or even a background. You created several button and card scripts that controlled the stack so that it could run almost completely on its own. You also learned how to protect a stack so that a casual browser wouldn't be able to modify the stack's contents or delete a card.

Specifically, you learned the following key information about HyperCard:

■ To create a stack from scratch, select New Stack from the File menu. You can copy the current background of the stack on your screen if you desire.

■ To create several cards in one stack that are similar, select Copy Card from the Edit menu.

■ When you copy a card, the card's script is also automatically copied to the new card.

■ Use the message handler `on idle` in a card's script if you want the card to perform some action without any intervention from the user.

■ To protect your stack from being modified or deleted, or to set a password, select Protect Stack from the File menu.

Let your imagination go and use the tools, practices, and samples to create your own HyperCard environment for you and your Macintosh.

10

Installing HyperCard

Before installing HyperCard, make a copy of each of the HyperCard diskettes. If you don't know how to make a copy of a diskette, refer to the Owner's Guide that came with your Macintosh.

Installing HyperCard on a Hard Disk

After you make a backup of your HyperCard diskettes, you are ready to install the program onto your Macintosh. It is assumed that your hard disk is set up and ready to use and that you are familiar with basic Macintosh procedures, such as opening, closing, and dragging icons and windows. Refer to Chapter 1 and the Owner's Guide that came with your Macintosh to familiarize yourself with these techniques.

Note: If you have been using Version 1.x of HyperCard and have modified either the Home stack or any other stack, DO NOT automatically copy the new stacks onto your hard disk. See the section on upgrading to 2.0 in this Appendix.

If you are installing HyperCard onto your hard disk for the first time, follow these steps:

1. Click once on your hard drive icon and choose Open from the File menu to open the hard drive onto the desktop. (You also can double-click the icon to open it.)

Here, Open is selected from the File menu.

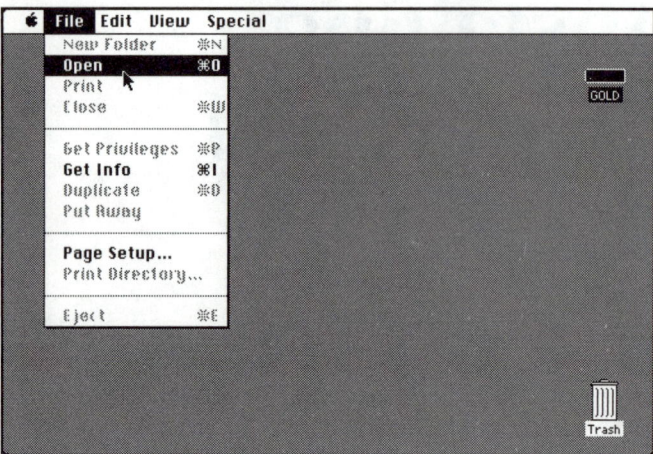

2. Choose New Folder from the File menu.

A folder named *Empty Folder* appears in the window.

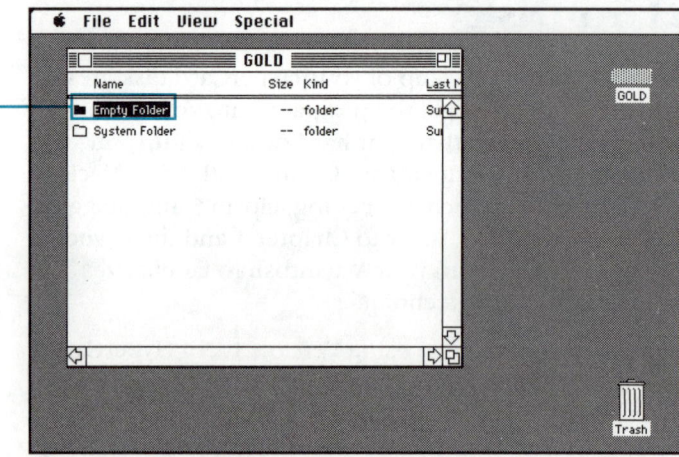

3. Change the name of the folder from *Empty Folder* to *HyperCard*.

4. Double-click the HyperCard folder you just created to open it onto the desktop.

5. Insert the HyperCard program diskette into the floppy disk drive.

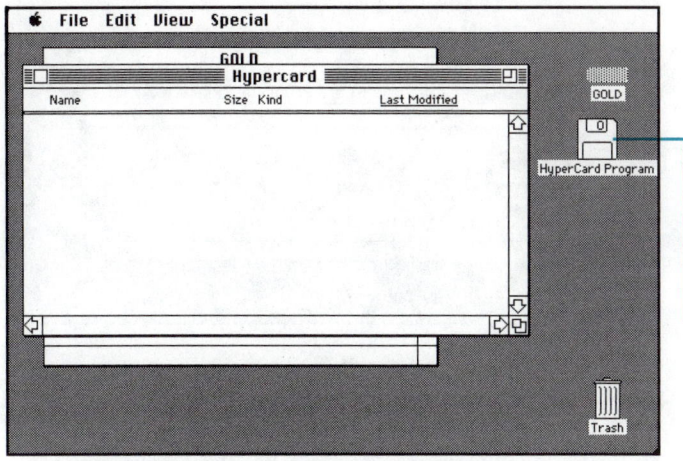

The diskette's icon appears on the desktop below the icon representing your hard disk.

6. Double-click the floppy disk icon to open its window.

7. Choose Select All from the Edit menu.

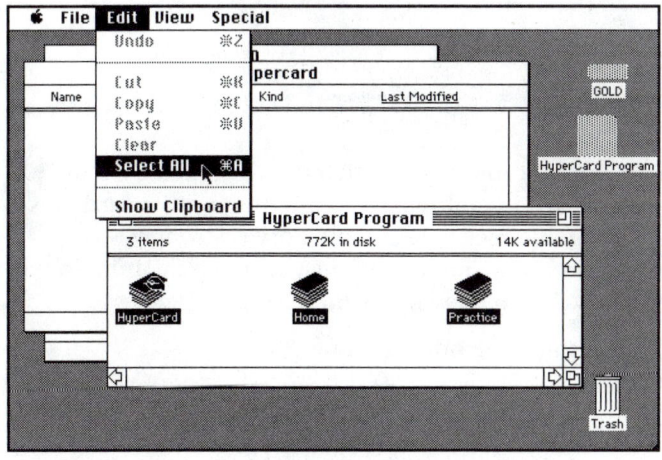

Here, Select All is selected from the Edit menu.

A

All the icons inside the floppy diskette window appear darkened.

8. Drag the selected items from the floppy disk window into your new HyperCard folder on the hard disk.

Your screen
should look like
this.

A dialog box shows the progress during the copy procedure.

9. When the copy procedure is complete, close the floppy disk window
   by clicking the box in the upper left corner. Drag the floppy disk icon
   to the Trash Can to eject the diskette.

   Dragging a disk icon into the Trash Can will not delete its contents.

10. Repeat steps 5 through 9 with each of the remaining HyperCard
    diskettes.

Running HyperCard in MultiFinder

If you are currently running applications in MultiFinder (or under System 7.0)
and would like to run HyperCard in MultiFinder, a minimum of 2 megabytes
of memory is required, although 4 megabytes of memory is strongly recommended. To run HyperCard in MultiFinder, you must set enough MultiFinder
memory aside for HyperCard. To do this, follow these steps:

1. Start your Macintosh with MultiFinder running.

2. Click the HyperCard application icon once.

3. Choose Get Info from the File menu.

4. Set the amount of the application memory size to 1000 (1 megabyte).

322

Upgrading to HyperCard 2.0 and 2.1

HyperCard 2 is a major upgrade. You must convert all 1.x stacks before you can use them with HyperCard 2. The Home stack has been changed as well as the Addresses and Appointment Book stacks. If you have been using version 1.x of HyperCard and have customized the Home stack or the Addresses or Appointment Book stacks, DO NOT automatically copy the new stacks onto your hard disk. First, look at the improved 2.0 or 2.1 stacks from the floppy disk and decide whether you would like to use the new Home stack (and others) or convert your old stacks. You either can convert your original Home stack and use it with HyperCard 2, or you may want to start using the improved HyperCard 2 Home stack instead.

Converting Your 1.x Stacks

Before converting your existing stacks to the HyperCard 2 format, make a back-up copy of each of them onto a floppy diskette. This is important to do because after you have converted a stack to HyperCard 2, the stack will no longer run in HyperCard 1.x.

To convert your stacks to the HyperCard 2 format, follow these steps:

1. Open the 1.x stack you want to convert with HyperCard 2.

Notice the little padlock icon located in the upper right corner of the stack.

A

The padlock icon indicates that the stack has not yet been converted into HyperCard 2.

2. Pull down the File menu and select Convert Stack.

Here, Convert Stack is selected from the File menu.

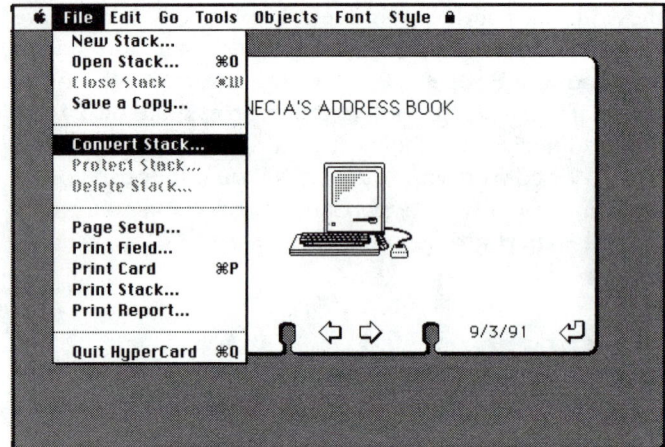

3. After the stack has been converted, pull down the File menu and select Compact Stack to optimize the stack's space.

A

Getting More HyperCard Stacks

B

One of the original goals in the development of HyperCard was the capability to access and share information with other Macintosh owners. This spirit of sharing still predominates the HyperCard community today. One of the best places to acquire HyperCard stacks is through friends and fellow "Mac Hackers" at user groups or on-line services such as CompuServe, GEnie, or America Online.

Another good place to look is in the classified section of several Macintosh magazines. *MacWorld*, for example, has a section in the Classifieds devoted specifically to HyperCard stacks.

To find out about Macintosh user groups in your area, call 1-800-538-9696.

To find out more information about CompuServe, call 1-800-848-8990.

To find out more information about GEnie, call 1-800-638-9636.

To find out more information about America Online, call 1-800-227-6364.

There are also several software companies that are called "redistributors" of shareware and freeware. Shareware programs are copyrighted programs that you can try on a trial basis. If you like the program, you send in a nominal cost to the program's author. Freeware is software shared without cost to the user, with the intention that the software will be shared by others and distributed throughout a large network of users. Several HyperCard stacks fall in this category.

Here are a few sources to contact for HyperCard shareware or freeware stacks:

1. ADVANTAGE COMPUTING
   1803 Mission Street, Suite 416
   Santa Cruz, CA 95060
   800-356-4666

2. BCS.MAC
   48 Grove Street
   Somerville, MA 02114
   617-625-7080

3. BMUG, INC. (Berkeley Mac User Group)
   1442 A Walnut Street, #62
   Berkeley, CA 94709-1496
   510-549-2684

4. DISCOVERY SYSTEMS
   7001 Discovery Blvd.
   Dublin, OH 43017

5. EDUCORP COMPUTER SERVICES
   7434 Trade Street
   San Diego, CA 92121-2410
   619-536-9999

6. GENIE ADMINISTRATION
   401 N. Washington Street
   Rockville, MD 20850

7. HEIZER SOFTWARE
   1941 Oak Park Blvd., Suite 30
   P.O. Box 232019
   Pleasant Hill, CA 94523
   415-943-7667

B

8. INTERNATIONAL DATAWARE, INC.
   2278 Trade Zone Boulevard
   San Jose, CA 95131
   408-262-6660

9. SOFTSHOPPE, INC.
   P.O. Box 3678
   Ann Arbor, MI 48106
   800-829-2378

10. SOFTWARE EXCITEMENT
    6475 Crater Lake Highway
    Central Point, OR 97502

B

Index

Free Catalog!

Mail us this registration form today, and we'll send you a free catalog featuring Que's complete line of best-selling books.

Name of Book _____

Name _____

Title _____

Phone (___) _____

Company _____

Address _____

City _____

State _____ ZIP _____

Please check the appropriate answers:

1. Where did you buy your Que book?
   - ☐ Bookstore (name: _____)
   - ☐ Computer store (name: _____)
   - ☐ Catalog (name: _____)
   - ☐ Direct from Que
   - ☐ Other: _____

2. How many computer books do you buy a year?
   - ☐ 1 or less
   - ☐ 2-5
   - ☐ 6-10
   - ☐ More than 10

3. How many Que books do you own?
   - ☐ 1
   - ☐ 2-5
   - ☐ 6-10
   - ☐ More than 10

4. How long have you been using this software?
   - ☐ Less than 6 months
   - ☐ 6 months to 1 year
   - ☐ 1-3 years
   - ☐ More than 3 years

5. What influenced your purchase of this Que book?
   - ☐ Personal recommendation
   - ☐ Advertisement
   - ☐ In-store display
   - ☐ Price
   - ☐ Que catalog
   - ☐ Que mailing
   - ☐ Que's reputation
   - ☐ Other: _____

6. How would you rate the overall content of the book?
   - ☐ Very good
   - ☐ Good
   - ☐ Satisfactory
   - ☐ Poor

7. What do you like *best* about this Que book?
   _____
   _____

8. What do you like *least* about this Que book?
   _____
   _____

9. Did you buy this book with your personal funds?
   - ☐ Yes   ☐ No

10. Please feel free to list any other comments you may have about this Que book.
   _____
   _____
   _____

— QUE —

Order Your Que Books Today!

Name _____

Title _____

Company _____

City _____

State _____ ZIP _____

Phone No. (___) _____

Method of Payment:

Check ☐   (Please enclose in envelope.)

Charge My: VISA ☐   MasterCard ☐
American Express ☐

Charge # _____

Expiration Date _____

Order No.	Title	Qty.	Price	Total

You can **FAX** your order to 1-317-573-2583. Or call **1-800-428-5331, ext. ORDR** to order direct.
Please add $2.50 per title for shipping and handling.

Subtotal _____

Shipping & Handling _____

Total _____

— QUE —

NO POSTAGE
NECESSARY
IF MAILED
IN THE
UNITED STATES

BUSINESS REPLY MAIL
First Class Permit No. 9918   Indianapolis, IN

Postage will be paid by addressee

que®

11711 N. College
Carmel, IN 46032

NO POSTAGE
NECESSARY
IF MAILED
IN THE
UNITED STATES

BUSINESS REPLY MAIL
First Class Permit No. 9918   Indianapolis, IN

Postage will be paid by addressee

que®

11711 N. College
Carmel, IN 46032